Fred Clarke

Fred Clarke

*A Biography of the Baseball
Hall of Fame Player-Manager*

Ronald T. Waldo

McFarland & Company, Inc., Publishers
Jefferson, North Carolina, and London

All of the photographs in this book were obtained from the National Baseball Hall of Fame Library, Cooperstown, New York.

LIBRARY OF CONGRESS CATALOGUING-IN-PUBLICATION DATA

Waldo, Ronald T., 1961–
    Fred Clarke : a biography of the Baseball Hall of Fame player-manager / Ronald T. Waldo.
    p.   cm.
    Includes bibliographical references and index.

    ISBN 978-0-7864-5933-9
    softcover : 50# alkaline paper ∞

    1. Clarke, Fred, 1872–1960. 2. Baseball players — United States — Biography. 3. Baseball managers — United States — Biography. 4. Pittsburgh Pirates (Baseball team) I. Title.
GV865.C437W35   2011
796.357092 — dc22   2010046573
[B]

British Library cataloguing data are available

© 2011 Ronald T. Waldo. All rights reserved

No part of this book may be reproduced or transmitted in any form or by any means, electronic or mechanical, including photocopying or recording, or by any information storage and retrieval system, without permission in writing from the publisher.

Front cover: Pittsburgh Manager Fred Clarke, 1915 (National Baseball Hall of Fame Library, Cooperstown, New York)

Manufactured in the United States of America

McFarland & Company, Inc., Publishers
  Box 611, Jefferson, North Carolina 28640
  www.mcfarlandpub.com

I would like to acknowledge a small group of people consisting of family and friends who in one way or another motivated me during the research and writing of this book. Special thanks go out to Arnold Waldo, Nancy Waldo, Randal Waldo, Jennifer Waldo, Susan Karpuszka, Mark Karpuszka, Christopher Karpuszka, Ryan McCoy, Jerel Patch, Alger and Big Champ.

Table of Contents

Preface   1
1. A Fall Day in Winterset   5
2. Two Passions Are Born   9
3. Fearless Youngster   18
4. The Original Boy Wonder Manager   29
5. Goodbye Louisville, Hello Pittsburgh   41
6. Pennant Flag Hangs from Corsair Craft   53
7. Pittsburgh Repeats in Spite of Johnson's Treachery   66
8. Historic Battle with an Old Friend   79
9. Clarke Trades Proven Performers to Improve Team   94
10. Twenty-Nine Game Loser Becomes Staff Ace   108
11. Pirates Come Close During Great Race   122
12. Championship Glory   137
13. Clarke Betrayed by Pittsburgh Fans   152
14. Marty O'Toole's Three-Ring Circus   165
15. A Great Career Winds Down   181
16. Can't Get Baseball Out of His Blood   196
17. A Full Life After Baseball   207

Appendix: Fred Clarke's Career Statistics   217
Chapter Notes   219
Bibliography   235
Index   237

Preface

As many readers know, offense in the Deadball Era was largely about strategy and guile. Home runs came only infrequently, so teams relied on the bunt, the hit and run and the steal to push baserunners home one at a time. Managers who were able to perfect this "small ball" style had great success. Those who did not usually became unemployed.

Around 1920, not long after Babe Ruth made his way from Boston to New York, the home run became the new strategy in baseball. Fans became less interested in steals and bunts, wanting instead to see prodigious blasts by the likes of Babe Ruth, Lou Gehrig, Rogers Hornsby and Hack Wilson. As time went by, rooters screamed for more and longer hits.

The bunt and steal are used in baseball today, and some managers adhere to small-ball policies when they need to manufacture runs. But the power game is still ascendant. Furthermore, new baseball ideas such as specialty pitching and platoons have replaced the player-manager and the Baltimore Chop. Starting pitchers are no longer expected to complete the game, and players who in the 1910s might have come out of the lineup only when injured are today given the occasional day off.

While baseball has changed dramatically during the past century, there are many facets of the national pastime that remain the same. Ballplayers still play for the love of the game as they did in 1900. They also play to win. Throughout history, the goal of most owners, managers and players has been to win a championship. For more than a century, players have gathered year after year with one purpose in mind: Play your best, defeat the competition and win the World Series.

A fiery competitor whose positive attitude rubbed off on everyone around him, Fred Clarke established himself as baseball's greatest left fielder while in Louisville during the rough-and-tumble decade of the nineties. He also received his managerial on-the-job training while playing in the Falls City. When Clarke moved on to Pittsburgh in 1900, he continued to build upon his resume as a great player, and he quickly proved that his managerial ability was equally deserving of praise. From 1900 to 1915, there was no manager in baseball who had greater success.

Clarke's achievements as both a player and manager were rooted in his desire to be the best through hard work, determination and dedication. He played a hard-nosed brand of baseball that alienated him from many opposing players throughout his career. Between the lines, he was willing to scratch and claw in order to win a baseball game. Away from the game, he was said to be a gentleman and devoted family man.

Clarke was more than just a baseball player. He was an inventor, entrepreneur, rancher and farmer. His love for life on the farm was in fact every bit as strong as his desire to play baseball. On more than one occasion, Clarke almost walked away from the game he loved so that he could nurture the Kansas farm and be with his family. Clarke had two callings which he answered in life. At times, it was difficult to give each its proper attention. In spite of this, Fred Clarke remained loyal to both.

During his time as manager of the Pittsburgh Pirates, Fred Clarke won four National League pennants and one world championship. He finished in second place five times, third place three times and fourth place two times. At a time when baseball success meant finishing in the first division, Clarke's Pirates did so every year but his final two. Pittsburgh owner Barney Dreyfuss expected such results, and Fred Clarke was able to deliver throughout their time together in Pittsburgh.

The Fred Clarke–Barney Dreyfuss partnership began in 1894. Dreyfuss was responsible for bringing Clarke to Louisville after the Colonel's treasurer scouted the outfielder during a minor league game in Memphis. Through the years, the relationship between Clarke and Dreyfuss grew as each moved up the ranks within the Louisville organization. In 1897, Fred Clarke was named to manage the Louisville Colonels. After the 1898 season, Barney Dreyfuss ascended to the presidency of the Louisville squad.

Both men were part of the Louisville transfer to Pittsburgh after the 1899 season. Fred Clarke became manager of the Pittsburgh Pirates when Barney Dreyfuss became the primary owner of the Smoky City squad. During their time together in Pittsburgh, Clarke and Dreyfuss had overwhelming success as the Pittsburgh Pirates quickly became a National League powerhouse. Fred Clarke was the ultimate warrior and field general, and Barney Dreyfuss was a shrewd mogul who supplied the fuel that kept the Pittsburgh machine running. Each did whatever was necessary to win.

Clarke and Dreyfuss were friends both on and off the field. At times, the two men had their differences. These differences of opinion never shook the strong bond which developed during their years together. Clarke and Dreyfuss were cut from the same cloth, driven men who demanded much of themselves and others.

The Pittsburgh Pirates are a big part of the Fred Clarke story, the majority of Clarke's baseball success having come in the Smoky City. Players like Honus Wagner and Ed Konetchy shaped Clarke's legacy in both a positive and negative way. Wagner's great play contributed to the success of Clarke's Pirate clubs during the glory years; Konetchy's disruptive behavior as a Federal League agent while still on the Pirates payroll in 1914 contributed to Clarke's first second-division finish in 15 years as Pittsburgh's manager. Events such as the war with the American League in 1901 and 1902 tested the young player-manager as he built a team which had few peers in baseball during the first decade of the twentieth century. If owner Dreyfuss had mapped out a blueprint of success for the Pirates, Clarke executed it masterfully.

My decision to write a biography covering the life of Fred Clarke was based on a desire to learn more about the man who brought glory to the Pittsburgh Pirates franchise during the twentieth century's first decade. Clarke was one of baseball's most popular and most quoted managers during that time. His willingness to talk with baseball writers during his career afforded me the opportunity to gather volumes of information during the research phase of this project. Articles and Fred Clarke interviews from both *The Sporting News* and *Sporting Life* were great research tools which made it possible for me to write this biography.

This work contains three elements that interact with each other. The first and most important of these is the story of Fred Clarke's life. The second is Clarke's relationship with owner Barney Dreyfuss during their time together in Louisville and Pittsburgh. The last element involves Clarke's Pittsburgh Pirates teams and specifically the interaction between him and his players. Throughout this book, I show how these elements remained intertwined each season during Fred Clarke's tenure as manager of the Pittsburgh Pirates.

History is kept alive through stories passed down by each generation. Unfortunately, as time has passed, some of the heroes from baseball's early days have been mostly forgotten. Fred Clarke first appeared on a National League diamond in 1894. Even in Pittsburgh, Clarke is sometimes a forgotten man as people talk about Clemente, Stargell, Mazeroski, Kiner and the Waner brothers while discussing Pirates baseball history. Fred Clifford Clarke's story is one that needs to be told in respect to both baseball and Pittsburgh history.

Chapter 1

A Fall Day in Winterset

After the Civil War, a new wave of settlers began pouring into the grand Midwest hoping to carve out an existence for themselves. Many of these people were European immigrants who came across the ocean looking for a better life in the land of opportunity. Whether it was a man from Germany hoping to enhance his station in life or a farmer in Illinois seizing the chance to improve his existence, the heartland of the United States was a popular destination for those chasing the American Dream. Places like Illinois were perfect for those who aspired to aid in the building of an industrial America. Iowa was a beautiful contrast for people who wished to remain close to the land while at the same time contributing to the great agricultural success of this country.

Iowa's population nearly doubled after the Civil War to about 1.2 million people. Many of these new residents were immigrants who had come from Germany, Sweden and Denmark. The Iowa legislature encouraged immigration and even published a ninety-six page brochure in 1869 titled *Iowa: The Home for Immigrants*. Great efforts were made to attract foreigners from all lands as the pamphlet was published in English, German, Dutch, Swedish and Danish.[1] Native sons stood side by side with their European counterparts as Iowa forged ahead during the late nineteenth century.

One of these native sons was a blacksmith named William Clarke who moved his family from West Point, Illinois, to a farm in Winterset, Iowa, during the late 1860s. Clarke was a Maryland native who settled in Illinois after his marriage to Lucy Cutler in 1852. When the Clarkes moved to Winterset, their family consisted of eight children. Anna, Edgar, William Jr., Mattie, Grace and Lucy were born while the family resided in Illinois. Prior to the Civil War, Hattie and Charley were born in Iowa.[2] Obviously, the Clarkes were not strangers to the beauty of Iowa. West Point was basically a stone's throw to the east of Iowa, so it was quite possible that William Clarke and his family had matriculated west for some reason during those years.

Winterset was a small city about 28 miles southwest of Des Moines. Designated as the county seat for Madison County, Winterset was founded in 1849.[3] By the time Clarke moved his family there twenty years later, the town had grown in size and stature. The Madison County Courthouse was completed in 1868 and some of the covered bridges which were the trademark of the county had been erected.[4] William Clarke worked hard as a blacksmith, and also farmed the land in an effort to provide a good life for his family.

In 1872, Winterset graduated from being somewhat of an outpost town to the status of viable city thanks to the railroad's arrival. The first train rolled into Winterset from Des Moines on February 28. The caravan, made up exclusively of construction cars, arrived at the Winterset station around 3 o'clock. Falling snow failed to put a damper on the proceedings as local citizens gathered to witness the gala event. A brass band was on hand for the celebration. Contractors and railroad men where honored at a huge banquet that evening inside the St. Nicholas Hotel.[5]

Passenger trains did not appear in Winterset until late spring. On May 13, 1872, the first passenger train arrived in the local station with the intention of taking riders to nearby Des Moines.[6] Not only did this event connect Winterset with surrounding communities, it also opened up new possibilities that would allow the town to grow in size and strength. As historian Herman Mueller described it, "The engine bell rang and for the first time the conductor called out 'passengers for Des Moines all aboard,' and Winterset was no longer an inland town, dependent upon wagons for communication with the outer world. During the summer of 1872, immediately following this event, seventy-three buildings were erected in Winterset, at a cost of over ninety thousand dollars, and within seven years next following it more than doubled its population."[7]

Another indication that Winterset was becoming prosperous was the birth of many newspapers throughout the area. In 1872 the *Winterset News* was born when Jacob Morgan, formerly a foreman with the *Winterset Madisonian*, bought the plant of the *Winterset Sun* from its owners.[8] Morgan changed the name and shifted the political content away from the pro–Republican material that the *Sun* printed. The first content was cranked out in a small rear upper room of the building where the plant was located.[9]

As the town of Winterset continued to grow throughout 1872, so too did the family of William and Lucy Clarke. On October 3, 1872, the Clarkes welcomed their ninth child into the world when Lucy gave birth to a baby boy on the family's farm. William and Lucy decided to name the newest member of the Clarke family Fred Clifford Clarke. With the birth of Fred in 1872,

1. A Fall Day in Winterset

the Clarke family legacy now spanned 18 years, from 1854 when oldest sibling Anna Clarke was born.

As the Clarke family grew in the autumn of 1872, a game that developed in the eastern part of the country was beginning to captivate youths in the Midwest. Baseball's popularity in America's heartland continued to grow as more people migrated westward. Young men like Adrian Anson of Iowa, Jimmy Galvin of Missouri, Charley Comiskey of Illinois, Sam Thompson of Indiana, and Abner Dalrymple of Wisconsin were cutting their teeth playing baseball as newborn Fred Clifford Clarke entered the world. Other Midwest youngsters such as James Holmes, Billy Sunday, Jake Beckley, Jack O'Connor, Perry Werden, Lave Cross, Charles Nichols, Frank Bowerman and Herman Long may not have embraced the game quite yet, but they would eventually be drawn to baseball's allure.

Baseball's popularity in the Midwest did not matter much to William Clarke. He had the basic day-to-day concerns of life to worry about as he provided for his wife and nine children, causing pleasurable recreation many times to be disregarded in favor of sweat and hard work. The Clarke children were responsible for doing their fair share of chores on the family farm. If any of the boys found time to get away and play baseball, it was done more for fun and exercise rather than preparation for this game to someday become a chosen profession.

William Clarke also had little concern for distant parts of the country which did not impact his everyday life. He no doubt cared very little that an eastern city in Pennsylvania was beginning to make a name for itself as an industrial power after the Civil War. By 1872, Pittsburgh had already begun charting the course that would allow the city to become America's king of the steel industry.

During the summer of 1872, a few months before Fred Clifford Clarke was born, the Isabella and Lucy blast furnaces became operational in Pittsburgh.[10] The Isabella, located in Etna, battled it out with the Lucy furnace across the river to see how many tons of pig iron each could produce. By the end of 1872, both furnaces were producing up to 500 tons per week.[11] In January of that same year, Mark Twain gave a lecture to a packed house at Library Hall about his experiences roughing it in the Nevada wilderness.[12] Two entrepreneurs named Henry John Heinz and L. Clarence Noble also moved their business to Pittsburgh in 1872. Heinz and Noble were food purveyors with a product line that included horseradish, pickles, celery sauce and vinegar.[13]

All of these events in Pittsburgh were of no consequence to William Clarke in Iowa unless he happened to purchase some of the Heinz-Noble products from time to time. In a way, these proceedings did relate to the newest member of the Clarke family. In 1872, nobody could have foreseen that Fred Clarke, who was only a baby at the time, eventually would become a baseball player whose destiny was to be fulfilled in Pennsylvania's Steel Town. Pittsburgh may have been insignificant to William Clarke, but it was the place where Fred Clifford Clarke ultimately achieved his greatest success as one of baseball's supreme player-managers.

Chapter 2

Two Passions Are Born

When Fred Clarke was two years old, his father William uprooted the family from Winterset and joined a covered wagon caravan that was making its way to southern Kansas.[1] Although the trip was not as perilous compared to a wagon convoy rolling through hostile Indian territory along the Oregon Trail, this venture wasn't quite like taking a Sunday buggy ride through Central Park in New York City either. The journey was long and arduous. Outlaws, angry Indians and a variety of unsavory characters still posed a threat to any wagon caravan moving through the prairie state.

The destination of the wagon caravan was a place called Cowley County, located in southern Kansas near the Oklahoma border. Lush bottomland was supposedly prevalent throughout the county.[2] William Clarke was intrigued with the prospect of making a better life for his family in a region which had so much untapped potential. Cowley County was named after Matthew Cowley, a first lieutenant from the Ninth Kansas Cavalry who was killed during the Civil War at Little Rock, Arkansas, in August 1864.[3] Kansas historian William G. Cutler explained how Cowley came into existence:

> It was carved out of Hunter County by the Legislature of 1867, which defined it as running thirty-three miles north from a point on the south line of the State, 103 miles west of the State line, and extending thirty-four and a half miles west. At this time, the county was comprised in the "thirty mile strip" or Diminished Osage Reserve, and the three mile strip on the south line which had been reserved as a pathway for the Cherokees on their hunting trips to their more western possessions. The great Osage trail ran east and west across the county, entering at the Flint hills on the east, crossing the Grouse about two miles above Dexter, the Walnut at Winfield, and the Arkansas at the mouth of the Ninnescah. The villages of the tribe were at the latter crossing and on Timber Creek, a short distance above Winfield.[4]

Such a strenuous journey across the plains was bound to toughen every participant in some manner. Even a small child like Freddie learned resilience, perseverance and hardiness in spite of his young age. The youngest member of the Clarke family certainly was not afforded the comforts and amenities that a two year old came to expect while residing in a permanent residence. A wagon caravan trip through semi-hostile territory molded and shaped a young child every bit as much as it did an older counterpart.

The trip ended for the Clarke family at a piece of farmland in Cowley, close to the city of Winfield. Here William Clarke decided to establish new roots for his wife and children. The Clarkes arrival in Winfield coincided with the departure of many settlers from that area who abandoned their claims to land after some tough times in 1874 and 1875. Drought issues were followed by an invasion of grasshoppers, which blighted the land and destroyed crops in the summer of 1874. Concerns arose for the 1875 growing season after the destructive swarm deposited eggs throughout Cowley and moved on to nearby fertile land.[5]

Farmers who feared for their survival cut and ran, feeling that the new horde of grasshoppers would be just as destructive after the eggs hatched. These worries were eventually proved to be invalid when the young hoppers left Cowley without inflicting any damage like their predecessors did in 1874.[6] If not for the troubled year of 1874 in Winfield, William Clarke may not have been able to acquire the piece of land that his family now called home.

Young Fred Clarke learned at an early age that hard work and dedication reaped immense rewards. Life on the farm was a sunrise to sunset endeavor, with chores consuming the bulk of the calendar week. It was through this type of life that the young boy was able to realize that goals were achieved with sweat and blood. Malingering on the farm was something that wasn't tolerated. Everybody had a job to do, and the family's ability to succeed depended upon each member completing their assigned tasks correctly and in a timely fashion.

Winfield in the 1870s was by no means a hostile area. Osage Indians had threatened and driven out early settlers in 1869. The tribe was eventually pushed aside when their lands were opened for settlement on July 15, 1870, and legitimate claims from settlers were accepted.[7] The town and young Fred Clarke grew up together as Winfield became more civilized each year. By the time Fred was of the age to attend school in the county's learning institutions, Cowley County's population had doubled to over 21,000 people by 1879.[8]

The U.S. Census taken in 1880 showed that William Clarke's real estate value totaled $2,000 and that he had additional personal wealth equaling $400.[9] The national population information regarding the Clarke family was entered into the record on June 21, which included the births of Mabel in

1875 and Joshua in 1879.[10] Some of the older Clarke children had moved on and were making a life for themselves. As tough times hit the Cowley area in 1880, it was William, his mother Sarah, Lucy and eight Clarke children contributing daily to the family's wealth and prosperity.

The summer of 1880 in Winfield was disastrous for farmers as another drought hit the area that was harsher than the one experienced by Cowley dwellers in 1874.[11] Farms big and small were affected as all people in the area suffered because of the crippled growing season. Whether it was the drought or some other unknown reason, William Clarke packed up his family in late 1880 or early 1881 and moved them back to Iowa. This time the Clarkes settled near the thriving metropolis of Des Moines.[12] Fred Clarke's father once again wore the dual moniker of blacksmith and farmer as the family took up residence in a fourth different city over the last 15 years.

During the family's days in Kansas, young Freddie grew to love the land around Winfield and its surrounding area in Cowley County. At times, the youngster did grow tired of the everyday tedium that went along with working on a farm. This was only natural for a child who had other interests. In spite of this boredom at times, Fred Clarke had formed a bond with the land in that area. After the family moved back to Des Moines, the youngster's burning desire to return to that place remained unquenched. Tiring of life in Des Moines, Fred hitched a train and ran away from home.[13] Many years later, a Udall, Kansas, newspaper chronicled the young lad's adventure:

> When a mere lad of 11 summers he grew tired of the monotony of farm life and, leaving his home in Iowa, started out to see the world. Everything went well until he reached Udall, where he was "ditched" by a heartless brakeman. His available cash assets at that time amounted to only 10 cents, which he judiciously invested in cheese and crackers. While waiting for another train Fred was sizing up the country hereabouts, and he resolved then and there to possess himself of a home in this immediate vicinity.[14]

Upon returning to Des Moines after his journey, he soon found a second thing that he was passionate about other than the prairies of Kansas. While working as a newsboy for Ed Barrow, a circulation manager for the *Des Moines Register*, Clarke was introduced to the game of baseball.[15] Most of the kids who had paper routes under Barrow were rambunctious lads who needed a positive way to channel all of their energy. Fred himself was one of the more pugnacious kids in the group. While waiting for papers in an alley one day, Clarke got into a fight with one of the other boys. He accidentally knocked out a window by pushing his antagonist through it. In order to teach Clarke a very important life lesson, Barrow made him pay every penny of the 35 cents required to replace the window.[16] The future baseball magnate introduced his seventeen paper route boys to baseball in an effort to keep them out of trouble. Barrow named the team the Stars and placed them in the local Des Moines City League.[17] Clarke played the outfield and quickly showed great ability on the diamond with his blazing speed and relentless hustling.

Finding time to play baseball was difficult at times considering the fact that Clarke had school, chores at home and various jobs to contend with. Besides having a newspaper route, Clarke also worked as a bellboy at the Savery Hotel, did odd jobs at the Foster Opera House and drove a delivery wagon for grocer C.C. Loomis.[18] While working for Loomis, he would sometimes stop the wagon, tie up his horses and participate in an inning or two of a game taking place on a sandlot park at Sixteenth and Woodland. Clarke was eventually fired for this practice.[19]

Baseball equipment was another issue that confronted Clarke in his quest to perform on the diamond. The young man certainly could not ask his father for money to buy items such as a glove or shoes. He had to scrounge around hoping to persuade other players in the area to donate equipment that was no longer being used. On occasion, Clarke could be seen hanging around the clubhouse of the Western League's Des Moines team.[20] His mission was twofold: He wanted to get a glimpse up close of professional players, and also hoped that someone would be willing to give him equipment that was no longer being used. A player from that team named Richard "Dad" Phelan did Clarke a good turn during the summer of 1888.[21] As Phelan told the story:

> It was back in '88 when I first ran across Clarke. I was with the Des Moines club that year and we won the Western League pennant. Clarke was only a kid and was playing with an amateur team called the "Stars." We had an off day and Clarke had just been chased from the clubhouse by several old players when I met him.
> "What is the matter, little fellow," I asked.
> "Oh nothing," replied Clarke. "I only wanted to see if I could get a pair of old baseball shoes from some of the players. But instead, they chased me off the grounds."
> I took a kindly feeling to the boy and brought him back to the park and gave him a pair of shoes.[22]

With new shoes in tow and the drive to become the best player that he could churning inside of him, Clarke once again decided to run away from home. Clarke had added the positions of catcher and shortstop to his repertoire on the Des Moines Stars team.[23] He was also performing quite capably for the Des Moines Mascots as well. When the opportunity arose to join an independent team in Carroll, Iowa, Clarke seized upon it. Comparisons to the prodigal son were not unwarranted even though Clarke wasn't about to ask for his share of the family fortune before he left:

2. Two Passions Are Born

My parents were opposed to my playing ball. I had learned my trade, that of a lather, and father and mother, and incidentally several aunts and uncles, thought I should devote more time to my calling. But I liked to play ball, and in this respect was just like every other kid. One day I received an offer from an independent club in a town in Iowa. They had an important game scheduled and were very anxious to have me take part in it. I knew it would do no good to ask for parental consent, so one night I went to my room, packed all my belongings in an old telescope bag, sneaked out the back way and started for the town where the club desiring my services was located. When I got there and we played the first game, in which they thought I did well at short, they made me an offer of $40 a month to remain. The team only played three games a week — Friday, Saturday and Sunday — and I was given employment at my trade for $3 a day; things were coming pretty easy for me. I drove nails into laths five days a week, getting off every Friday, and drew my little $10 per week for playing ball. I remained for two months, and when I started back for my own fireside I was rich — had $114 in my pocket.... Once inside the house I ran to mother and before saying a word, or before she could say anything, I handed her the $114. She looked at the money, and I guess she thought I had been a pretty good boy to save so much in two months, for she did not scold me. Instead I was accorded a real motherly welcome."[24]

There definitely was no use in trying to stop Clarke from realizing his dream of becoming a professional baseball player. When the time came for young Clarke to pursue his ambition, William Clarke begrudgingly gave his consent. Clarke's father gave his son sound advice which the youngster heeded throughout his career.[25]

Clarke was able to embark on his career in professional baseball because of an advertisement he placed in the want column of *The Sporting News*. A club in Hastings, Nebraska, that was looking for players answered his ad in 1892 and offered the youngster $40 a month in salary.[26] Clarke jumped at the chance, packed his gear, and made the trek to Nebraska. He received Ed Barrow's seal of approval as one of his first "finds" debuted in baseball's professional realm. "Fred Clarke played one of the outfield positions and from the start displayed a real knack for hitting the ball," said Barrow. "My brother, George, caught for the Stars. I managed, and also tried to pitch, and played first base. Around 1892, Fred and George Barrow decided they were good enough for a try at pro ball, and landed in the old Nebraska State League. Fred made it, but my brother soon returned home and obtained what he thought would prove a steadier job."[27]

Clarke showed strong ability with the bat as he hit .302 during his brief time with the Hastings team. His play in the outfield was a bit suspect at times, though, leading the youngster to doubt his ability as a ball player. Clarke had made a smooth transition as a hitter, but he found that what worked for him in the field as a Star or Mascot in Des Moines was not good enough to get the job done at the true professional level. The young player was concerned that this shortcoming could halt his baseball career before it had even started. "They put me in the outfield," stated Clarke, "and I was lucky to catch half of the drives hit to me. Looking back, I still wonder how a manager, even in a league way down in the sticks, could have put up with such a terrible outfielder. An old-timer told me I could improve by practice, so I went out to the field at 8 o'clock in the morning and practiced until game time in the afternoon. After a while, I got so I could catch fly balls pretty well."[28]

Clarke's hard work and practice paid off as he honed his fielding skills every day. By summer, Clarke was a highly capable flycatcher who knew the nuances of the position so well that the youngster now made plays that he had been unable to execute at the beginning of the season. Unfortunately, the Nebraska State League folded in July and Clarke's baseball career in Hastings came to an abrupt end.[29] Because the season's sudden and unexpected end left him in a monetary bind, Clarke needed to ask a favor in order to get home. "The league blew up in July," Fred commented, "and when it did I had overdrawn my small salary by $7. The manager told me if I would give him my personal note for $15, he would give me a ticket home. After he got my signature on the note, he told me I could go to the hot place. Was I sore!"[30]

In spite of the shortened season, Clarke had done a good job during his first year of professional baseball. Buoyed by this positive experience in 1892 and the belief in his own mind that he could make it as a baseball player, Clarke signed a contract to play for the Western Association's St. Joseph, Missouri, team in 1893. Joining him on the Saints was fellow Des Moines resident James "Ducky" Holmes.[31] When the season began, Clarke found himself batting leadoff and playing left field for the Saints. His play was so impressive that it was not long before he received an offer to hook up with Montgomery of the Southern League.[32] Clarke jumped at the opportunity to climb another notch on baseball's ladder. Future New York Giant pitcher Joe "Iron Man" McGinnity was already making a splash for Montgomery when Clarke was signed. Manager John McCloskey offered Fred $100 in advance money when the former Saint reached Alabama. This brought great joy to Clarke. He remembered the sting of his financial status the previous summer in Hastings. As a precaution, Clarke put some of this newfound wealth in an account at a local Montgomery bank.[33]

Manager McCloskey altered Clarke's responsibilities once the youngster joined the Colts. McCloskey decided to place him in the fourth spot of the batting order. Clarke didn't disappoint as he batted .292 in 32 games. The outfielder was still finding his way as a left fielder in the outer garden's confines.

2. Two Passions Are Born

Even though Clarke was a young man with a slender build, he had a cannon for an arm and showed better accuracy with his throws each game. He did commit five errors for the Colts, but he also threw out seven runners from left field that season.

Just as Clarke was finding his groove on the diamond, bad luck struck once again. This time it was a health epidemic in the city of Montgomery, which caused a league which he was playing in to disband for the second consecutive season.[34] To make matters worse, Clarke's prudent move of putting money in the bank when he arrived in Montgomery backfired:

> When I landed in Montgomery, I received $100 in advance on arrival, and put $50 in the bank to be sure I would have a ticket home. While we were playing in New Orleans, yellow fever broke out in Montgomery. We started back, but were forced off the train in Mobile. Armed men were preventing anyone from going into Montgomery. We stayed in Mobile, and played there for ten days. When we finally were able to take a train for Montgomery, the train was not allowed to go into the station. However, a bus met us ten miles out of town. We got back on a Monday, only to find that the league had folded because of the yellow fever scare; and the bank in which I had deposited my $50 home money had closed the preceding Saturday.[35]

Clarke's luck took a turn for the better when St. Joseph's sent him train tickets with instructions to rejoin the Saints. He remained with the Western Association team until the season's close.[36] After the season, Clarke made a decision that almost altered the course of his life. Disgusted with the economic setbacks that were prevalent during his first two years as a professional baseball player, Clarke turned to something else he loved in an effort to achieve stability in his life.

On September 16, 1893, the Cherokee land strip in Oklahoma was opened for people who wished to file land claims in that area. Clarke was among the first group of people who arrived in Oklahoma to make the run by horseback, hoping to acquire a beautiful section of land in the untapped Oklahoma territory. Clarke's luck in this venture worked out no better than his misfortunes the past two years in baseball. Fred's mount was not fast enough and the youngster was beaten to the prime Cherokee real estate by other riders.[37] Clarke may have fared better if the horse's speed was comparable to that which Fred possessed in his nimble legs.

Had Clarke secured a claim during the run, it could have meant that he was through as a baseball player for the time being, since it would have been necessary for Clarke to remain in Oklahoma to establish the validity of his claim. Since the Iowa native had failed in this particular business enterprise, he could now turn his attention back to securing a spot on the baseball diamond in 1894.

The roller coaster of fate presented a positive ascension for Clarke in 1894 when the Southern League reorganized. John McCloskey, named to manage the Savannah Modocs, hadn't forgotten Clarke's stellar play during their time together in Montgomery. McCloskey asked Clarke to join him in Georgia.[38] Clarke picked up where he left off the previous season. He batted .311 in 54 games and continued to show off his rifle arm in left field. Clarke gunned down 14 reckless runners, an average of about one every four games.

Once again, the Southern League began to run into financial difficulties as the season reached midsummer. If things continued to go bad for the league, Clarke was looking at the prospect of having a third consecutive season cut short for reasons beyond his control. Savannah was in such dire financial straits that McCloskey didn't have the necessary money for train fare home after a series in Memphis.[39] It was here that fate finally favored Clarke.

While the Modocs were stranded in Memphis, the treasurer of Louisville's National League team was attending to business in the Tennessee city. Barney Dreyfuss was the Louisville ballclub's treasurer, who also scouted players. There was one player with Savannah who had made a favorable impression on Barney when he took in a few games between Memphis and Savannah.

At some point during his stay in Memphis, Dreyfuss had a discussion with the downtrodden McCloskey, who told Dreyfuss that the current road trip had been a disaster and the team was hemorrhaging red ink. When he explained to the Louisville treasurer that the Savannah team was without financial means to return home, Dreyfuss offered a solution that he believed was advantageous to both parties. "I'll try to help you Mac," said the sympathetic Dreyfuss. "You have a young outfielder named Clarke, who looks like he might develop into a good ball player. Now I'll pay the fare for your entire ball team from here to Savannah, if you are willing to turn this boy over to me."[40]

McCloskey quickly agreed to this deal, and Dreyfuss bought Savannah's railroad tickets for about $200.[41] Clarke and pitcher Harrison Peppers headed to Louisville while the remainder of the Modocs returned home to Georgia. Clarke was guaranteed to receive a $100 bonus if he reported to Louisville within five days.[42] Dreyfuss was quite ecstatic that he was able to acquire Clarke only days after he had entered the outfielder's name into his little scouting dope book. Barney Dreyfuss later explained why he was so captivated by Clarke's play:

> A young, thin, rawboned little fellow was playing left field for Savannah; going after everything in sight and hitting the Memphis pitcher, Wadsworth, out of the lot, but unfortunately for his team he seemed to be the only man who tried to and did play ball, the rest of the nine acting as if the ghost had not "walked" for some weeks. Suddenly the catcher of the Savannah team

became ill. No one else being on hand to do the windpad work the young left fielder came in and volunteered to do the backstop work, and he did it well, though three times he threw the ball into center field endeavoring to catch base runners, for the simple reason that infielders were too tired to cover the bag.[43]

Clarke's hard work and perseverance had paid off, as his hustling and win-at-all-costs attitude left an immediate impression on Dreyfuss, whose Louisville squad was one of the National League's bottom feeders. The addition of dedicated players such as Clarke was bound to improve the listless team. Amazingly, he had made it to the big leagues without playing a full season for any minor league team. Clarke officially became a member of the Louisville Colonels on June 28, 1894. How far Clarke was ultimately destined to progress as a major league player would be answered in relatively quick fashion.

Chapter 3

Fearless Youngster

With a guaranteed $100 bonus waiting for the youngster if he was able to join the Colonels by July 3, Fred Clarke immediately hustled off to Louisville and arrived in town well ahead of the designated time. Once in Louisville, he reported to the ballpark and met with Colonels manager Bill Barnie in the team's clubhouse.[1] Barnie handed the rookie player a baggy, oversized jersey. Clarke put on the huge tent-like uniform and joined his new teammates for practice. When the pre-game preparation concluded, Clarke went up to the Louisville manager and reminded him that the club still needed to fulfill its $100 bonus obligation.[2] He wanted to be sure that the bonus promise was kept since the rookie would only be pulling down $175 a month in salary.[3]

Barnie wrote out a check for that amount and handed it to Clarke. He refused to accept the piece of paper. Clarke had experienced financial hardship many times during the past three years. Useless paper was of no consequence to a person like Clarke who had seen monetary funds disappear in the past through unfortunate circumstances beyond his control. The rookie outfielder decided that he would accept legitimate coin of the realm and nothing else.[4] Barnie tried to appease the youngster by explaining that a Louisville Colonels check was as good as gold. "But Mr. Dreyfuss' name is on the check," said Barnie. "All the same I want it in money that I can feel," persisted Clarke.[5]

Barnie begrudgingly acquiesced to Clarke's wishes. The Louisville manager had to scrounge around for the money, but Barnie eventually was able to accommodate John McCloskey's prodigy as he paid Clarke his bonus in small bills. Clarke pinned the cash in the pocket of his baggy uniform pants, since he needed to keep the money close at hand.[6] Clarke didn't know any of his new teammates well enough to trust them. The youngster also did not yet feel comfortable with his new Louisville surroundings to the point that such cash could be left at his place of lodging.

When Clarke joined the Louisville Colonels on June 30, 1894, the team stood in last place in the National League standings with a pathetic 14–40 record. The thriving Kentucky town which he now would call home throughout the baseball season was famous for its bourbon and whiskey distilleries. Louisville treasurer and part-owner Barney Dreyfuss had amassed his fortune acting as a wholesaler moving the product that such distilleries produced. Dreyfuss followed a much more circuitous route to Louisville than his new outfielder encountered. While Clarke's origins were rooted in the plains of the Midwest, Barney Dreyfuss was a European immigrant who came to the land of opportunity with high hopes and little money.

Dreyfuss left Germany in 1882 at the age of 17 and made the journey to the United States by boat hoping to realize the American Dream. With help from relatives in Paducah, Kentucky, Dreyfuss was able to obtain work at the Bernheim distillery. Dreyfuss worked his way up from cleaning whiskey barrels to become head bookkeeper for the company.[7] Barney's strong work ethic was something to be admired, but the long hours working and learning English contributed to a decline in his health at a relatively young age.

A doctor in Paducah recommended that Dreyfuss find some means of recreation that would afford him the opportunity to exercise. He believed that Barney's health would improve if the youngster had some fun and did not work so hard. The doctor sold Dreyfuss on the merits of baseball. Barney took a quick liking to the game and saw his health improve as he played recreational ball for a semi-pro team in Paducah.[8] By no means was Dreyfuss a baseball star, but he became enchanted with the game that was gaining popularity across the country. As time went by, Dreyfuss soon became fascinated with baseball's inner workings. Dreyfuss may not have been destined for stardom on the diamond, but his analytical mind made him a perfect candidate to perform a front office role within the game.[9]

Dreyfuss was able to align himself with the Louisville franchise when the Bernheim distillery moved there from Paducah. In 1890, Dreyfuss was elected treasurer of the club after he purchased a small percentage of stock in Louisville's American Association entry. Two years after he was selected to this post, Louisville joined the National League. In 1892, Dreyfuss became secretary-treasurer under Harry Pulliam who was chosen as president of the National League's newest team.[10] Slowly but surely, Dreyfuss continued to purchase large chunks of Louisville stock. By 1894 he was working his way toward becoming the team's majority owner. His job description at that time permitted him to handle team financial matters and scout for young phenoms like Fred Clarke.

Louisville was a city in transition when Clarke arrived in 1894. Churchill Downs, made famous through horse racing and the Kentucky Derby, was experiencing some financial difficulties. The New Louisville Jockey Club took over day-to-day operations of the facility in an effort to nurse the track back to economic health.[11] In 1894, the Louisville Slugger trademark was established after John "Bud" Hillerich changed the name of the Falls City Slugger baseball bats he produced at a local factory. Hillerich started making bats for major league players after Pete Browning requested a specific model in 1884.[12]

As Clarke prepared to participate in his first big league game on June 30, his Louisville teammates began to taunt and ridicule the rookie outfielder. The object of their scorn was the bat that Clarke had brought with him from Savannah. The Colonels players compared the wooden cudgel to a peashooter and claimed that the opposing pitcher would knock it out of Clarke's hands.[13] Louisville was playing a Philadelphia team on that day which included star players such as Sam Thompson, Ed Delahanty, Billy Hamilton, Lave Cross and Tuck Turner. Veteran stalwart Gus Weyhing was slated to oppose Louisville in Clarke's inaugural game.

Clarke's first game in the Falls City was nothing short of unbelievable. Four days prior to his arrival in town, a vicious electrical and wind storm had torn through Louisville. Houses were destroyed and roofs were torn from the town's dwellings. The devastating winds uprooted trees and numerous citizens were injured by downed power lines.[14] On June 30, Clarke tore through Gus Weyhing in similar fashion. The rookie outfielder had a historic debut as he devastated and annihilated the Phillies veteran to the tune of four singles and one triple in five trips to the plate at Eclipse Park. Undeterred after his magnificent performance, the rookie responded to his teammates as he reflected on his first major league game:

> Gus Weyhing, one of the better Philadelphia pitchers, was warming up, and some of the older Louisville players were encouraging enough to remark that Gus would knock my little bat right out of my hands. They used to make it real tough for a rookie breaking in. I was half inclined to believe them, but I cracked Weyhing for a hit my first time up. Well, that made me feel pretty good, but before the game ended, I had five in five times up, one a triple. When the game was over, I took the bat into our clubhouse, patted it fondly, and remarked so everybody could hear: "Well, they had a helluva time knocking this bat out of my hands today, anyway." There was nothing but silence — and a lot of it — after that.[15]

Clarke also commented about not needing a big bat to hit bushers like Weyhing.[16] The 21-year-old youth showed brass and guts standing up to teammates who had ridiculed him only hours earlier. Rookie players who joined a major league baseball team during the rough and tumble era of the 1890s

3. Fearless Youngster

usually kept their mouth shut and didn't offer unsolicited opinions or observations to veteran teammates. Clarke probably felt justified since most of his teammates had failed to deliver the goods. In spite of Clarke being perfect at the plate, Louisville lost to the Phillies 13–6.

It was not long before Clarke was imposing his hard-nosed will upon opposing National League players as well. He knew that the road to success was paved through determination and hard work. If Clarke planned on succeeding in the National League, the youngster realized the game would have to be played on his terms. At times, this meant that Clarke was the instigator when events on the field took any ugly turn. Fred Clarke found out the hard way that being prepared to retaliate when one initiates an action was crucial to long-term baseball survival during the rough and rowdy baseball played in 1894.

In a game against Brooklyn on July 10 in Louisville, Clarke drew the ire and anger of Bridegrooms catcher Con Dailey. The incident occurred when he tried to score from second base on a single by teammate Sam Dungan. Dailey was guarding the dish as Clarke tore around third base and headed toward the plate. Since the Louisville rookie arrived at home plate just as the throw from center field reached Dailey, Clarke decided that his only option was to run over the Brooklyn catcher.[17]

Fred Clarke slammed into Dailey and knocked the catcher down. Before the dazed Clarke was able to touch home plate, Dailey came over to where Fred was standing and smacked him on his back with the baseball. Dailey's left hand then connected with Clarke's face, before he countered with a crushing right that dropped Clarke to the ground. Clarke was declared out both literally and figuratively. As the umpire told Dailey to leave the grounds as hissing Louisville fans hollered, Fred Clarke laid motionless on the field.[18]

Clarke fared much better when he and Adrian "Cap" Anson had an unforgettable encounter when the two met on a baseball diamond for the first time. Clarke knew to be wary of veteran players tripping him or giving a hip check when he rounded the bases. The first time Clarke played against Anson's Chicago Colts team, the all-star first baseman tested the rookie's mettle when he reached base. Clarke responded in a manner which made his veteran teammates take notice. "I remember my first run-in with Cap," Clarke once told an interviewer. "First time I faced his club I made a hit apparently good for two bases. As I rounded first, Anson tripped me, and I had to scramble back to first. I didn't say a word, but the next time I deliberately hit an infield out and as I got to first I landed on his shoes with my spikes and ripped the shoe open. He was a rough man, with a good punch, but I knew he could never catch me. Anson was slow, and had to hit for his reputation. He let me alone after that."[19]

Clarke's speed, which had allowed him to get out of this tight situation with Anson, was the strongest asset that the outfielder possessed during his rookie campaign. Clarke appeared in 76 games for the Colonels, hitting .274 during his first season in major league baseball. Clarke's blazing speed directly led to 55 runs scored, 11 doubles and 7 triples. He also stole 26 bases during his debut season. After a few learning experiences on the basepaths in 1894 and 1895, Clarke found a proper basestealing technique that caused his body the least harm.

"Billy Hamilton of Boston was the most daring base-stealer in the league when I was at Louisville," Clarke recalled. "He was a headfirst slider and I copied his style. But not for long. One day in Washington I stole second, but the second baseman — I forget his name — tagged me to black both my eyes and break my nose. While I lay there, semi-stunned, their center fielder Tom Brown, walked in and said: 'What do you care, you got a stolen base, didn't you? Get on your feet and lets get going.' After that generous display of sympathy, I learned to slide feet first."[20]

Clarke's successful rookie season did little to improve Louisville's position in the National League standings. The Colonels placed last in the league with a 36–94 record, finishing a whopping 54 games behind the pennant-winning Baltimore Orioles. Non-descript players like John Grim, Fred Pfeffer, Danny Richardson, Larry Twitchell, Farmer Weaver and Luke Lutenberg manned positions on the 1894 Louisville team.

Manager Bill Barnie was not brought back to direct the Louisville Colonels in 1895. A man familiar to Clarke was tapped to replace Barnie. John McCloskey was signed by Louisville in an effort to pull the team out of the depths of despair. Clarke would once again be working under a man who had supreme confidence in the Iowa lad's play. This gave Clarke an even stronger advantage of gaining a spot on the 1895 team. Amazingly, pre-season prognosticators did not feel that Clarke would be part of the Louisville team when the season opened.[21]

During exhibition games played at Galveston and New Orleans, McCloskey moved Clarke throughout the batting order. He was given the responsibility of hitting fourth or fifth during most of the practice games. When the regular season opened, McCloskey once again tapped Clarke to be Louisville's starting left fielder. Batting either sixth or seventh in the order, he jumped out of the gate strong and was hitting .327 after 12 games. Clarke's strong early season play didn't go unnoticed by other National League managers. When Louisville offered pitcher Fred Knell and $400 to Cincinnati for catcher Morgan Murphy, Buck Ewing demanded Clarke and the money instead.[22]

Clarke continued to sizzle for the Colonels, even though Louisville had assumed its customary last place position in the National League standings. By the middle of June, he was hitting a solid .333 for the Falls City squad. As summer progressed, it was noted by Louisville scribes that Clarke, Frank Shugart and Mike McDermott were the only Colonels players putting up the solid article of ball that was expected from major league players.[23] McDermott's inclusion in this group seemed strange since he delivered miserably on the mound that year with a 4–19 record and an unsightly 5.99 ERA.

As Clarke progressed through his first full season of big league baseball, Louisville writers began comparing the young outfielder to other accomplished National League players. A writer from the *Louisville Times* believed that Clarke was a small version of Charles Comiskey. He felt that Clarke compared favorably to the recently retired Cincinnati Red in both appearance and demeanor on the baseball field.[24]

Clarke continued to roll as the season wore on. By the end of July, he was hitting a blistering .346. While Clarke began to show dominance at the plate, he was going through some growing pains in the outfield. The youngster played the left field position very aggressively. Clarke used his blazing speed to advantage at times as he ran down fly balls that seemed to be out of reach when they left the opposing player's bat. His overaggressive nature also caused the young outfielder many problems during the 1895 season. When the year ended, Clarke topped all outfielders with 413 chances but he also committed 49 errors in left field.

As Clarke finished his first full season of big league baseball, the youngster had an epiphany which helped to shape his attitude and demeanor toward baseball and life. Clarke began following a path of destruction that had ruined the careers of many young players before him. To gain acceptance from his teammates, he hung out with them and mimicked their behavior. Since Louisville was a team loaded with veterans who liked to pass time drinking alcohol, Clarke quickly became a master at the art of boozing.[25] In an effort to become one of the boys, Clarke was mortgaging his future as a baseball player.

> It was still a time when young ball players were supposed to be seen — not heard. I would sit and drink and would never say a word until it became my turn to order another round of drinks. But I realized I was going badly, and not helping myself.
> Barney Dreyfuss recognized it, too, and he called me into his office. He didn't lecture me, merely said: "Fred, you know if a man goes into any kind of a business and neglects it, it will surely go to the dogs." Then without saying another word, he left me.
> I couldn't get it out of my mind and I lay awake thinking about it most of the following night. Then at last I got its full meaning. I went to see him the next day and said: "From now on, Mr. Dreyfuss, it will be business." And

from that day on I never again neglected business, whether it was baseball or any other activity. I do not think any employer ever gave a young player better counsel.[26]

From that point on, Clarke cut out the nighttime carousing and decided to make baseball his only business while not allowing outside influences to interfere. This was a bold decision for a youngster of only 22 years to make. By refusing to socialize with his teammates in local gin joints, Clarke risked being ostracized by fellow Louisville players. It was his unwavering confidence in his own ability that made such a decision easier. Most of his league counterparts were rough and ready fellows. Clarke decided that he would follow their lead on the baseball diamond and not in social circles.

Clarke sizzled as Louisville secured another last place finish in 1895. The young outfielder led the team in hitting with a .347 average. Clarke also hit safely in 35 straight games during the season. He banged out 191 hits, scored 96 runs, drove in 82 and stole 40 bases. He played every inning of Louisville's 132 games and basically led the team in each offensive category. The team actually won one less game under John McCloskey than it did in 1894, but there seemed to be a sense of hope in Louisville for the first time in years. In spite of Louisville's poor showing in the standings, McCloskey seemed to be building a team that could make its way into the first division before long.

An infusion of new blood came courtesy of players such as Ducky Holmes, Tom McCreery, Frank Shugart, Jack Warner and Bert Cunningham. Jimmy Collins was loaned to the Colonels from Boston and did exceptional work for Louisville before the Beaneaters requested his return. McCloskey converted Collins from an outfielder into a crack third baseman who had few peers on the team other than Clarke. Collins liked Louisville so much that he refused to report back to Boston late in the season and went home instead.

Emboldened by the fact that Collins impressed Louisville management while playing in the Falls City, Boston offered to trade him straight-up for Fred Clarke at season's end. The Colonels ownership passed. When Dr. Thomas Hunt Stucky went to New York for the November league meetings, the Louisville magnate was hammered with offers for his star left fielder. Cincinnati offered four players and $4,000 to secure Clarke's services. New York supposedly made two offers in an effort to obtain Clarke. Giants management gave Stucky the choice of $7,000 in cash or five specific players from New York's roster.[27] Stucky rejected all offers from his league counterparts. This buoyed the hopes of Louisville fans who were happy that a rising star like Fred Clarke would remain in the fold.

As Clarke gained popularity in baseball circles, scribes began arguing over who was responsible for bringing the left fielder to Louisville. Writers from Cincinnati and the Falls City weighed in with their opinions regarding the matter. Savannah resident De Jay See rejected the notions of each city's writers when he shed new light on Clarke's discovery in a letter that appeared in a January 1896 issue of *Sporting Life*:

> In reading your valuable columns in last week's issue I was rather amused at the controversy between your worthy "scribes" of Louisville and Cincinnati in regard to the discovery of Fred Clarke. If you will allow me a little space I will throw some light on the discovery of this shining star. As both of the above gentlemen have told you that Clarke was playing in our city up to the time that he went to Louisville, the next question is how did he get to Louisville and who recommended him. The way was thus:
>
> Mr. John J. Horrigan, of this city, on perceiving that the Southern League would not last, recommended Clarke to Manager Manning, of Kansas City, but at that time Manning had three good outfielders and did not want another, so he told Manager Cushman, of Milwaukee, that Clarke was recommended to him by Mr. Horrigan, and as he (Manning) had no place for him and Cushman was at the time strengthening his team Manager Manning advised Mr. Cushman to secure Clarke at once on Mr. Horrigan's recommendation. So Cushman at once wired here for Mr. Horrigan to get Clarke's terms and sign him for Milwaukee.
>
> Everything then was arranged for Cushman to secure Clarke and it was only left for Cushman to send the advance money and the transportation ticket for Clarke; but Cushman in place of wiring the necessary ticket sent it by mail, and as Clarke counted on receiving it by wire, when it did not come as was expected he, of course, thought Cushman had given him up.
>
> In the meantime a player by the name of Wolfe, who had played with the Macon team that season, had gone to Louisville before the disbanding of the Southern League, and told the Louisville magnates that Clarke was a fast man and it would be well for Louisville to sign him. So they at once wired Clarke for his terms, and when they received an answer they immediately wired Clarke a ticket to Louisville.
>
> All the time the Louisville deal was going on while Clarke was waiting for his ticket from Milwaukee; and Clarke would have waited on Milwaukee had not Mr. Horrigan advised him to accept the offer from Louisville. The next day the ticket arrived from Cushman, but it was too late — the bird was caged.
>
> While I admit that McCloskey was the first one that discovered Clarke, I say the real one to put him where he is was Mr. John J. Horrigan, of this city. Mr. Barnie did not in any way bring Clarke to Louisville, nor can he be accredited with any part in his discovery. The Cincinnati writer was wrongly informed on this subject. The Louisville writers have good grounds for contention, when they say that McCloskey was the discoverer; but Mr. Horrigan has the best claims, and Fred Clarke will not doubt tell you so.[28]

It is hard to say if Mr. See's description of events leading to Fred Clarke's discovery has any validity. His theory regarding who helped bring Clarke to Louisville eliminated Barney Dreyfuss as being a major player in the signing.

This seemed very unlikely since Dreyfuss actually did scout Clarke, watched him play in Memphis and subsequently closed a deal with McCloskey. During a time in history where importance was given to the person who discovered a great baseball player, inconsistencies were bound to arise when someone was not given his due.

For the second year in a row, Clarke spent his off-season at home in Des Moines helping out on the family farm. Clarke believed that hard work was the proper tonic for remaining in good shape during the winter. Prior to the start of spring training, his optimism was bubbling as he talked about Louisville's prospects in 1896. "Well; anybody who thinks we will be last can get a $100 suit of clothes at my expense. I am confident we will give a good account of ourselves. All the new men Manager McCloskey has signed are winners, and, take my word for it; the Colonels will be heard from. We have a good man in McFarland. Given a proper show he will make his mark in fast company. I have played with him and know just what he can do. When he gets his eye on the ball he can hit with any them in the big league."[29]

Clarke's hopefulness was quickly dashed once the 1896 season commenced. Louisville got off to a horrible start, costing McCloskey his job on May 9 as the Colonels lost 17 of their first 19 games. Bill McGunnigle, who had previous experience managing Brooklyn and Pittsburgh, was chosen to replace McCloskey as Louisville's new leader. McGunnigle walked into a tough situation. When he assumed control of the team, the Colonels were already firmly entrenched in last place, 11½ games behind league leading Philadelphia.

Things did not go as smoothly for Clarke either during his third big league season. Louisville fans were becoming disgusted with the wretched play of the team and quickly turned on the players. Clarke received his fair share of roasting during an August series against Brooklyn when he muffed two fly balls in left field. The hissing bleacher dwellers booed their favorite son and demanded that he be removed from the game.[30]

Clarke's luck only became worse when Louisville rolled into Cincinnati for an August series against the Reds. During the final game of the series on Sunday, August 9, Clarke let his anger get the best of him. Players from the Louisville team believed that umpire Bud Lally was in Cincinnati's "back pocket" throughout the series, due to many questionable calls that seemed to favor the Reds. Rumors abounded that Lally was hand picked to umpire a string of home games in order to help Cincinnati in the pennant race.[31]

Three days prior to this game, Lally and star pitcher Frank Killen of the Pittsburgh Pirates had come to blows on the diamond after a questionable call. Cincinnati police came on the field and arrested Killen.[32] History repeated itself on August 9 when Fred Clarke struck the umpire after he became enraged when Lally made an unfavorable decision. Once again, Lally retaliated and punched Clarke. Players from both teams interjected before the fight gathered steam. Local law representatives entered the picture, escorting both Clarke and Lally to a nearby jailhouse.[33] Clarke was subsequently chided in the newspapers for placing his good name at risk by striking an umpire. Lally received criticism for demeaning himself by engaging in such pugilistic tactics.[34]

Despite some of these less memorable moments, Clarke still had a solid season for the Colonels in 1896. His average did drop off a bit from the previous year as he hit .325. Louisville's star player scored 96 runs, smacked 15 doubles, hit 18 triples and stroked nine home runs while knocking in 79. Clarke made 30 errors in left field, but gunned down 18 mischievous baserunners.

Louisville made it a perfect last-place trifecta during Clarke's time there as the team once again finished at the bottom, with a 38–93 record. More new players such as Charlie Dexter, Billy Clingman, Bill Hill and Charles "Chick" Fraser were brought in to improve the team's fortunes. Fraser did yeoman's work on the mound during his rookie season, although his 12–27 record and 4.87 ERA indicated that the youngster did experience some growing pains. Clarke and Fraser quickly became good friends during the 1896 season and were inseparable companions throughout the year.

When the season ended, Clarke joined Fraser in Chick's hometown of Chicago. Clarke went into business with another man in the Windy City and began dealing in butter, eggs, rice and sugar.[35] In order to stay in shape since he would not be working on his father's farm, Clarke played indoor baseball while his new business venture blossomed. Clarke quickly became a favorite of the Chicago fans.[36] When Fred had spare time, he usually hung out with Fraser and some of the pitcher's Chicago acquaintances. In November, Louisville team president Harry Pulliam invited Clarke and Fraser to join him at the National League meetings, which were being held in the Windy City.[37]

Rumors preceding the meetings indicated that New York was willing to offer pitcher Amos Rusie to the Colonels for Fred Clarke.[38] This trade didn't have much basis since it seemed very unlikely that Pulliam would have invited Clarke to join him if the Louisville executive intended to trade the star outfielder. Pulliam's purpose in allowing Clarke and Fraser to join him was twofold. He wanted some familiar faces nearby to make the trip more enjoyable. He also wanted Clarke to experience what the league meetings were all about so the youngster could get a taste of how baseball looked from management's perspective.

While Clarke was in Chicago, Louisville publications were roasting the outfielder because he hadn't yet come to terms on a contract for the 1897 season.

It was intimated that Clarke intended to holdout until he was guaranteed the salary limit befitting a man of his talent and ability. Many scribes claimed that Clarke should be happy with his present salary situation since the youngster's play had dropped off slightly in 1896.[39]

All of these accusations were without merit. Clarke had told one newspaperman before he left for Chicago that when the proper time arrived, he would sign his contract for 1897 without any further incident. Clarke believed that Louisville management was treating him fairly and he really enjoyed playing in the Falls City.[40] Little did Clarke know that many changes in the young outfielder's life were looming on the horizon. More responsibility would soon be placed on his shoulders and expectations were destined to reach immeasurable proportions.

Chapter 4

The Original Boy Wonder Manager

Clarke did not come to terms with the Louisville club until Pulliam went back to Chicago and hammered out contract details with the outfielder in late March. It seemed that Clarke was slated to make $1800 for the 1897 season. After much discussion between player and magnate, it was rumored that Clarke received a contract that called for the player to receive $2100 during the upcoming season. He signed the contract and stated that no one would work harder to further Louisville's cause in the National League and that the club's success was his top priority.[1]

Before Clarke went to Louisville's West Baden spring training site to sign his contract, he attended to an important life-changing event in Chicago. His new best friend, Chick Fraser, was settling down and marrying the daughter of a prominent Chicago glass maker.[2] Fraser had become smitten by the charms of one Mina Gray and the two exchanged vows on St. Patrick's Day.[3] The ceremony was a gala event that included a small contingent of family and friends. Clarke was one of the invited guests. Since Fraser was a ball player, the event did receive some press coverage:

> Chick Fraser, the Colonel's pitcher, will not reach Louisville until about April 1, for the reason that he is now on his bridal tour through the South and does not expect to reach Louisville until the time mentioned.
>
> Fraser was married Wednesday evening, March 17, at the home of the parents of the bride, Miss Mina Gray, Clybourn Place, Chicago. The Rev. E.M. Griffin was the officiating clergyman. After partaking of an elegant lunch and when the hand-shaking was over the couple started on a tour of the South. Mr. and Mrs. Fraser will make Louisville their home in the future.
>
> The bridesmaid was Miss Annette Gray, a sister of the bride, and the best man was Mr. Joseph Luby, the pitcher, who formerly played with the

Louisville team and who has been Fraser's chum for years. Only a few friends and the members of both families were present. The house was prettily decorated with flowers and potted plants, and Tomasco's orchestra furnished music for the occasion.[4]

Just as Fraser had fallen for Mina, so too was Clarke attracted to Annette Gray, the maid of honor in this ceremony. Clarke and his business partner had been with Fraser on many occasions when the pitcher visited the Gray residence. As time went by, Fred and Annette began to kindle a relationship that the Louisville player preferred to keep private.[5] Clarke was always willing to talk baseball. He just didn't believe in baseball writers infringing on his private life.

When Clarke reported to spring training, the youngster found that he would be playing for his fourth manager in as many years. McGunnigle's services were not retained and 25-year-old Jim Rogers was named to manage the Louisville Colonels. This choice seemed odd since Rogers only had one season of big league baseball under his belt, splitting the 1896 season playing for both Washington and Louisville. Faithful fans figured that if the Louisville front office wanted to experiment by the turning the reins over to a young manager, that man should have been Clarke.

What the Falls City fans didn't know was that Clarke had been considered as a viable replacement for McGunnigle during the winter. Louisville's ownership hierarchy gave the matter much thought but then decided that his off-field activities indicated Clarke was still too immature to be trusted with such responsibility.[6] It probably hadn't helped Clarke's cause any when he refused to sign his 1897 contract in an expeditious manner. For the time being, Clarke would continue to provide leadership as a player and help the team any way that he could as captain of the Louisville team.

As the 1897 season moved into the hot days of summer, Rogers actually had the Colonels in ninth place with a 17–24 record on June 15. Rogers seemed to have Louisville headed in the right direction, but there was one major problem — he was a lousy ballplayer. Through 42 games of action, the second baseman was only hitting .144. Louisville ownership needed a manager who could lead the team both in the clubhouse and on the field. Because Rogers was sadly deficient in one of these areas, he was abruptly shown the door.

On June 16, 1897, Clarke was named to replace Rogers as manager of the Louisville Colonels. Since Clarke was the best player on the squad by far, it stood to reason that he should be given an opportunity to the lead the charges as its manager. The local fans loved and adored Clarke.[7] They believed that Stucky, Dreyfuss and Pulliam made the correct decision by naming Clarke to manage Louisville. Writer C.L. Moore certainly believed that Louisville made a wise choice. "Fred Clarke, if given proper support by the President and Directors of the Louisville Club will undoubtedly get together a lot of

4. The Original Boy Wonder Manager

Fred Clarke was appointed to the Louisville Colonels managerial post on June 16, 1897. Honus Wagner was one of the first players Clarke added to his squad when he purchased the Flying Dutchman from Paterson, New Jersey, in July. In this 1897 team photograph, Clarke and Wagner are third and fourth from the left in the second row.

fast ball players and win a good per cent of the games yet to be played," wrote Moore. "Besides being one of the greatest players on the diamond, Fred Clarke knows a player when he sees one. Every fan in the city was glad to see Fred get the place and we feel that he will in a few days have the boys playing good ball and making a strong fight for every game. Everybody will admit that Fred knows the game from A to Z and all believe him capable of imparting his knowledge of the game to the other boys with great results."[8]

Clarke received a $500 salary bump after he was named to manage the Louisville Colonels.[9] Managing must have agreed with him since the left fielder had his best season to date on the baseball diamond. Clarke finished second behind Willie Keeler for top batting honors in 1897 with a .390 batting average (it was recorded at the time that Clarke hit .407, but this was adjusted at a later date). He banged out 205 hits, scored 122 runs, hit 30 doubles, smashed 13 triples and stole 59 bases. Clarke did everything in his power that season on the field in an effort to set a proper example for his teammates.

From a management standpoint, Clarke began to assemble the type of team that was fast and could hit. In July, John Henry Wagner was purchased from Paterson, New Jersey, of the Atlantic League. Wagner was a big man who had a chest of iron, long arms, bowed legs, and hands the size of steam shovel buckets. The German outfielder from Carnegie, Pennsylvania, was an Ed Barrow discovery who could clout the ball and catch it with equal precision. Wagner made a quick impression on Manager Clarke by hitting .335 in 62 games. Good fortune during a series in New York had given Clarke a player who seemed to possess the tools that would make him a star someday. "The state Sunday blue law was in effect then," Clarke said, "and we had the day off. I went over to Paterson with Barrow to see Wagner play. That night Barrow put Wagner on the train for Louisville with a sack of bananas to keep him happy. Wagner came to Louisville as an outfielder. That meant nothing. He was a player who could do everything, play anywhere and be a star."[10]

Louisville management continued to scour the country looking for baseball talent. In August, a diminutive infielder named Tommy Leach was purchased from Auburn of the New York State League for $650. On August 25, Louisville signed a husky free agent southpaw pitcher from Butler County, Pennsylvania, named Rube Waddell. The young twirler recently had been given a trial with the Pittsburgh Pirates that didn't last past breakfast after Manager Patsy Donovan tired of the youngster's incessant babbling during the morning meal. Waddell's first encounter with his new manager had a lasting effect on Clarke when Rube reported for duty aboard Louisville's baseball craft.

"We were in Washington and I was awakened about 1:30 one morning by a pounding on the door. I opened the door to see a tall, well-set-up chap," Clarke remembered.

"He said: 'Don't you know me Fred? I'm Rube, your new pitcher. Can you let me have $2?'

"I didn't know whether to fine him right then. But I found myself laughing instead. Maybe it was the 'Rube' business. It fitted him.

"I told him to go see the secretary for the two bucks. I couldn't help adding, ironically, 'And why don't you go around and meet all the boys, as long as you are here?'

"He did it. The whole team told me the next day about the hick screwball who had got them up in the middle of the night. But none of them were mad at Rube, in a day when a new boy couldn't find out what time it was from a regular. The Rube had that charm from the start."[11]

Waddell only saw action in two late-season games before Louisville shipped him to Detroit of the Western League in November. The free spirit was probably proud of his manager when Clarke pulled the kind of late-season stunt against Chicago that would typify Waddell's career. After Clarke stole second base in a loss to the Colts, he proceeded to knock the bag loose. He picked up second base and continued his journey to the third base bag. When

4. The Original Boy Wonder Manager

Clarke was tagged out near third, he stopped dead in his tracks and claimed he was still on second base since his hands were wrapped around the bag.[12]

The umpire did not agree with Clarke's logic and called the Louisville manager out. The Chicago fans howled with delight as they watched the spectacle. Clarke himself had a good laugh as he returned to the dugout. Unfortunately, the next Colonels batter recorded a hit that would have scored Clarke and a subsequent blast that came from the following player at the plate would have brought home the deciding tally.[13]

Earlier in the season, a few weeks after he was named to the managerial post, Clarke showed compassion to a youngster in this same Chicago ballpark. Clarke's generous nature brought back memories of Richard "Dad" Phelan from 1888 in Des Moines when Clarke secured his first pair of baseball shoes. W.A. Phelon described how Clarke made the dream of a lifetime come true for a boy who came from Clarke's same prairie background by giving him a chance to play for Louisville.

> There was a 16-year-old prairie boy named Frank Martin, who used to come around the park mornings and chase balls for the players. He was petted considerable by Griffith and Ryan, and showed himself, for a small boy, a wonder in catching and throwing. On the morning after the great victory, he came to the park, practiced awhile, and then, figuring the groundskeeper would throw him out when it was time for the game, hid behind the bleachers. He sent out another kid for a pie, and was sitting there eating the pie when Fred Clarke approached him.
>
> "I want you to play in the game this afternoon," said Clarke.
>
> The kid looked at him in a dazed way. "Watcher giving me?" said he. Clarke assured him that he meant it, and uniformed him without delay. He went in, and played a hot game, subsequently going to Louisville with the team. Thus did the youngest infielder ever seen in the National League break into the game—from kid peeping through the fence to second baseman of the Louisvilles.[14]

Young Frank Martin only played in two games for the Colonels, recording two hits in eight trips to the plate and committing three errors at second base. Martin would see minimal action with Chicago in 1898 and New York in 1899 before his baseball career ended. If it had not been for the kind heart of Clarke, the teenager may never have realized his dream of playing in a big league baseball game.

Clarke guided his troops to an eleventh place finish in 1897 as Louisville crossed the finish line with a 52–78 record. Clarke himself posted a mark of 35–54 and saw the team drop two spots in the standings after the left fielder replaced Rogers. As the season was concluding, Dr. Stucky decided to give Pulliam total control over player procurement for the upcoming season.[15] Stucky also wanted Clarke to be heavily involved in cultivating Louisville's roster. The doctor was happy that Fred was guiding the squad, but he pondered what the team would have done if McGunnigle and Clarke had been leading the charges.[16]

"We have given Pulliam full control," said Dr. Stucky, "and he is privileged to do as he chooses in regard to engagements and releases. The directors are well satisfied with the way the club has been handled and the present arrangement will be continued in 1898. In Fred Clarke the club has at last found a capable manager and he will be retained. I wanted Clarke made captain last year. I still have confidence in McGunnigle's judgment of ball players; and believe that if Mac had been retained with Clarke as his right bower Louisville to-day would be up in the first four."[17]

Clarke did briefly hand over the managerial reins to a subordinate in September so he could attend the wedding of his business partner in Chicago. The bride was another member of the Gray family, John and Ellen's oldest daughter Mary. Rumors swirling around Clarke himself indicated that he was engaged to Annette Gray and the two were expected to get married sometime in 1898.[18] When pressed to give details regarding this matter in his private life, Clarke remained silent, refusing to offer any information which denied or corroborated the tales of love and romance.

Clarke once again attended to his business interests in Chicago during the off-season. While he was selling rice, sugar, eggs and butter, Pulliam was determined to make changes that would improve Louisville's team. Reports from the National League meetings stated that Cincinnati wanted to trade infielder Claude Ritchey to the Colonels for Fred Clarke and pitcher Bill Hill.[19] Another story claimed that Reds management had offered Louisville $10,000 for Clarke's services earlier in the year.[20] Neither deal was seriously considered from Pulliam's side of the table.

Louisville and Cincinnati did make a deal on February 3, 1898, when the Reds shipped Ritchey, outfielder Dummy Hoy and pitcher Red Ehret to the Falls City for Hill. In Ritchey, the Colonels received a young infielder who would solve their second base problem. Hoy was a veteran outfielder counted upon to strengthen the center field position. Honus Wagner was one player who responded happily when newspapers reported that he hadn't been part of this deal. Rumors had circulated to the effect that Cincinnati demanded Wagner once they realized attempts to acquire Clarke were futile. "I would hate to leave Louisville," said a relieved Wagner, "as I have many good friends in that city and the kindly treatment I received makes me have a warm spot in my heart for the Kentucky metropolis, but I suppose if the club people want to chase me away I will have to go. If I can benefit the team any by being traded, I am perfectly willing. If I remain it will get my best services, for I am not ungrateful and appreciate good treatment."[21]

If Wagner hoped to remain in the outfield for Louisville, he was destined to be sadly disappointed. As Clarke prepared to oversee his first training camp at West Baden Springs in Indiana, the manager made it clear that many of the spots on the roster were wide open. "There is no certainty about the position of hardly any of our men," said Clarke. "What I want to do is make up a team of the best batters. That trade did a whole lot of good and will go far toward bracing up our weak spots. I don't know how the rooters feel in the matter, but I think we got decidedly the best of the Reds in the dicker. While Bill Hill is a good pitcher and will be of splendid service to Ewing's crowd, we get in exchange for him a good fielding and hard-hitting shortstop, a fine outfielder and a pitcher who is equal to the average in the league at least. This leaves us only second base and right field to look after. If we can not do any better, either Wagner or Smith will be good enough men to take care of the middle bag. If Dillard lacks the ability to hold his place in league company, that old war horse, Jimmie Stafford, is a pretty fair candidate for the position. I feel confident with the men we have now we ought to be able to make a good stand against any of them."[22]

Things did not start off very well for Clarke and his Colonels once the season began. Wagner, Ritchey, Hoy and Clarke himself struggled mightily at the plate during the early months of the campaign. By the end of June, Louisville stood in its customary last place position with a 21–42 record. Wagner's slump at the plate was attributed to the fact that he was constantly being moved around to every infield position but shortstop. Louisville fans believed that Clarke's troubles on the field directly correlated to pressure from his responsibility as team manager.

Critics quickly turned on Clarke, saying he was a disappointment as a team leader who had not achieved the success that was expected of him. Many felt that the worries which came with the job affected his performance on the diamond.[23] It was also surmised that Clarke was derelict in asserting his authority when men like Chick Fraser and Bill Wilson did as they pleased and interfered with him running the team properly.[24] Baseball scribes believed that Fraser had the tools that would make him a star pitcher someday. They just didn't foresee this happening while he was playing on a team run by one of his best friends.[25] Clarke was so inundated he supposedly considered relinquishing his managerial responsibilities during the summer.

Clarke did have a lot on his plate during the 1898 season. This was his first full season as manager of the Louisville club. With expectations high for the first time in years, the pressure to succeed was great. Fred Clarke was now the clear-cut, bonafide star of the Falls City team and had become a fan favorite after only a few seasons. Great things were expected of Clarke both as a player and manager. It was also possible that he felt a little stressed since the rumors regarding summertime nuptials were actually true.

It was announced that Fred Clifford Clarke and Annette Bertilla Gray would wed on July 5. The Colonels were in Cincinnati on July 4. The plan called for Clarke to leave the team after the game and arrive in Chicago for his wedding. After the ceremony, bride and groom would then head to Pittsburgh and join the team for its next game on July 7.[26] The gala event received much press coverage, given the fact that Clarke was now considered one of the top stars in baseball:

> Fred Clarke is a benedict. He was married in the city yesterday afternoon to Miss Annette B. Gray. The ceremony was performed at the Church of the Annunciation, the Rev. Father E.M. Griffin officiating. The whole wedding party assembled about 3 o'clock at the house and proceeded in carriages to the church, where the couple were united. The wedding profession from the house to the church was headed by John Carlson's band of 20 pieces. The presents were many and handsome. Among them was a silver table service from the directors of the Louisville Club. The members of the club sent a handsome silver ice cream service. A silver water set was presented by Chicago friends, and there were numerous other handsome gifts in silver. The groom presented the bride with a valuable set of diamond earrings. Congratulatory telegrams were received from all the base ball clubs in the League, as well as many private messages. Mrs. Clarke is a sister of Mrs. "Chick" Fraser.[27]

Later in the summer, Clarke received accolades of a different sort from Cap Anson. The star National Leaguer who retired in 1897 wasn't giving out congratulations for the Louisville player's recent marriage to Annette Gray. He was bringing to light the fact that Clarke was indeed the best player in the National League. Anson also pointed out that Clarke had earned the dubious distinction of being the league's dirtiest performer as well.[28] "He used to keep me busy getting out of his way when he would come tearing down the first base line," remarked Anson. "Once he tore my shoe off with his spikes. After he left the field, though, he was as gentlemanly as one could wish. But that boy does try too hard to win. In my opinion he is the best ball player in the world to-day, though Bill Lange runs him a close second."[29]

Anson was correct when he assessed Clarke's psyche and temperament. Clarke did try very hard to win. He put it all on the line both as a player and manager each and every day. Things hadn't gone well for the Colonels during the early stages of the 1898 season. This all changed as the team hit stride when the summer heat began blazing through the Falls City. From July through season's end, Clarke guided his troops to a 49–39 record. This brought Louisville up to ninth place with a final mark of 70–81, 33 games behind the pennant-winning Boston Beaneaters.

At one point during the season, Clarke's average was floundering around the .250 mark. He righted the ship and finished the season at .307. Clarke recorded 184 hits, scored 116 runs, pounded 23 doubles, stroked 12 triples and stole 40 bases. Wagner also pulled out of the depths of early season batting despair, hitting .299 and leading the team with 10 home runs and 105 runs batted in.

Youngsters like Clarke's little brother Josh were given trials throughout the season. The 19-year-old outfielder saw action in only six games for his older brother's team. Josh's .167 average proved that the younger Clarke was not quite ready for professional baseball. Another late season addition named Billy "Will" Taylor only played nine games for the Colonels in September, but that was enough time for the Pittsburgh native to realize that Clarke possessed strong leadership qualities.

"Manager Clarke of the Louisville club is an excellent manager and when it comes to playing the outfield he has them all beaten with ease," said Taylor. "I never saw a man who could go back with the ball and take it while running at full speed with the ease and grace that characterizes Clarke's performances. He is certainly the greatest in the business. He also played a wonderful game for the Colonels. Yes, I look for the Louisville club to be an important factor in the league race next season. It is one of the fastest team's in the country."[30]

Louisville's on-field success during the second half of the season did not translate into a huge triumph at the box office. The Colonels had so many financial difficulties that many National League executives believed Louisville would be one of the teams to go if the 12-team aggregation should be pared down. Financial disaster was averted when Stucky and the other Louisville owners reached into their own pockets and paid off team debt. Barney Dreyfuss was the most generous of the group, putting up $6,000 in order to pay bills and insure that every player received his salary.[31]

Dreyfuss now was considered the majority owner of the Louisville club. With this designation also came a new title. The Louisville Board of Directors decided that Dreyfuss would become the team president for 1899. He was permitted to represent Louisville in this capacity at the 1898 December league meetings in New York.[32] Barney remained in the Big Apple after the meetings, hoping to sell his club to Giants owner Andrew Freedman. Dreyfuss, however, quickly realized that Freedman wasn't interested in his plight.

"As a final offer I suggested that Freedman exchange Rusie for Dexter, but I absolutely refused to sell Clarke," Dreyfuss said. "The latter receives $3600 a year from Louisville for his services as a player, captain and manager. If we should let him go our club would not be worth a cent. If the League wants to cut the circuit down to eight clubs Louisville can be bought out. Otherwise we are prepared to continue in the twelve-club league. Including $6700 paid out for players the Louisville Club finished $13,000 behind on last season."[33]

Freedman was willing to pay Louisville $10,000 to secure Fred Clarke's services.[34] The New York owner just didn't want to buy the whole team. Dreyfuss was not interested in selling his only box office draw. Freedman's decision not to purchase Louisville was wise since players from that team could be available if Louisville was eliminated from the National League. Dreyfuss showed prudence by not handing over Clarke. If the Colonels were to push onward in 1899, they would need their fearless leader and strongest player.

While Dreyfuss was attempting to sell the Colonels in New York, Clarke was spending the winter in Chicago. He broke away from the Windy City for a few weeks to go hunting in Kansas and the Oklahoma territory.[35] Upon returning to Chicago, Clarke once again attended to his lucrative business enterprises. He also planned to finalize deals for pieces of land in Iowa and Kansas for which he had placed down payments years before. The chunk of Kansas land was located near Udall where young Fred Clarke had been put off a train when he ran away from home 15 years ago. Clarke had vowed on that day to make this place his home someday.

Minor changes were made to the Louisville team for 1899. Clarke's brother-in-law, Chick Fraser, had been sold to the Cleveland Spiders the previous September. With a spot in the rotation needing to be filled, Dreyfuss made two moves hoping to improve his pitching staff. Walt Woods was acquired from Chicago for future considerations in January. Louisville also selected Charles "Deacon" Phillippe from Minneapolis of the Western League as part of the 1899 major league draft. Phillippe came highly recommended, although it did not look as if the young twirler would be signing anytime soon. There was a large gap in salary between both parties which only was eliminated through divine intervention before Louisville left for spring training.

"Deacon Phillippe," said Dreyfuss, "was with the Minneapolis Club when I purchased his release and sent him a contract for $1,000 for the season. Phillippe answered that he would not sign for less than $1,500, and I did not pay any attention to him for awhile. When I next wrote him he answered that he would not come to Louisville for less than $2,000. I made up my mind there and then to pay no more attention to him. Well, on the morning that the team was to start for its training grounds a young fellow walked into my office and introduced himself as Phillippe. I told him I had no business with him and he said: 'Well, I am here, and want to sign with you at your terms. What I wrote to you don't go. I have lost all I have in a fire, and so I concluded to come to you at your terms.' Phillippe has never regretted that."[36]

Dreyfuss and Clarke certainly didn't regret the fact that Phillippe came to terms with Louisville. Deacon started 38 games for the Colonels, posting a 21–17 record with an ERA of 3.17. Two other youngsters who had previously seen minimal action in Louisville also became a more vital presence on the team in 1899. Tommy Leach split time between shortstop and third base after a brief trial in 1898. Leach hit .288 in 106 games. Night owl Rube Waddell came back in September, courtesy of the Columbus–Grand Rapids team. Waddell showed much better form than in his first trial with the Colonels, going 7–2 for the month with a 3.08 ERA.

Dreyfuss and the board of directors were indignant early in the year when Louisville lost 11 Sunday dates from the schedule during a league meeting in March.[37] This freeze out policy also included three other teams that the league seemed intent on eliminating. A compromise was eventually reached with owners Hart, Robison and Brush where Sunday dates were added involving Chicago, St. Louis, Cincinnati and Louisville.[38] This slightly appeased Dreyfuss, but the fact remained that Louisville's National League franchise was hanging by a thread. The 1899 season followed a usual pattern for the Louisville team. They started slowly and found themselves in tenth place with a 22–40 record on July 1.

Clarke had some problems of his own regarding the manner in which some of his players felt about the Louisville manager. A faction had developed that believed that he was much too loyal to ownership. They felt that Clarke was managing with his employer's interests in mind rather than their own.[39] This group only included a few players. The vast majority of the team was determined to stick by Clarke and do anything that their manager asked.

Catcher Malachi Kittridge was believed to be one of these dissenting players. A rift between catcher and manager had supposedly developed after the team started poorly. Dreyfuss released Kittridge during the summer. On June 9, veteran catcher Chief Zimmer was purchased to replace the malcontent player. Zimmer quickly became a calming influence on the team and was a great aid to manager Clarke. Louisville finished strong during the last three months of the season, concluding with a record of 75–77. While this was still only good enough for a ninth place finish, Louisville had achieved its greatest success in years.

The season was not a total disaster for Clarke. On August 2, wife Annette gave birth to a baby girl who was christened Helen Louise Clarke. Clarke was a happy father for the first time. Louisville's faithful presented Clarke with a baby buggy when the team returned home from an eastern trip on August 22.[40]

Clarke also returned to dominating form on the baseball diamond. After a less than stellar performance at the plate in 1898, he bounced back nicely and batted .340. That average was good for second on the squad behind Wagner's team-leading .341 mark. Clarke also banged out 206 hits, scored 122 runs, smacked 23 doubles, recorded nine triples and stole 49 bases. Clarke's cannon arm from left field threw out 20 opposing runners who were reckless on the basepaths.

Unfortunately, Louisville's strong season-ending performance could not be enjoyed by the loyal Falls City faithful. On the morning of August 12, the grandstand at Eclipse Park was destroyed by fire. Lightning was the culprit as Western Union lines were hit, sparking the blaze that reduced part of Louisville's ballpark to ashes.[41] When the Colonels returned home on August 22, they attempted to play and make do with squalor conditions at the park. Attendance sagged as patrons objected to having to stand or sit in positions that caused discomfort. They were also subjected to the blazing August sun since there was no longer a roof cover.[42]

After the Colonels played Washington at Eclipse Park on September 2, Dreyfuss decided that it would be prudent to transfer the remaining home games to other cities. Dreyfuss claimed that the team was running a net loss of $200 per game since fire destroyed the grandstand.[43] Dreyfuss had to act against his loyal patrons in order to pump some capital into the fledgling franchise.

Louisville closed out the abbreviated home schedule on September 2 when they obliterated Washington, 25–4. Clarke contributed to the rout, going five-for-seven at the plate. He also scored three runs and smacked a home run. Many fans in attendance believed that they were witnessing the last major league game in Louisville history. A majority of National League magnates were intent on reducing the league from 12 teams to eight. If this occurred, Louisville was a prime candidate to be eliminated.

Rooters who attended this final game were entertained by Clarke in typical fashion. The youngster who had started his Louisville career like lightning by recording five hits on September 30, 1894, blazed his way out of town by duplicating that feat in grand style. Although big league baseball would soon be dead in Louisville, Clarke had loyally entertained the Falls City faithful for six years, leaving a strong imprint on the national game.

Chapter 5

Goodbye Louisville, Hello Pittsburgh

After the 1899 season, Fred Clarke headed for his farm in Kansas, where it was his intention to enjoy his whole off-season hunting with dog in tow and gun close at hand. Clarke also spent some time with his wife and baby daughter. Because Clarke had been thrifty with his money since he entered the arena as a professional athlete, he could ably provide for his family. In addition to a farm near Winfield, Kansas, and another in Iowa, his interests in a few Chicago business ventures were bringing Clarke nice monetary returns that supplemented his earnings from baseball.[1]

While Clarke was enjoying the fruits of his labor, Barney Dreyfuss continued to search for a way to remain in major league baseball as an owner. As expected, the National League had decided to eliminate four teams from the 12-team league: Baltimore, Cleveland, Louisville and Washington. Dreyfuss had correctly anticipated that his team was to be one of the four to go, so the magnate put a plan in place to avoid being squeezed out of baseball.

When it became apparent to Dreyfuss that his Louisville club would be placed on the chopping block, he began negotiations with other magnates. Louisville players like Fred Clarke and Honus Wagner were his biggest bargaining chip, which would be used to secure the best deal. Dreyfuss negotiated with various teams in the West before making the Eastern swing from Louisville. Chicago and St. Louis looked like the early favorites to strike a deal with Dreyfuss, but it was Pittsburgh owner William Kerr who structured a deal that interested Dreyfuss the most.

Kerr and Dreyfuss hammered out a deal that seemed amenable to both sides. Dreyfuss was going to make the trip to Pittsburgh on November 3 and pay Kerr the option price of $70,000 which would allow Barney to become a partner within the Pirates ownership hierarchy.² Kerr then had a change of heart. When the Pirates owner found that the National League was being condensed to eight teams, he decided that selling was no longer an option.³ Dreyfuss was surprised when he reached Pittsburgh and found that Kerr had changed his mind.

"I am sorry that I cannot leave the sum of money I have with me in Pittsburgh," said Dreyfuss. "But Mr. Kerr does not want it, and I guess I'll take it home. I brought it on to pay off the balance on the purchase of the club. Mr. Kerr, however, would not give me a guarantee that there was more than 850 shares of club stock issued, or that the club debts exceeded $586. He admitted that if he were the buyer in such a deal he would want such a guarantee. He said my agreement as drawn was all right, but still he wouldn't sign anything. So the deal is off."⁴

Ostensibly, Kerr initially killed the deal because Dreyfuss wanted guarantees regarding debt and issued shares of stock since Dreyfuss was handing over a large sum of money.⁵ Many believed that Kerr used these pre-conditions as an excuse. The truth of the matter was that Kerr did not like the stipulation which stated Dreyfuss would be permitted to run the Pirates without meddling or interference from other board directors.⁶ Such an agreement would have stripped Kerr of the authority he now enjoyed.

This setback did not mean that the deal was dead. Kerr and partner Phil Auten had hemorrhaged heavy monetary losses during the past few seasons and were desperate for an infusion of cash. Dreyfuss had plenty of greenbacks which would help make the Pittsburgh Pirates fiscally solvent once again. The Louisville owner was also able to offer star players like Clarke along with the monetary capital. It was the inclusion of Louisville's best players in the transaction that sealed the deal as Kerr agreed to Dreyfuss' proposal.

Clarke left his farm in Kansas and joined Dreyfuss and Pulliam in Pittsburgh. The biggest deal in baseball history was consummated on December 8, 1899 at Kerr's office in the Arbuckle Building. Louisville shipped pitchers Rube Waddell, Bert Cunningham, Patsy Flaherty, Walt Woods and Deacon Phillippe; first baseman Mike Kelley; second baseman Claude Ritchey; third baseman Tommy Leach; catchers Chief Zimmer and Tacks Latimer; and outfielders Honus Wagner and Fred Clarke to Pittsburgh. In return, the Pirates sent Jack Chesbro, George Fox, John O'Brien, Art Madison and $25,000 to Louisville.⁷

Clarke quickly gave this trade his ringing endorsement. Many baseball pundits believed that a deal had already been struck which would make him the Pittsburgh Pirates manager in 1900. If this were the case, Clarke would have an abundance of riches from which to choose when constructing a team for the season. Pittsburgh was a team that had performed only slightly better

5. Goodbye Louisville, Hello Pittsburgh

than Louisville during the nineties. Like the Colonels, they too had begun to stockpile young ballplayers who seemed to display much potential. Clarke was looking forward to molding both groups into a strong, pennant contending outfit.

"I am more than pleased with the deal," said Clarke after the announcement. "Yes, I consider myself most fortunate — in fact, I can not recall an instance where a manager of a National League club had so much excellent material from which to select a team. I do not anticipate any trouble when it comes to the task of placing the men, and if nothing happens I am satisfied that the Pittsburgh Club next season will become one of the strongest ever known in the National League. Look at the pitching talent we have at our command; then glance over the list of players for the other positions."[8]

Everybody in Pittsburgh seemed delighted that the deal with Louisville was finalized. The same could not be said for fans and owners in other parts of the country. Rooters in Chicago who believed that stars like Clarke, Wagner, Leach and Phillippe could be headed to the Windy City were disappointed. In St. Louis, Cardinal owner Frank De Haas Robison felt betrayed. He wasn't thrilled with the course of events which transpired during December 1899. He was so confident that an agreement had been reached with Dreyfuss that St. Louis passed on signing some minor league prospects they were interested in.[9]

"So certain am I that the deal was practically closed that I went so far as to consult Clarke about coming to us and found him pleased," said Robison. "We agreed on salary and he gave me encouragement to believe that we would have no difficulty in getting the signature of each of the other players we were after to a contract.... When Mr. Dreyfuss was reported by the newspapers as going from city to city to dispose of his players, I did not know what to think. That deal with Pittsburgh convinced me that he had violated his promise and prevented us from adding four of the best players in the profession to our team."[10]

Dreyfuss denied that an agreement was ever in place with Robison and the St. Louis Cardinals. Dreyfuss admitted that discussions took place wherein Robison said he would like to purchase Clarke, Wagner, Leach and Phillippe, but never gave any assurance that Robison would be given first choice if these men were actually sold. Dreyfuss also said that all negotiations with Robison ended when the St. Louis magnate told Pulliam that payment for any Louisville players would be deferred until the spring.[11]

Now that a deal with Kerr was finalized, the only matter left to Pittsburgh's ownership group was the designation of authority throughout the organization. Dreyfuss, always wanting to make the business transaction which benefited him the most, reaped the ultimate reward when it was announced that he would become president of the Pirates.[12] Pulliam joined Dreyfuss from

Louisville and assumed the position of team secretary. Kerr was relegated to the post of treasurer.

This change of the team's officers became legally binding when Pittsburgh held its annual team meeting in Atlantic City. The evening before this conference, a celebratory dinner was hosted by Dreyfuss during which the owner assured newspaper writers that he was not taking total control of the team. He was only a partner, although it seemed apparent to all in attendance that he would be responsible for major team decisions. Dreyfuss' first order of business as Pittsburgh's magnate was the confirmation that Clarke would replace Patsy Donovan as manager of the Pirates.[13]

Clarke left the celebration early so that he could return to his wife and child in Kansas and attend Sunday evening church services. He vowed that he would come back in January to begin the task of sorting out what players would comprise the Pirate team in 1900.[14] Former Louisville players like Wagner, Leach, Phillippe, Ritchey and Waddell were expected to mesh nicely with Pittsburgh holdovers Clarence Beaumont, Jimmy Williams, Jack Chesbro (back after Louisville was eliminated), Sam Leever and Jesse Tannehill. Tannehill was the star twirler of the Pittsburgh staff in 1899, posting a 24–14 record with a 2.82 ERA. He believed the Louisville transaction had made the Pirates a pennant contender overnight.

"That deal with Louisville will make the Pittsburgh team one of the strongest in the league," said Jesse. "A team can be selected from that brace of material which will be one, two, sure. Why, when you look over the players from which the team is to be chosen, it is hard to figure how it can finish lower than that. Look at the infield, will you? There are Williams, Wagner, Leach, Ely and Ritchey, not to speak of others. Williams is really a better shortstop than he is a third baseman, though it is not generally known. He can be played at short, Leach at third, Ely or Ritchey at second and Wagner at first. Then there is the outfield, Clarke, Donovan, Beaumont and McCreery — a quartet of stars that can't be beaten. The pitching and catching departments will compare favorably with the best in the League when you sum them up. Mark my word, we'll be in it next season."[15]

Tannehill showed great clairvoyance when giving his prediction about Pittsburgh's starting lineup in 1900. Clarke decided to place Ritchey at second base, Ely at shortstop, Williams at third base and Dillon at first. The outfield consisted of Clarke in left, Beaumont in center and Wagner playing right field. Leach was designated as a utility player and Zimmer was chosen to work behind the dish. Tom McCreery was relegated to the bench. Former manager Donovan was sold to St. Louis for $1000 in January.

C.B. Power, writer for the *Pittsburgh Leader,* certainly wasn't shocked when Donovan packed his bags and moved on to the Mound City. Power believed that Clarke was a great ballplayer. However, the Pittsburgh scribe didn't feel that Clarke had any ability as a manager.[16] "Fred Clarke is one of the grandest ball players the game has ever known," wrote Power as he quoted an anonymous man high up in baseball, "but I have serious doubts as to his abilities as a manager. Unfortunately Fred has never had the opportunity of playing under a competent National League manager, and when he was placed in charge of the Louisville club he had no very clear idea of what constitutes the duties of a manager. He had not had much National League experience — a serious handicap."[17]

Power cited the fact that Clarke received assistance from veteran Perry Werden after he was appointed to the Louisville managerial post in 1897.

Fred Clarke came to Pittsburgh after the 1899 season when Barney Dreyfuss consolidated most of his Louisville team before the Colonels were eliminated from the National League. Dreyfuss assumed the presidency of the Pittsburgh Club and Clarke was installed as the team's manager, replacing Patsy Donovan.

Later, Malachi Kittridge became a right hand man until a coolness developed between catcher and manager in 1899. Clarke also did not have Billy Clingman nearby for advice that season since the infielder spent time on the disabled list.[18]

"Zimmer was then secured," continued Power, "and the Louisville club promptly profited by his experience and a grand finish was the result. Of course, those not on the inside gave Manager Clarke credit for the good showing of the team. Much of this was deserved, but the valuable assistance of his lieutenant's was overlooked. Now, I do not wish to be understood as trying to belittle Clarke's abilities as a manager, but the facts as related are there and cannot be ignored. I want to see Fred made a success in his new position but the lack of training under a manager of experience is going to be a serious handicap.... There is no question of his ability to handle his men off the field, but when it comes to inside work in a game the old managers and captains can and will, I fear, outgeneral him."[19]

Many of the local baseball experts were ecstatic that Pittsburgh had acquired Clarke — the ballplayer. They just weren't as enthused over the fact that Clarke was chosen to manage this new, thrilling aggregation. Clarke paid no attention to the criticism. He had supreme confidence in his ability as both a player and manager. Clarke knew that he already had made a name for himself as a star performer in the National League. Clarke now realized that the opportunity presented itself in Pittsburgh for him to quiet the naysayers through achieving equal greatness as a field manager as well.

Clarke's philosophy when dealing with his troops was very simple. The Pittsburgh manager treated his players like human beings and not slaves.[20] He didn't enact a strict set of rules or guidelines. Clarke expected his men to perform to the best of their ability on the field. He also wanted his players to conduct themselves like adults away from the diamond as well. There would be no booze clauses in player contracts, but Clarke also wasn't going to tolerate players showing up at game time with a hangover.[21]

> Now, I don't mean by this that we are going to offer prizes for the men who can get outside the greatest quantity of malt extract within a given time, nor are we going to keep any man in our employ who fills his hide to such an extent at night that he is unfit for duty the next day.
>
> All we will ask is that our players report every day fit to perform the duties for which they are paid. No employer of men will put up with an individual who drinks to excess, though where will you find the employer who demands of his men that they shall refrain from a social glass of lager at their own firesides if they see fit? They are mighty few and far between. I have noticed that the man who grants to his employees the right to think and not for themselves usually gets the best results. His men will honor and respect him, and are at all times willing and anxious to advance his interests. Now, why should not the same policy be pursued in base ball?
>
> Ball players are no better and no worse than any other class of men, and I am not one bit afraid of any member of the Pittsburgh team taking advantage of us. If any should interpret our policy as meaning that he has full license to make a pig of himself he will find that we can rule with an iron hand, and that we do not intend to put up with any foolishness. Why, with the Louisville Club we found only one man who filled his hide just because he knew he was privileged to take a glass of beer occasionally. But I guess he is convinced by this time that he made a mistake.[22]

Clarke arrived in Pittsburgh prior to spring training so that he could set up a local domicile in the Allegheny section of town.[23] Mrs. Clarke and young Helen did not join him immediately. The Clarke family decided that it would be best if Annette and the baby stayed with Chick and Mina Fraser at their boarding house residence in Philadelphia.[24] This way, Mina could help Annette care for the infant, leaving Fred Clarke to concentrate on his new duties in Pittsburgh.

Once spring training began, local writers quickly noticed that Pittsburgh's current squad seemed to make boneheaded plays on the diamond. Balls were thrown to incorrect bases, runners were being reckless and fielders couldn't make plays that the average ballplayer usually handled with ease. Pittsburgh scribes believed that Dreyfuss and Kerr had assembled the largest number of brainless players in Pittsburgh Pirate history.[25] Because he knew that the mental lapses could be attributed to players who hadn't played together trying to become accustomed to one another, Clarke was confident that the squad would come together once the regular season began.

On April 26, the Pittsburgh Pirates opened their home schedule at Exposition Park after splitting the first six games of the season in St. Louis and Cincinnati. When Clarke trotted out to left field in the top of the first inning against the Reds, bleacher fans booed him heartily.[26] Pittsburgh's rooters were unhappy that Donovan had been shown the door, and Clarke was a convenient villain in their minds. Clarke was unfazed by the treatment. "Before this season is over you'll stand up and take off your hats," Clarke hollered back at them.[27]

As the season moved into May, Clarke became involved in an incident that brought back memories of his early days as a rookie in Louisville. In a 7–6 loss against Chicago on May 6, Clarke became involved in a scrap with Orphans infielder Clarence "Cupid" Childs. Clarke roll blocked Childs on a play at second base, which prevented the Chicago second baseman from completing a double play. When Childs jumped the unsuspecting Pittsburgh manager, a short scuffle ensued in which neither man was able to claim victory.[28]

In most instances, such animosity usually died on the field. As luck would have it, the Pirates and Cubs were scheduled to play each other in Pittsburgh the following day. When players from both teams encountered one another at the railway station that night, Childs and Clarke resumed their fight in much more aggressive fashion.[29] The tale of the tape showed Clarke was five foot ten inches, 165 pounds, while Childs carried a 20-pound advantage and was two inches shorter. Cupid seemed to get the upper hand in the fracas as he consistently punched away at Clarke's body. When the battle ended, Clarke was badly bruised on the face and shoulders. Childs seemed to only suffer the humiliation of having his clothes torn.[30]

When the train carrying the Pirates entourage rolled into Pittsburgh, Clarke received word that he was to report immediately to Dreyfuss' office. When Clarke arrived, Dreyfuss explained that the Pirate manager needed to cut out his rowdy tactics. The Pittsburgh owner also extolled the virtue of playing clean baseball. Dreyfuss even threatened to get rid of Clarke if the Pittsburgh manager didn't changes his ways. Clarke listened intently to Dreyfuss, never saying a word in response during the little magnate's speech.[31]

That day, a crowd over three times the average for a Monday at Exposition Park attended the game. Everyone came hoping to see Childs and Clarke continue their battle from the previous day. Pittsburgh claimed victory over the Orphans without any such incidents occurring during the game. On Tuesday morning, Clarke returned to Dreyfuss' office in order to drive home the point that Monday's game had drawn an unusually large crowd. Clarke then jokingly said that rowdy tactics would become the death of the Pirates magnate. Dreyfuss never criticized Clarke's aggressive, hard-nosed style again.[32]

Clarke's team played uneven baseball throughout the season's early stages. As June ended, Pittsburgh found themselves in third place with a 29–28 record, 7½ games behind league-leading Brooklyn. Realizing that the catching department had been quite deficient during the months of April and May, Dreyfuss rectified this problem by purchasing Jack O'Connor from St. Louis for $2,000. O'Connor came to Pittsburgh with the reputation of being a great handler of pitchers and a chatterer behind home plate. Although O'Connor's heady guidance began paying immediate dividends, the results still were not apparent in the standings.

As a new batterymate entered the scene, another fell into disfavor and quickly became entrenched in Clarke's doghouse. Clarke had grown tired of pitcher Waddell's unreliability. Rube was prone to take unexcused absences which left the Pirates manager in a bind on more than one occasion. Everyone on the team loved Waddell. He was a jokester and prankster whose child-like antics helped to keep the troops loose. Clarke was fond of Rube as well, but he realized that he needed to make an example of the southpaw pitcher so that team discipline could be maintained.

"We all loved Rube, as I said," continued Clarke. "but I knew I couldn't stay manager long if I let him take French leave whenever he wanted. During one of his absences I went to Barney Dreyfuss and said: 'Life is too short to monkey around with this guy. Suspend him and mail him his check.'

"The next day Waddell came into the clubhouse with the afternoon paper which showed a big picture of him and which carried the story he was suspended.

"'Is this true Fred?' he asked.

"'It sure is, so get your stuff out of here and never come back,' I answered.

"'Fred, I never had an idea you felt that way,' retorted Rube. 'Next time I see you I will shoot you full of holes.'"[33]

Waddell packed his bags and went to pitch for a semi-pro team in Punxsutawney, Pennsylvania. Manager Connie Mack of the American League Milwaukee team got wind of this and asked Dreyfuss if the Pirates would loan the southpaw to his squad. Dreyfuss agreed and Mack sent Waddell a letter which stated that Rube would receive $250 per month in salary plus expenses.

5. Goodbye Louisville, Hello Pittsburgh 49

After a short delay, Waddell approved the terms and joined Mack's Milwaukee team.³⁴

The key word regarding this transaction was that Waddell had been loaned. Clarke probably would have preferred to make the situation permanent. Clarke was not a taskmaster, but he managed his team in an orderly and disciplined manner. Waddell was definitely a player who had no use for such things. He was happy playing marbles with the local kids or chasing fire engines. Rube believed that if doing these things meant missing the start of a ball game or his turn in the pitching rotation, then so be it. Waddell marched to his own beat and no strict regulations were going to change that.

Waddell did fine work for Milwaukee. He probably would have finished the season under Mack's employ if not for a brilliant performance in an August doubleheader against the Chicago White Stockings. Rube went the distance in a 17-inning affair and defeated Chicago in the first game. Waddell followed that up by throwing five shutout innings to claim victory during the shortened second game. He pitched all 22 innings in both games and allowed only 11 hits.³⁵

When Dreyfuss heard of Waddell's great pitching feat against the White Stockings, he realized the Pirates needed Rube back to help out during the stretch drive. Mack saw the potential in the big left-hander and was sick over the fact that there was nothing he could do to keep Dreyfuss from reclaiming Rube since he was indeed Pirates property. However, Waddell balked at returning to Pittsburgh.

Rube met the Milwaukee team for a series in Indianapolis instead of reporting to Pittsburgh (as reward for winning the second game of the Chicago doubleheader, Mack gave Waddell permission to go fishing rather than join the team for a series in Kansas City). Dreyfuss wired Mack to inquire as to why Waddell had not reported back to Pittsburgh. Mack in turn told Dreyfuss to come and get him.³⁶

> We needed Rube for the last eastern trip of 1900, and I sent Chief Zimmer, a catcher, to get him. Zimmer was a diplomat and, besides, Rube liked all catchers.
>
> Zimmer sent me a telegram. It said Waddell wouldn't come back because he would have to shoot me full of holes.
>
> I wired back to Zimmer that I would take my chances, but that he shouldn't fail to bring back his man.
>
> When Rube joined us in Buffalo, all he said was: "Hello there, Freddie."
>
> I had an idea that I could keep him straight by rooming with him, so I arranged for adjoining rooms with a connecting door.
>
> The next day I asked him if he had a spare button. I had lost one from my ball pants.
>
> He told me he would look around and began digging in his trunk. I heard

several clicks. Rube was in front of a mirror snapping the trigger on a huge pistol.

I got a little worried, and asked him again about the button. When I looked up again, he was coming through the door with a bowie knife in one hand.

I was frightened. Just plain frightened. He had changed his mind. He wasn't going to shoot me full of holes. Just dig me full of holes.

"Lookit here, Rube, you can't do that," I objected.

"Thought you wanted a button," he said. "I just cut one off my pants for you."

He had slashed off a button from his uniform pants, so he was in the same fix I was.[37]

Despite the tension between Waddell and Clarke, Rube had a fairly decent season for the Pirates in 1900. His 8–13 record was a bit misleading as he led the team with a 2.37 ERA. Phillippe became the leader of the staff, fashioning a 20–13 record with an ERA of 2.84. Holdovers Tannehill (20–6, 2.88 ERA), Leever (15–13, 2.71 ERA) and Chesbro (15–13, 3.67 ERA) rounded out the resurgent Pittsburgh pitching corps.

The Pirates work at the plate also improved significantly in 1900. Playing in front of the hometown Pittsburgh fans certainly agreed with Honus Wagner, as the Carnegie native led the National League in average (.381), doubles (45) and triples (22). He also topped the team with 100 runs batted in. Ritchey (.292), Beaumont (.279) and O'Brien (.290) complemented the Flying Dutchman with solid stick work. Third baseman Williams struggled through a season that was shortened by injury and illness. He saw his average drop from .355 in 1899 to .264 in 1900 and his RBI total plummeted from 116 to 68.

Clarke had a tough season of his own at the plate. He fell below the .300 mark for the first time since his rookie year. Clarke hit .276, recorded 110 hits, scored 84 runs and stole 21 bases. All of these figures were well below the norm Clarke had established throughout his baseball career. Clarke only appeared in 106 games as he missed time in September with a leg injury.[38]

Clarke's personal numbers didn't put a damper on the fact that he had succeeded beyond expectations as a field general. Pittsburgh rebounded after its early season mediocrity and finished with a record of 79–60. The Pirates squad gained momentum during the summer and eventually settled into second place, 4½ games behind the first-place Brooklyn Superbas. New blood from Louisville helped the team jump five spots in the standings from the previous year. Clarke had quieted his critics as Pittsburgh came close to winning the National League pennant.

Pittsburgh and Brooklyn did play a post season series that was sponsored by the *Pittsburgh Chronicle-Telegraph* newspaper.[39] The Pirates offered little resistance as Brooklyn won the series, three games to one. Many local scribes believed the Pirates were severely overmatched while others felt Pittsburgh failed to put forth the necessary effort. Just weeks earlier, Dreyfuss had accused some players of loafing in a series against St. Louis.[40] Clarke didn't believe that anyone laid down on the job against Brooklyn. "We lost the cup series on its merits and have no explanation to make," said the Pirate manager. "It is great satisfaction to know that we rank as the second team in the official standing at the close of the race. That is something for a one-year team to be proud of. Then again we made more money than any other club, so I am told a number of new players will be added to our roster in 1901 and it will be a surprise to me if we do not do better in the next race than we did this year."[41]

Rumors began making the rounds about potential players that Clarke and Dreyfuss were targeting. The names of possible Pirates who would act as trade fodder were proposed by the press. Williams even requested that Dreyfuss send him to a new team. The star of the 1899 Pirates team when he hit a blistering .355, sadly, looked like a burned out supernova in 1900. "I made a terrible showing here last summer," Williams was quoted, "and I think a change would do me good. I was treated royally by the club owners and public, but for some reason I could not make good on the home ground and would like to get away."[42]

Another bizarre rumor circulated as 1900 came to a close. It was reported that Treasurer Kerr had proposed a trade that would send pitcher Tannehill to Cincinnati for pitcher Noodles Hahn. Cincinnati rejected this deal and the Pirates responded with a counter offer of Tannehill for pitcher Ed Scott.[43] The odd thing about this news was that Dreyfuss' name was not connected to it. When Dreyfuss was named president of the team, it was understood that he would be responsible for all personnel decisions. Under the new three-pronged ownership entity, Kerr did not have the authority to propose or finalize trades.

Fans were a little surprised that Tannehill's name was being thrown about in trade discussions considering his 20–6 record in 1900. One rumor had made the rounds that Clarke and Dreyfuss were not pleased with Tannehill's work, and for this reason, he did not pitch in the post-season Cup Series against Brooklyn. Another story stated that Jesse refused to pitch. Tannehill quickly responded to this allegation. "During the cup series with Brooklyn there was a statement published to the effect that I had refused to pitch in any of the games. This was not true, because I was never asked to pitch," responded Tannehill. "In justice to me I think that Manager Clarke should have denied the story at that time, but he did not see fit to do so. As far as a portion of the public souring on me is concerned that is all bosh. Nobody has soured on me save Dreyfuss and Clarke. So long as a pitcher wins a majority of his games the public is satisfied. I did that, and I can't see what kick there is coming against me or my work."[44]

Clarke probably didn't use Tannehill in the Cup Series because there were indeed times when the southpaw pitcher was not receptive to doing yeoman's work on the mound. Tannehill always claimed some malady had afflicted him, but whispering behind the scenes indicated something else. It seemed that Tannehill became disinterested in working when the point in the season was reached in which he believed he had done enough to earn his salary. This was the kind of problem that Clarke did not need given the high expectations that were being placed on his Pittsburgh squad. Many writers and fans were already dreaming of a pennant in 1901, which placed an enormous amount of pressure on Clarke's shoulders.

Chapter 6

Pennant Flag Hangs from Corsair Craft

After the very successful 1900 baseball season, Pittsburgh players scattered about the country and returned to their off-season residences. For Fred Clarke, this meant another winter working on his farm in Kansas. Many of Clarke's teammates who came from America's heartland would be following his lead by cultivating their individual homesteads. One player who dared to be different during the winter was "Rube" Waddell. He decided to follow the thespian call and became an actor. Rube's new profession evidently didn't pay well since the southpaw contacted Barney Dreyfuss and requested monetary assistance.

"Oh yes," said Dreyfuss, "I had a letter from 'Rube' Waddell the other day. He told me about having become an actor, and incidentally requested me to send him money. Did I send it? Certainly. No, it was not advance money. You see 'Rube' saved me some money last season without knowing it, and I am now going to give it to him in dribs. During the season 'Rube' would draw a dollar or two almost every day, and when the season closed he had no idea how he stood with the club and was greatly surprised when I told him he had $198 due him on account of salary. Of course he wanted it all right away, but I could not see it that way. Having saved the money for 'Rube,' I concluded I had a right to act as custodian of the fund, and have been sending the money to 'Rube's' wife in installments. By this method I have fixed it so that the big twirler can not ask for advance money, and at the same time I know that the money goes where it will do the most good."[1]

One had to wonder if Waddell was a good actor on stage. He was probably looked upon as a bad actor by Clarke, even though that phrase had nothing to do with Rube's theatrical endeavor. Players who didn't adhere to team rules and caused their manager grief were usually tagged with the bad actor moniker. Many fans in Pittsburgh wondered if Clarke would continue to tolerate Waddell's behavior. If Rube did not change his ways, it was likely that the curtain would soon be closing on Waddell's Pittsburgh baseball engagement.

As Clarke kept himself busy during the winter, bizarre rumors were given undue credence in the city of Pittsburgh. Some baseball scribes were reporting that the Pirates were interested in Brooklyn first baseman Hughie Jennings. Dreyfuss dismissed this report, saying that Kitty Bransfield, a player he had just purchased from Worcester, would man the initial sack for Pittsburgh in 1901.[2] Even after Dreyfuss rejected the notion that Jennings was headed to the Pirates, writers continued to claim that Hughie would be joining the team. They also speculated as to whether Jennings was slated to replace Clarke as Pittsburgh's manager.

This contention on the scribes' part seemed odd since Clarke quickly signed a multi-year contract after he guided the Pirates to a second-place finish in 1900. It was also unusual that Kerr was the first member of Pirates ownership to issue a statement denying that Clarke was being replaced. Kerr had beaten Dreyfuss to the punch regarding this unfounded gossip.[3] This was the second time that Kerr had overstepped his authority as Pittsburgh's treasurer. Previously, he had offered Tannehill to Cincinnati in a trade even though Dreyfuss was explicitly responsible for all personnel decisions.

Kerr probably felt that he was doing Dreyfuss and Clarke a favor when he offered Tannehill to the Reds. Tannehill had caused problems for Donovan in 1899 and issues resurfaced once again in 1900.[4] One thing seemed certain as Kerr continued to operate outside his realm of authority. Changes within the ownership hierarchy of the Pittsburgh Pirates carried a strong likelihood as the 1901 season approached.

Rumors that a faction of the ownership led by Kerr was trying to squeeze out Dreyfuss and Pulliam had surfaced in the winter of 1900.[5] Kerr, probably realizing that the Pirates had the potential to become a future powerhouse, did not like taking a back seat to Dreyfuss. With success on the horizon, he wanted to be center stage in order to bask in the glory of any potential championship. The showdown between both sides occurred when Kerr's group attempted to fire Pulliam. They felt that the team secretary was much too loyal to Dreyfuss.[6] The little magnate was able to avert disaster when he turned the tables on the rebellious Kerr at Pittsburgh's annual team meeting in New Jersey.[7]

Kerr and Auten made a horrible mistake when they refused to hold the annual election of officers for the club at this December summit. Dreyfuss, in accordance with team by-laws, called for a vote to take place. Kerr and Auten refused. Both men were apprehensive to do anything until after the league meetings, which were simultaneously going on in New York, concluded. To make matters worse, Kerr's faction then attempted to hold a special election at a later date.[8] This was in direct violation of legal precepts that were established by Pittsburgh ownership years earlier.

Dreyfuss had the courts on his side in this instance. Kerr and Auten's attorney was told that their only recourse would be to let New Jersey's Supreme Court hear the case sometime in the fall.[9] This was not a feasible alternative for the traitorous partners. With their attempt to eliminate Dreyfuss and Pulliam foiled, the Kerr-Auten faction decided to force Dreyfuss into a corner with a buy or sell proposal. Dreyfuss would either sell his interests to Kerr and Auten or he would have to buy his associates out at a very high price. Dreyfuss called the bluff of his two partners and elected to purchase the Kerr stock.[10] In February 1901, it was announced that Dreyfuss paid $35,000 for the Kerr-Auten block of stock, which allowed him to assume full control of the Pittsburgh club.[11]

Had Kerr prevailed in this matter, it was quite possible that Clarke may have been relieved of his managerial duties. Clarke and Dreyfuss did the same thing in 1900 when they took the managerial title away from Donovan and shipped him to St. Louis. If Dreyfuss had been forced out, there was no guarantee that Clarke would have stayed on in his capacity of player or manager. Kerr initially denied the rumors surrounding Jennings leading the Pirates in 1901. One had to wonder if Kerr would have stood by that statement if Dreyfuss were out of the picture.

Clarke arrived from his home in the West to be on hand for the big announcement regarding Pittsburgh's ownership realignment.[12] Spring training in Hot Springs, Arkansas, was only a few weeks away, so Clarke decided to remain in Pittsburgh. No trades were made during the off-season, although reports stated that Pittsburgh had pursued a deal for shortstop Bobby Wallace. The names of Tannehill and Ely commonly popped up when potential transactions were discussed.[13]

Even though no deals were forged between Pittsburgh and other National League combatants, the Pirates did lose one player under a very strange set of circumstances. First baseman Tom O'Brien passed away in early February. O'Brien had been suffering from the lingering effects of an illness he contracted while traveling with other players for an exhibition series in Cuba after the 1900 season. Someone recommended to O'Brien that he drink salty sea water in order to combat seasickness. O'Brien evidently drank about three quarts of the sodium potion. This decision had tragic repercussions as O'Brien became seriously ill while making the trip to Havana. O'Brien eventually passed away in Arizona on February 3 from tuberculosis, or consumption, as it was sometimes referred to.[14]

O'Brien was expected to assume a utility player role in 1901. Since Bransfield was going to be given every chance to claim the first base job, O'Brien's loss wouldn't be that dramatic from a baseball perspective. As Clarke was solving his first base dilemma, another issue quickly arose which required his attention. A second Pittsburgh player was lost through strange circumstances that were not quite as tragic as O'Brien's but still penalized the Pirates heavily.

Pittsburgh's loss of a star player to defection could be directly attributed to the new climate which now prevailed within baseball. Barney Dreyfuss had taken care of the enemy from within by buying out Kerr and Auten. Unfortunately, Dreyfuss and his fellow league magnates soon faced a new challenge presented by the American League. It was an all-out war as Ban Johnson's new league began raiding National League team's rosters for players with the promise of higher salaries for those who jumped to the American League.

Teams were established in Chicago, Philadelphia and Boston to compete head-to-head for fans with National League entries in those cities. Johnson planned to offer rooters a viable second major league to battle the established National League. It was rumored that new American League teams were told not to pillage the Pittsburgh roster. The idea behind this strategy was that if Pittsburgh remained unscathed, they would win the National League pennant with such relative ease that fan interest would wane. Someone must have forgotten to send John McGraw of the Baltimore club this hands-off memo toward Pittsburgh players because he quickly scooped up third baseman Williams for his team.

McGraw swooped in and plucked Williams for the Baltimore squad while Jimmy was doing some early training at Hot Springs. The Baltimore manager gave Williams his best salesman pitch. After McGraw presented his proposition to the third baseman, Williams was given little time to mull over the offer. He quickly agreed.[15] Williams was escorted to a train and sent on his way to Baltimore before he could second guess his decision. Many were surprised when reports reached the Smoky City that Williams had defected. Back in Pittsburgh, Jimmy's wife was shocked when she heard the news. The new bride was also worried since McGraw kept Williams in seclusion for two days.[16]

If Williams hadn't arrived at Hot Springs early to train on his own, the Pirates third baseman probably would have remained Pirates property. It seemed that McGraw wouldn't have been likely to tamper with Dreyfuss' property while the whole Pittsburgh contingent was training under Clarke's guidance. Dreyfuss was particularly angered by the fact that McGraw stole his player after Williams' train fare from St. Louis to Hot Springs had been paid by the Pittsburgh club.[17]

A few weeks after his defection to Baltimore, a remorseful Williams headed back to Pittsburgh. He was having second thoughts and wanted to meet with Dreyfuss so the matter could be rectified. Williams had to wait a few days while Dreyfuss recovered from an illness. When the meeting did occur, Dreyfuss said that he would only pay Williams his salary amount from last year. That would not be a problem for Williams if the Pirates were willing to protect him from any legal action that Baltimore might take.[18] Dreyfuss pondered over whether he wanted to take such action.

"I may not take legal proceedings if Williams plays in Baltimore," said Dreyfuss. "My course will be decided later by my attorney, who is out of the city. I may not enter a suit. I do not want to force Jimmy to come back here, and as much as I would like to prevent him from staying with McGraw, I may have to keep that matter out of court, as a verdict in my favor might force me to give the player employment when I would not want him.... There is not the slightest truth in the report that I offered Williams a big salary to return to Pittsburgh; the one club that has a moral right to his services. If Williams had proved loyal he would have received exactly the same salary that he got last year, and not a cent more. I could not have afforded to take him back at any other terms."[19]

Dreyfuss decided that he would not pursue the matter even though Williams wanted to return to Pittsburgh. The precedent which Dreyfuss set in this case was that any player disloyal to the Pirates team in regards to dealings with the American League would not be welcomed back with open arms. Clarke wasn't concerned that Williams had jumped to the new league. The Pittsburgh manager was confident that Leach would step in as the new third baseman and do a marvelous job in 1901.

Chesbro remained loyal to the Pittsburgh club when he spurned an offer from Boston of the American League.[20] Another player was snagged by the new league's wide net when catcher Harry Smith signed with Connie Mack's Philadelphia team. Pirates center fielder Beaumont didn't feel these defections would ruin the National League's quality of play. "The National League has a good many extra players it can fall back on," said Beaumont, "and every one is pretty fair at that. I would like to see the two leagues on an equal basis and working in harmony, as I think it would help the game. I feel certain that I will sign again with Pittsburgh, as my treatment there in a season is all that could be desired, and I am sure the same will be accorded me this season. I see that hardly any of the Pittsburgh players have been claimed by the American League, which shows that the boys have been well treated by Mr. Dreyfuss."[21] Clarke agreed with Beaumont about the National League's strength. The Pirates manager did not believe that competing clubs were severely weakened by defections. He contended that an infusion of young talent would help keep these squads in the running.

Pittsburgh opened the season behind Sam Leever's strong pitching performance with a 4–2 victory against Cincinnati on April 20. Clarke had decided on a 1901 lineup of himself, Beaumont and Wagner in the outfield.

Manning the infield from first to third were Bransfield, Ritchey, Ely and Leach. O'Connor and Zimmer were expected to split time behind the plate. Many of the same twirlers from 1900 were back performing the pitching duties.

No changes were made to the Pirates squad until Waddell was sold to the Chicago Orphans on May 2. Clarke felt that Waddell was too much of a distraction. When the southpaw pitcher started the season by losing his first two starts and was hammered by opposing batters to the tune of a 9.39 ERA, Pittsburgh's manager decided that Rube's potential no longer outweighed his glaring deficiencies. Clarke never asked any of his players to do any more than he was willing to undertake himself. He also did not need any jollying he did not hand out.[22] On this occasion, Waddell didn't threaten to shoot Clarke full of holes.

Three days after the trade, Rube faced his old teammates in Chicago and lost the game by a score of 4–2. Waddell did not have much success against the Pirates that year as the southpaw failed to win in all three starts against Pittsburgh. A special strategy devised by Wagner helped the Corsairs conquer their old friend. In one game where Rube definitely seemed to have the upper hand against Pittsburgh, Clarke followed Wagner's advice and destroyed the Chicago pitcher's concentration. "Rube was a notorious talker, and in fact was told he would be fined if he gabbed with the other side," related Clarke. "Our job was to get him talking. Honus Wagner came up with a plan. 'As you go by him Fred,' Wagner said to me, 'invite him up for the pheasant shooting with us next month.' I did, and it worked. Waddell was a fan whenever anybody mentioned anything concerned with guns, and he got to talking pheasants and forgot to pitch, and we scored six runs. That's the kind of talk that counted."[23]

This four-game series in Chicago turned out to be a rough one for Clarke. During one of the games, Chicago third baseman Fred Raymer gave Clarke the shoulder and then tripped him when he was rounding third base. Clarke fell hard to the ground, was removed from the game, and missed some playing time.[24] Pitcher Tannehill, who was also a terrific hitter, subbed in left field during Clarke's absence.

It was determined that Fred Clarke had a caved-in breastbone. Despite the fact that Clarke had a broken bone in his chest, he did not remain out of the lineup for long, even though he was unable to get out of bed without assistance from someone. On the field, Clarke couldn't make throws from the outfield after he caught the ball. He flipped the ball underhanded to Beaumont instead. The reason Clarke returned so quickly was that he didn't want some other player showing ownership that he could do a better job in left field.[25] Even though the eight-year veteran was a league star, he knew that any hotshot could come along and make even a great player expendable.

Clarke never commented about the incident in Chicago. Clarke believed the game of baseball should be played with reckless abandon, so he couldn't fault Raymer for knocking him down. Collisions were bound to occur in baseball. Clarke never complained when he came out on the bad end of one. Other players would scream and holler when victimized, but Clarke was always willing to take his lumps. The same could not be said when Clarke inflicted pain upon first baseman John Ganzel during a June series against New York.

New York newspapers roasted Clarke over an apparent spiking incident that occurred when Pittsburgh played the Giants. Scribes accused Clarke of intentionally cutting Ganzel as the Pirates manager slid hard into first base on a close play. Writers Sam Crane and John Foster referred to Clarke as "Spiker." Clarke claimed these accusations were totally false and that infielder Charlie Hickman had botched the play and was playing the martyr card for his teammate.[26] He also believed Hickman was acting like a baby. Clarke ignored the stinging barbs that came from New York baseball writers.

When Pittsburgh left New York on June 21, the Pirates stood on top of the National League standings, three games in front of the second-place Giants. Clarke knew his team was ready to make a pennant run and Dreyfuss quickly made moves that were designed to help the Pirates reach this goal. Outfielder Alfonzo "Lefty" Davis was purchased from Brooklyn on June 23 and southpaw pitcher Ed Doheny was acquired from New York on July 25. Both players had been left for dead by their previous teams, but Clarke thought Davis and Doheny would give Pittsburgh's cause a boost.

Doheny had failed to deliver the goods during five-plus seasons in New York. His best season was in 1899 when he went 14–17 with a 4.41 ERA. Many baseball experts said that Doheny had one of the best curve balls in the National League. Clarke quickly realized this was not true and advised his new pitcher to make adjustments which would benefit both him and the team. "At New York," said Fred, "Ed was always wild, and the Giants were willing to sell him to us. Ed was supposed to have one of the best curves a lefty ever had, but he simply could not get it over. But I could see nothing wrong with his live fastball. When we brought him in, I watched him pitch in practice. I said: 'Ed, let's pitch my way for awhile and see if we cannot control that wildness. Give up the curve and throw only the fastball.' That overhand fastball was a beauty, and as I had suspected, Doheny didn't need a curve."[27]

While Davis didn't see action initially when he joined the Pirates, events quickly evolved which changed that when shortstop Ely became a problem both on and off the field.

> In Philadelphia one day, our shortstop, Fred Ely, told me he could not play. He had a little scratch on the finger. That was no excuse; we played with broken fingers in those days, I explained and pleaded with him, but he refused.

I said: "Fred, if you don't play for me today, you will never play for me again." Ely was a great favorite in Pittsburgh. But the great players would not think of quitting unless they could not get on the field, and I could not let Ely do it, no matter how it would hurt us at the gate in Pittsburgh.

I played short that day for the only time in my life. The first chance I got I threw over first, and kept right on going to try retrieve my own overthrow.

The next day I asked a little fellow named Louie Carr, who wasn't with us long, to try his best at short. He did his best, but in our final road game, when we had the bases loaded and needed a run to win, Carr stuck his arm over the plate to be hit, and get to base to drive in the run. When we got back to Pittsburgh the next day, the arm was swollen high as a bee-hive.

I had to have another shortstop. At that time Ely came up to me and said he would play if I needed him.

It hurt, but I had to tell him, "What I said goes, Fred."

I went to Dreyfuss in the front office and said: "I want to release Ely." Barney argued with me. He explained how popular Ely was in Pittsburgh, and wanted to know where I would get a shortstop anyway.

I said: "It's either Ely or me."

I got his release and ten days' pay, but Dreyfuss said: "Fred, I am going with you, but you are to blame if anything goes wrong."

I told Ely to get out. Then I went to Leach who was playing third at the time, and to Wagner, and told them: "You fellows came here with me and you have to stick by me. Honus, you have to play shortstop today."

Wagner objected, and said he thought Leach could play short better, and he would go to third. I let that stand. In the meantime the papers and the fans were on me something awful.

The fans began chanting: "Ely, Ely, Ely!" After a few games I went to the Dutchman. "Dutch," I said, "there is no use breaking up two positions for one. You go to shortstop."

After practice the Dutchman was still reluctant, but I told him: "Dutch, you will never see the time they take you out of there."

With Wagner at short the clamor for Ely died down, and after he was at the position three days the papers came out and observed what wonderful judgment I had used.[28]

With Wagner being moved to short, Davis was given a chance in right field. Davis acquitted himself nicely, hitting .313 in 87 games. Speed was one of his strongest assets and this helped Lefty steal 22 bases and score 87 runs during his abbreviated year with the Pirates. This was a strong upgrade to the stats put up by Ely in the 65 games he played. "Father Time," as he was referred to by teammates, could only muster a .208 average with 18 runs scored during that time.

When Ely was released in late July, many fans figured it was the result of his anemic statistics. Many Pittsburgh patrons were not aware that Ely had refused duty because of a cut on his finger. These fans were further surprised when one of Ely's local friends claimed that the shortstop was cut adrift since he reportedly acted as an agent on behalf of Ban Johnson and the American League. "Probably the principle cause for the release of Ely was the connection of his name with an American League team in this city next year," said Ely's newspaper friend. "If the National and the American leagues do not amalgamate or come to an amicable understanding at the close of this season it is certain that Pittsburgh will be represented in the opposition league next year and Ely is slated for manager. Local capitalists with plenty of money are ready to buy an American League franchise and put the strongest team in Pittsburgh that money can obtain. It is said that grounds have been located within five minutes' ride from the down-town section and if the American League does not consolidate with the National, there will be two big league clubs in Pittsburgh next season."[29]

The new combination with Wagner at shortstop and Davis in right field clicked nicely as Pittsburgh continued to fend off second-place Philadelphia throughout August. Many writers and opposing players noticed something different about Pittsburgh's squad in comparison to other National League teams. It was a tight, close-knit unit. The players always seemed to hang out together when the Pirates were on the road. They were focused on the task at hand and didn't let outside influences distract them. Clarke's men always talked baseball, slept baseball and breathed baseball.

Such an atmosphere also made it easier for Clarke and his players to interact. He was a strong proponent of a manager voicing his opinion on the baseball diamond when a player made a mistake. When one of his players seemed to lose focus, Clarke would yell, "Get in the game!" to the guilty party. He believed in reprimanding a player openly so that nothing festered beneath the surface. Of course, when Clarke did this, he yelled so loud that everyone in the ballpark heard him.[30]

Clarke was not exempt from such treatment when he, too, made a mistake. In a late summer game, Clarke made a dash for third in an attempt to steal that base, hoping to catch the opposing catcher napping. He would have been safe if Tannehill was not already occupying that bag. Clarke took his punishment like a man as every member of the squad chastised their manager for making such a boneheaded play.[31] Such incidents were dealt with on the field, although Clarke was probably subjected to some good natured ribbing that evening.

A loose baseball club also finds unique ways to handle adversity. In late August and early September, the Pirates played a string of six doubleheaders in nine days. Home games against Chicago were followed by another batch of games in Boston and New York. The games in Pittsburgh were played in intense heat. Clarke's brigade seemed to be tiring as the Pirates lost the first game of a doubleheader on August 31. Clarke pulled out a bottle of brandy and allowed each player to take a swig.³² One Pirates player suffered a detrimental reaction to the tonic.

"About the second inning Claude Ritchey, my second baseman, called me in from the outfield," said Clarke. "'Fred,' he said 'is that bridge over there moving?' He pointed to a bridge outside the park. I saw he probably had taken a drop too much brandy, but I refused to take him out. No sooner than I returned to my position in left than a pop fly was hit. Ritchey was absolutely the funniest sight I have ever seen as he staggered under the ball, and when it finally hit him smack on the head, everybody on both sides roared with laughter."³³

Ritchey may have suffered from injured pride, but his head was fine and the second baseman didn't miss any games. The Pirates played stellar baseball during this rough stretch and recorded a 10–2 record during these six doubleheaders. This began a run which saw the Pirates set a blazing September

In 1901, the Pittsburgh Pirates captured their first National League pennant in team history. Pittsburgh's 90–49 record supplied a 7½ game cushion over second-place Philadelphia. In this team photograph, Manager Fred Clarke is sitting in the middle of the second row.

pace. Pittsburgh's 25–7 record that month was good enough to guarantee that Pittsburgh would win the 1901 National League pennant. As the Pirates were putting distance between themselves and second-place Philadelphia, a distressing story was circulating in the City of Brotherly Love. It seemed that Ely may have been successful while acting as an American League agent.

Information coming out of Philadelphia indicated that Ely hadn't bungled his work and did convince some Pirates to desert the National League. As the season wound down, Philadelphia papers were reporting that Wagner, Leever, Tannehill and Beaumont planned to jump to the American League for the 1902 season. Of course, the Philly publications chose to ignore the fact that all of these Pirates players were already signed for the 1902 season as they spread this incorrect information.[34] Dreyfuss was able to bring all of his players aboard for the next season because he gave them fair treatment, not something that could be said about other National League magnates.

While the rumor about player defections had no basis, information regarding a possible American League entry in Pittsburgh for the 1902 season had validity. There was a movement afoot by some businessmen in the Smoky City to pool monetary resources together to attract an American League team to Pittsburgh.[35] One of the money backers for this team was alleged to be Kerr, Dreyfuss' former partner. Dreyfuss certainly did not want an American League team competing head-to-head with him in Pittsburgh.

Despite all of the rumors, nobody was able to stop Pittsburgh as they completed their banner season. The Pirates clinched the National League pennant on September 26 when they defeated Brooklyn, 4–3, at Exposition Park. Pittsburgh finished the season with a record of 90–49 and topped second-place Philadelphia by seven games. Besides the Williams defection in March, Pittsburgh remained unscathed in regard to having their roster raided by American League teams. Whether this was the result of a hands-off policy toward Pittsburgh by the new league or just plain luck, no one could be sure.

Pittsburgh's rise to the top of the National League was accomplished due to the rapid development of the overwhelming talent that manager Clarke had at his disposal. Wagner once again led the team with a .353 average and paced the National League with 126 runs batted in. Supporting Wagner with strong performances at the plate were Beaumont (.332), Ritchey (.296), Bransfield (.295) and Clarke himself (.324). Swift baserunning supplemented the strong hitting as five Pirates stole over 20 bases, with Wagner's 49 thefts leading the league.

Solid pitching complemented the hitting accomplishments of Wagner and Company to play a major role in leading Pittsburgh to its first pennant. Phillippe once again paced the Pirates hurlers, posting a 22–12 record and an ERA of 2.22. Chesbro (21–10, 2.38 ERA), Tannehill (18–10, 2.18 ERA) and

Leever (14–5, 2.86 ERA) supported the staff ace quite well and made life difficult for opposing batters throughout the summer.

Clarke's managerial style also played a huge role in Pittsburgh's pennant-winning season. Clarke never was shy when making a game-strategy decision on the field. He showed nerve and made brash moves when the team played at home or on the road.[36] His intensity and passion rubbed off on the other players. As a result, Clarke's team followed his lead and worked just as hard and confidently behind him.

After the season, a big celebration was arranged by railroad moguls throughout the country that honored the Pittsburgh Pirates. Fred Tristam of the Wabash and J.R. James of the Missouri Pacific were the originators of this reception idea. Sydney Van Dusen of the Frisco line joined this committee and the idea was proposed at a meeting of the Railroad Club, where donations were solicited. After only one day the members raised $500. This was more than enough money to buy the Pirates a beautiful loving cup.[37]

The celebration took place as part of the Pirates' season finale at Exposition Park on October 2. Railroad officials from Buffalo, Cincinnati, Cleveland, Erie, Wheeling and Columbus were in attendance. Dreyfuss, Pulliam and Clarke accepted the trophy on behalf of the Pittsburgh Pirates from Railroad Club president S.P. Woodside. Pirates officials and players then issued a proclamation of thanks for the railroad men and Pittsburgh baseball fans.[38]

Celebrations and banquets continued over the next few weeks before the players scattered for the off-season.[39] Clarke returned home to Kansas for the winter, where a few business matters needed his attention back on the farm, but his mind still was in Pittsburgh. As Dreyfuss prepared to attend the league meetings, Clarke corresponded with the little magnate in order to receive assurances that no trades would be made in New York.

No player moves occurred, but other league matters caused Dreyfuss to become concerned. Two factions of magnates had reached a stalemate while trying to choose a league president. The choices came down to incumbent Nick Young, or the man that Dreyfuss backed, Albert Spalding.[40] At times, the debate became heated and the voting was tenuous. Dreyfuss had even considered a compromise candidate that he knew pretty well.

"Pulliam is on friendly terms with both factions and could have been elected without a dissenting vote," said Dreyfuss. "'Don't give up a single player. Have just bought a farm for $12,600,' wrote Fred Clarke to me from Kansas. I wired Fred not to worry; that I have no intention of letting any of his stars get away while he is looking after the property interests in Kansas. I used the wires because I knew that if Fred did not get some assurance that the champion team would remain intact another season he would not enjoy Christmas."[41]

6. Pennant Flag Hangs from Corsair Craft

Fred Clarke was able to celebrate Christmas knowing that his championship team was still together. Clarke managed a squad that was the class of the National League and had the potential to become a future baseball dynasty. The American League raids were only a minor inconvenience to the team during this championship season. Dreyfuss had also won the battle with the enemy from within prior to the start of the 1901 season. It would become a little tougher for Dreyfuss and Clarke in 1902 as Ban Johnson's new league began to target Pittsburgh players more aggressively. This, coupled with a new threat from National League magnates, would truly test the mettle of the Buccaneer leaders.

Chapter 7

Pittsburgh Repeats in Spite of Johnson's Treachery

Knowing that his pennant-winning combination from 1901 wouldn't be altered in any way, Fred Clarke was able to relax and enjoy life at home for a few months after the 1901 season. He spent several weeks hunting in the Indian territory, and also stayed in game shape by laboring exhaustively on his Kansas ranch. Clarke left his prairie home comforts and returned to the Smoky City in early January, to get his family's residence in the Oakland section of town ready for Mrs. Clarke and young Helen.[1]

Clarke was so busy working that many Pittsburgh citizens did not know he had slipped into town. After a few days, local writers caught up with the Pirates manager and quickly noticed that he looked in top condition.[2] Three months of hard work on the farm had kept him in great shape for the upcoming season. Weeks of walking through the Oklahoma territory hunting for game also worked wonders in strengthening Clarke's legs and improving his stamina. While talking about that particular area of the country, Clarke also reminisced about the time he coached an Indian team in the Territory.

The team that Clarke oversaw could run and field like nobody's business. Unfortunately, their hitting ability was suspect.[3] All of the players from the Indian squad were fast. It was only a matter of time before Clarke was challenged by the fastest member of the squad in a 100-yard race.

> I did a little sprinting in those days and the boys at school got to hear about it. They were proud of their own fleetness of foot and finally the best boy in the bunch challenged me to run 100 yards for $25 a side. I accepted and won the race, but the superintendent of the school would not allow me to keep the money. Later the defeated sprinter insisted upon another trial for $25 a side upon the condition that the terms be kept secret. He was so persistent that I finally agreed to meet him, in another sprint, as I supposed, but when

he talked business I found that the Indian wanted to make the second race from the school to town and return, a distance of 15 miles. I declared the match off at once, I would not have been in sight at the finish of a long race with that Indian. He could put a mail bag across his shoulder, run 7½ miles to the post office with his load, fill the bag up with letters for the school and run all the way back. I might as well have given him the money as to have started in the race he proposed."[4]

Clarke didn't use running as a means of exercise while he spent part of the winter in Pittsburgh, but he did other things to stay in shape. He was a strong proponent of using ice skating as a means to keep the legs sturdy and strong during the off-season. Star pitcher Deacon Phillippe joined him almost daily as the two stayed in shape skating at Duquesne Gardens.[5] It was here that Fred Clarke was attracted to another game where physical confrontation was a key element. Clarke, a solid all-round athlete who was already a proficient wrestler, boxer and golfer, decided to add ice hockey to that list of accomplishments.[6]

Playing hockey on his own for exercise wasn't a suitable option for Clarke. He craved competition and desired to be part of a team. He found a squad which consisted of Pittsburgh bankers that needed players. Clarke was drawn to hockey because of its raw speed. He also enjoyed the physical contact aspect of the game. Clarke could use the same mentality that was prevalent on the baseball diamond when he played ice hockey. Clarke's hockey debut may not have been as monumental as his first baseball game in Louisville, but it certainly did interest Pittsburgh people enough that it was chronicled in various publications.

Fred's debut as a hockey player was successful. He played with the Banker's team of the Western Pennsylvania League against the Quaker City team of Philadelphia. The Eastern seven was made up of crack college players, but was no match for the locals. Clarke was green, of course, but made a remarkably good showing for a man who had practiced only a few weeks and had never played a real game before. Some of the fans were afraid that in the roughing Clarke would be hurt, but the boss Pirate showed that he was able to take care of himself on the ice as on the diamond; while he received several hard bumps he managed to give as good as he got.[7]

Clarke used ice hockey as a means to keep his body strong and durable. Clarke found another activity which supplied hours of pleasurable leisure and also aided his sharp batting eye. He loved to test his marksmanship skills by shooting targets at a Carnegie facility. Clarke was usually joined by Phillippe and Honus Wagner at the range daily during the winter of 1902. All three became so good that they fostered the idea of holding a live-bird event of their own.[8]

Of the three, Wagner was the best of the bunch. This did not mean that Honus possessed the best shooting marksmanship skills on the Pittsburgh Pirates team. That honor belonged to Sam Leever, who was a crack shot and a demon trap shooter.[9] Not surprisingly, when guns were mentioned, Rube Waddell's name just naturally popped up in the conversation. Everyone knew that Rube loved guns, and Clarke hearkened back to when Waddell was under his guidance. While Clarke didn't miss the aggravation that Rube subjected him to, he and his fellow marksmen did pine for the endless amusement that Waddell supplied for his teammates in the clubhouse.

"Rube Waddell furnished fun for the entire team and for that reason I was sorry to see him leave," related Clarke. "I never had much trouble with him while I was with Pittsburgh because Harry Pulliam always saw that Rube got what was coming to him, and in return Eddie would do anything that Harry suggested. When Cliff Latimer was with us I put him and Eddie together in the hotels that we put up at on the road. One morning Cliff knocked at my door about 1 o'clock and I had to let him in.

"'Say, Cap, can't you make Rube quit pointing that big revolver at me?' demanded the catcher. 'Eddie is only joking, but I can't see the fun of it.'

"The request seemed reasonable, and I promised to do something, so after breakfast I called Waddell aside and asked him why he indulged in a practice that was so dangerous.

"'I'll put the revolver away if you'll keep Latimer from holding his razor against my neck,' said Rube.

"I let the matter drop, but was thankful to know that I had another room. But Eddie and Cliff had few quarrels. Any time that Cliff would not do as Rube desired the southpaw would say, 'I won't let you catch for me any more,' and that usually wheeled Latimer into line, for he would do anything to escape bench duty."[10]

As Clarke was staying in shape and thinking back to days gone by, Barney Dreyfuss was dealing with some issues that threatened his current status as a baseball magnate. Dreyfuss was looking at the prospect of another war if the stalemate at the 1901 National League meetings in New York was not resolved. Dreyfuss was forced into a battle with fellow magnates as he tried to maintain absolute control of the powerhouse team that he and Clarke had built in Pittsburgh. New York owner Andrew Freedman, with the backing of Cincinnati owner John T. Brush, introduced a proposal at the league meetings that seemed to specifically target Dreyfuss' team.

The Freedman measure called for the National League to become one large syndicate in which money and resources would be shared among the eight teams. Profits that the league grossed would be divided among owners at fixed percentages which were not exactly equal. Under the plan, Freedman would receive the largest piece of the pie.[11] The initial plan put forth by Freedman did not mention the moving of players from one team to another.

Many believed that this had strong possibilities in the future since players technically fell under the category of team resources. If such a plan were to be implemented, star Pittsburgh players such as Wagner or Clarke could be moved to another team without reservation. Freedman finally would be able to bring Clarke to New York and there wouldn't be anything that Dreyfuss could do about it. Ironically, the rival American League would operate under the syndicate concept for the 1902 season as Ban Johnson moved money and players around to keep the league running.

Freedman's syndicate plan also called for club owners to share in any losses that might be incurred during the 1902 season.[12] As one of the few owners who made a significant profit each season, Dreyfuss was strongly opposed to this plan. Dreyfuss did not want to put his profits into a league pool and believed that he should not have to assume the financial burden of teams who had been mismanaged horribly by their respective magnates. Freedman was one such owner. He angered New York fans with second-division finishes year after year and suffered huge monetary losses as well. His plan, on the surface, was put forth as a counter to the American League and their raid on National League rosters. Dreyfuss knew this proposal was presented for the sole purpose of reducing the Tammany-Hall-affiliated owner's red ink.

Dreyfuss' counter attack against Freedman in this incident was to propose that Albert G. Spalding, former owner and manager of the Chicago White Stockings, be elected to the presidency of the National League. Owners from Chicago, Philadelphia and Brooklyn supported Dreyfuss in this endeavor. New York, Boston, St. Louis and Cincinnati backed incumbent president Nick Young who had been on the job since 1885. Many of the Young dissenters felt that a change was necessary because Nick had gone through the motions during the past few years.[13]

With his nomination going nowhere fast, Spalding lashed out at Freedman and Brush. Spalding saw these two as the principle detractors who blocked him from being elected to the presidency.[14] Unless one of the eight magnates were willing to change his position, it looked as if the stalemate was destined to continue each time the owners took a vote. Magnates from both sides of the aisle continued their posturing with the hope that someone would jump to the other side. Harsh accusations were made. This led Freedman and Brush to pack their bags and leave before a decision was reached.[15]

When Brush and Freedman left the proceedings for good, the other magnates who supported Nick Young also exited the meeting room. Before that, twenty-five votes had been taken and twenty-five times the tally stood at four for Spalding and four for Young. After the Young supporters left, another vote was quickly called for by Colonel John I. Rogers of the Phillies who was monitoring the proceedings. Dreyfuss of Pittsburgh, Ebbets of Brooklyn, Hart of Chicago and Reach of Philadelphia voted for Spalding a twenty-sixth time.[16]

Since Fred Knowles, a secretary for the Giants under Freedman was still present in the room, the vote was valid with a majority of the clubs being represented. Spalding made a quick acceptance speech, the meeting was called to order, and Freedman's syndicate plan was shot down by the same four to zero vote that made Albert president. Knowles, still considered a representative of the Giants, abstained from the vote.[17]

The Freedman-Brush faction refused to recognize Spalding as the new league president and filed suit in court to overturn his election. It was in March 1902 that a New York judge ruled against Spalding and his backers. Spalding quickly resigned from the post and new candidates were put forth to assume the presidency.[18] Harry Pulliam's name was even tossed into the ring as a possible replacement for Spalding.

On April 2, a compromise was reached by all the owners as Nick Young once again assumed power, this time as secretary-treasurer under a new format of leadership. It was decided that the league itself would be run by a three-man executive committee. Brush from Cincinnati would act as chairman with Hart of Chicago and Soden of Boston functioning as subordinates. Dreyfuss only had one ally on the board whereas Freedman had two plus Nick Young.[19] Freedman's syndicate plan would never be proposed again, but the board did make life difficult for the Pirates as the 1902 season played out.

Whether it was suspensions handed out to rowdy players on the ball field or the reducing of roster limits to 19th century levels, Dreyfuss felt that Brush was prejudiced when the board made decisions regarding the Pirates. When punishment was doled out to players, it seemed like those under contract to Pittsburgh were treated more harshly than those from the other seven National League squads. Rumors began to surface that the Pirates intended to move to the American League in 1903 because Dreyfuss felt that Brush and his cohorts had a personal vendetta against him.[20] These rumors were eventually proven to be false, but one had to wonder how far Dreyfuss could be pushed as the board continued to make life uneasy for him throughout the summer.

Clarke also felt the wrath of league jurisprudence once the 1902 season began. He was involved in an incident with Boston first baseman Fred Tenney in May which saw both players receive suspensions. Clarke was not the perpetrator, but only defended himself when Tenney attacked the Pirates skipper. It was Clarke's first outburst of the season, and even though he hadn't started the fight, he apologized to local fans for losing his cool.[21]

7. Pittsburgh Repeats in Spite of Johnson's Treachery

Clarke was accused of playing dirty once again in June. This time there was no suspension as Clarke denied that he had spiked an opposing first baseman. On this occasion the controversy swirled around Clarke and Cardinals first baseman Roy Brashear. Manager Patsy Donovan believed that Clarke had torn Brashear's stocking with his spikes during a close play at first base in a game at Exposition Park. Clarke claimed that nothing happened and stated Brashear pulled John Ganzel's common stunt of looking down at his shoe after a play in order to receive sympathy from the crowd.[22]

During the traditional handshakes after the game, Donovan wouldn't let the incident die. Patsy acknowledged that Clarke was at fault when the St. Louis manager talked to some Pittsburgh friends. When the usually docile Dreyfuss heard this, he threatened to fight Donovan if the former Pirates manager visited his office and brought this libelous accusation before him. Dreyfuss had seen the play in question and was convinced that Brashear faked the whole incident.[23] In one of the few times that Dreyfuss actually showed a violent side, he proved that he always would support Clarke to the bitter end when vicious allegations were false.

Clarke's problems did not affect the play of his team one bit. By the end of June, Pittsburgh stood in first place with a blistering 41–12 record. Second-place Chicago trailed the Pirates by 11 games. Pittsburgh was practically unbeatable and matters could have been worse for National League foes if Rube Waddell was on the Pirate team. Waddell had been on Clarke's radar ever since the pitcher matriculated West after being suspended by Chicago manager Tom Loftus near the end of the 1901 season.

Rube went to Los Angeles after the suspension and did good work for a barnstorming aggregation put together by Joe Cantillon. Waddell eventually tired of life in California. During the winter, Clarke had sent Rube a check for $100 and a train ticket from San Francisco to Pittsburgh.[24] He hoped to bring Waddell back aboard the Pirates craft. Waddell was never heard from, but Rube also didn't return the check or ticket. When news reached Pittsburgh that Waddell had signed with Connie Mack for the 1902 season, many believed this was not true. Local rooters alleged that Rube yearned to be close to his Butler county roots.[25]

Waddell didn't report to Philadelphia in expeditious fashion. Those who believed that Rube was headed to Pittsburgh because he did not report to the Athletics hadn't quite figured the pitcher out when he played in the Smoky City. Waddell could just as easily be Florida bound intending to wrestle alligators as he was likely to resume pitching for the Pirates. With Rube anything was possible. Waddell did fulfill his obligation and reported to the Athletics, though, as the big lefty had a breakout season, leading Philadelphia to the American League pennant by going 24–7 with an ERA of 2.05.

Corsair hurlers were so dominant during the 1902 season that the possible addition of an eventual twenty-four game winner like Waddell wasn't necessary. Chesbro had a breakout season of his own, pacing the National League with a record of 28–6. His 2.17 ERA was only good enough to rank him third on the Pirates in that category. Clarke had four other reliable starters who ably complimented "Happy Jack." Tannehill (20–6, 1.95 ERA), Phillippe (20–9, 2.05 ERA), Doheny (16–4, 2.53 ERA) and Leever (15–7, 2.39 ERA) rounded out a quintet that was one of the best in league history.

With so much dominant pitching at his disposal, Clarke could have contended for the pennant with a hitting detachment that performed below expectations. Of course, Pittsburgh's work with the bat in 1902 was every bit as strong as the team's pitching. Beaumont took top honors in the league hitting department with a .357 average. Following the center fielder on the hit parade were Wagner (.330), Clarke (.316), Bransfield (.305) and Leach (.278). "Tommy the Wee" also topped the National League charts with six home runs. None of Leach's leading shots left the yard as he became Pittsburgh's first power champion by virtue of the inside-the-park home run.

Pittsburgh's total dominance in the National League race allowed the Pirates players to have some fun as the season progressed. On July 4, the Pirates had a morning-afternoon doubleheader scheduled against Brooklyn. Pittsburgh easily won the first game behind Tannehill's two-hitter, besting the Superbas by a score of 3–0. No clouds dotted the skies as the sun glistened brightly on Exposition Park's field. The only water in sight was that from the swelling Allegheny and Ohio Rivers, which could be seen beyond the center field wall by grandstand spectators. The culprit seemed to be a backed up sewer which ran near ballpark.[26]

It was still sunny as the second game commenced that holiday afternoon. As Chesbro methodically went through the process of shutting out Brooklyn, water began to seep under the grandstand near Pittsburgh's bench. Water also began to ooze beneath the outfield fences and quickly flooded different areas of the field. Center field quickly became an area of concern as the water rose to waist-high proportions. This didn't bother Ginger Beaumont who treated the unexpected lake like a minor inconvenience.[27] As John Gruber described, Beaumont took it all in stride and enjoyed the conditions in childlike fashion.

"Clarence Beaumont, in center for Pittsburgh, was also active," stated Gruber, "though not to such a degree as his rival. He had but two put-outs, and was obliged to break a way through the water after only three hits. He considered the unusual conditions as a huge joke, and ran races with himself, holding his hands high and making the water boil prodigiously with his kicking feet. He had the last put-out of the game, a fly from Bill Dahlen's bat. After making the catch he held the ball aloft and then plunged into the water.

The dive took him out of sight, and when he emerged, he blew hard and punched his fists into his eyes like a real swimmer."[28]

Fun and strong play continued to be Pittsburgh's mode of operation throughout the summer. Given Pittsburgh's solid balance of hitting, defense and pitching, it would have taken a monumental effort by another National League team to prevent the Pirates from repeating as league champions. In spite of the actions taken against his squad by John T. Brush and the new executive committee, Clarke's Pirates barreled through the National League like a runaway freight train. The pennant race was never in doubt as Pittsburgh dominated the competition, going 103–36 and finishing 27½ games in front of second-place Brooklyn. National League foes knew they would be choking on Pittsburgh's dust after the Buccaneers stormed to a 30–6 start.

A possible chink in the armor of the team's success began to rear its ugly head. A mid-summer rumor stated that Dreyfuss and Pulliam had received word of a meeting in a Pittsburgh hotel involving Ban Johnson, agents who were working on his behalf and Pirates players. Johnson and his people barely escaped detection by sneaking out through a freight elevator as the Pirates owner stormed into a room where the meeting was being held. As this report gained credence, people speculated on who was being targeted by the American League and whether there were any traitors who were working as agents to Johnson within the Pirates organization.

As the season wound down, stories began to surface stating that Pirates players had indeed signed contracts to play for American League teams in 1903. It was also reported that Johnson had once again infiltrated the Pirates ranks with agents who did his dirty work. The first player discovered by ownership to be acting in accordance with people from the American League was catcher Jack O'Connor. Dreyfuss acted swiftly when he received this information by releasing the former St. Louis catcher.[29]

Dreyfuss contended that O'Connor acted as a liaison for Ban Johnson and Charles Somers when the two men came to town in August intending to sign Pittsburgh players for their league in 1903. O'Connor brought several teammates to Johnson and Somers' room at the Hotel Lincoln. After a few meetings there, the talks shifted to Tannehill's room in Allegheny. O'Connor herded two more players to this room so that they could meet with the American League agents. By early evening, the operatives were discovered. Johnson and Somers ran for the hills and reached the train station just in time to leave town without any confrontation.[30]

Dreyfuss seemed to believe that none of his players were turncoats. He was confident that most of his men were loyal to a fault. Many of the players on his squad had already signed contracts to play in 1903. The only men who hadn't returned contracts were Tannehill, Chesbro, Conroy, Burke, Davis and

Leach.[31] Dreyfuss wasn't overly concerned since Chesbro and Leach both stated that they intended to stay in Pittsburgh.

"I don't believe they signed any of our players, and I hope the net results of their efforts will be shown in the future to be nothing," said Dreyfuss. "I have treated our men well and am willing to pay them as much as anybody can honestly promise to pay. If, notwithstanding, any of our players at the expiration of their contracts chose to leave the Pittsburgh club, well and good. But I will not stand for treachery or disloyalty from anybody while in my employ. No player can be a stool pigeon for the American League and draw salary from the Pittsburgh club at the same time."[32]

Dreyfuss referred to Johnson and Somers' trip to Pittsburgh as a "gum shoe mission" because of its sneaky and deceitful nature. Johnson quickly began to work the spin machine through the press, stating that the nature of his trip to Pittsburgh was for inspecting grounds in case an American League team moved into Dreyfuss' back yard. The president of the rival league also stated that a meeting was held with Pirates players, but he took offense to Dreyfuss' comment regarding the devious fashion in which the whole affair was conducted.

"Sure we were in Pittsburgh," said Johnson. "I see Mr. Dreyfuss says he had no objection to our coming after his players and bidding fairly for them, but he did object to what he claimed were gumshoe methods. What did he expect — that we were going to have several brass bands at the station to meet us, that we should have let him know a week in advance that we were coming? His remarks surprise me."[33]

Johnson and Somers continued playing it close to the vest regarding which Pittsburgh players had been approached when the two were in the Smoky City. The fact that they didn't even admit that O'Connor was complicit in their plan mattered little to Dreyfuss. He had suspected O'Connor's traitorous motives for some time and firmly believed the catcher was the specific American League enlister. One of O'Connor's friends, a local politician, even explained to the papers why Jack had turned on his employer. The friend stated that money made O'Connor do it and that he believed the catcher did wrong without intending to.[34]

American League agents made bringing Honus Wagner into the fold their top priority when they visited Pittsburgh. Johnson failed in this venture as Wagner had already signed a Pittsburgh contract for 1903. Clarke's name never received any mention in connection with American League overtures. Knowing that Clarke was deeply loyal to Dreyfuss, American League magnates quickly came to the conclusion that efforts to sway Clarke would prove futile.

In September, the *New York Sun* revealed the names of Pirates players who had jumped to the American League. Smith, O'Connor, Tannehill, Chesbro,

7. Pittsburgh Repeats in Spite of Johnson's Treachery 75

Conroy, Leach and Davis all signed to play for New York's American League franchise in 1903. Each player supposedly received $1,000 in advance money to desert the Pirates ship.[35]

One man who remained loyal to Clarke and Dreyfuss was Beaumont. He spurned an offer to leave Pittsburgh and jump to Detroit. With all the secretive cloak-and-dagger meetings going on between players and American League owners, it was difficult to get a handle on who was going and who was staying. Compounding the situation was the fact that some players were having misgivings about their decision to desert.

After Johnson and Somers visited Pittsburgh, Ban intimated that the players who were recruited by O'Connor would be playing for an American League entry in the Smoky City. A week after this trip, it was announced that these defectors would be headed to New York. Some of these players were willing to play for a Pittsburgh team in the American League because they liked the city. A few of the traitors may have felt betrayed by Johnson when their rights were awarded to New York. O'Connor and Davis would be playing for New York since Dreyfuss had already released both players. Tannehill would also be free to go. He was handed his unconditional release, paid in full to October 15, and told to remove his belongings from Exposition Park immediately.[36]

There were reports that Leach would remain with the Pirates for the 1903 season. The status of Chesbro still seemed up in the air as the 1902 season ended. Chesbro wanted to stay if Dreyfuss was willing to offer the pitcher a two-year $17,000 contract. It was rumored that Chesbro would receive $8,000 a year from the American League. When it came time to prepare for a special post-season series between the Pirates and an American League all-star squad, Clarke decided to use only Phillippe and Leever as his pitchers for the series.[37]

It was rumored that Clarke decided not to use Chesbro in the series against the all-stars at the request of other Pirates players who questioned Jack's loyalty. Chesbro's teammates also felt the pitcher should not be permitted to share in the monetary proceeds from this exhibition. Before the series, Chesbro was second guessing his decision to leave Pittsburgh. Many believed that his exclusion from participation in this event eliminated those misgivings and swayed him in his decision to make the jump. This seemed like a viable possibility until it was learned that Dreyfuss told Chesbro to leave. "Chesbro is gone, and I am glad of it," said Dreyfuss. "I wish the Americans all kinds of luck with him, but no more of him in Pittsburgh."[38]

Dreyfuss also accused Chesbro of throwing games by claiming sickness and refusing to pitch.[39] Chesbro was permitted to join Tannehill, Davis and O'Connor in New York with the owner's blessing. As the dust settled, it became apparent that O'Connor received assistance as he enlisted Pirates players into the American League ranks. Tannehill confided to some friends that he actually ran the American League operation in Pittsburgh with help from O'Connor. Dreyfuss hadn't been in the dark regarding these dealings even though the little magnate kept his silence for a long time.

"I have known for many weeks that Leach, Smith, Conroy, Tannehill, Chesbro and O'Connor each accepted a draft of $1,000 from the American League," said Dreyfuss. "Some of these players were deceived by the syndicate agent and when they came to their senses decided that they could not afford to sell their reputation, so they returned the drafts uncashed. I saw the drafts given to Leach, Conroy and Smith. These were returned to Somers. Some of the drafts were on the Hanover bank of New York and others upon a Cleveland bank. Somers knows that our players are all under contract. He should have known it in the summer, and he has no excuse for not knowing it now."[40]

Leach also sent Dreyfuss a letter which indicated that he would be playing in Pittsburgh in 1903 despite all the rumors that stated otherwise.[41] Leach's decision to ignore advance money he received from the American League and make the jump back to Pittsburgh opened deep wounds that had been festering for some time. Ban Johnson believed that Leach was American League property since he had signed a contract and received $1,000 in advance money. Dreyfuss felt that Leach's rights were bound to Pittsburgh through the reserve clause. He also thought that the third baseman showed loyalty by rejecting Johnson's tempting offer. Dreyfuss considered the whole affair closed. "Johnson is too much of an artistic prevaricator for me," remarked Dreyfuss. "I do not care about wrangling with him when he will not stick to the truth — does not, in fact, show any inclination of ever hovering near the same. I will show a few documents which will prove that Leach has returned the advance money sent him by the American."[42]

Dreyfuss may not have wanted to engage Johnson in controversy, but that is exactly what the Pittsburgh magnate did. It certainly didn't help that Dreyfuss accused the American League president of being a liar. Johnson reacted quickly to Dreyfuss' comments. He believed that Leach had signed a valid contract to play in New York, and contended that the document did not suddenly become null and void because Tommy returned the advance money. To enforce his statement Johnson exhibited documents which included Leach's autograph at the bottom of an ironclad contract, and a receipt for $1,000 in advance money.

"I see it is claimed Leach has returned the $1,000 to Mr. Somers of Cleveland and that releases him from his contract with us," Johnson said. "He might have sent the money to President Roosevelt or J. Pierpont Morgan just as well so far as this case is concerned. I signed Leach personally to that contract, and

7. Pittsburgh Repeats in Spite of Johnson's Treachery

I sent him his advance money through Mr. McRoy, my secretary. I have not received any returned advance money. Dreyfuss knows it and is going beyond the limit when he makes an assertion to the contrary. As far as Mr. Somers is concerned, he was connected with the transaction only as a witness to the contracts. I suppose if I had been alone at the hotel and called in a hall boy to witness the signatures Leach would have returned the advance money to him and claim release from the contract on that ground."[43]

The case involving Leach became the fulcrum for all the desertions that occurred during the war between both leagues. Both sides decided that this would be the pivotal point where each made their final stand. In a way, the waters had been very murky during the past two seasons as players jumped from one league to the other. How the Leach case was resolved would go a long way in determining how future situations would be dealt with. Each league believed they had a valid claim to the third baseman. Whether he liked it or not, Leach's set of circumstances took on a symbolic tone that became much larger than the player himself.

Johnson tried to turn the tables on Dreyfuss. He accused Barney of supporting contract jumping since the Pittsburgh owner was attempting to bring Leach back even though he signed an American League contract. Johnson and his operatives smeared Leach by claiming that it was him, rather than O'Connor and Tannehill, who acted as a spy relative to American League interests.[44] Dreyfuss didn't buy any of this for a minute.

"I have known for weeks, in fact, ever since Leach decided he would not jump his contract, that the American League was going to try make him unpopular with the Pittsburgh rooters, simply for revenge," said Dreyfuss. "He was the man that the trust wanted and now that it knows that he can't be bribed, it is trying to make trouble for him.... We know other details about the conspiracy that convince us that we did not make any mistake in blaming O'Connor and Tannehill, but I have mentioned enough to prove that Johnson had trumped up the latest charge against Leach to punish Tommy for being too honest to jump his Pittsburgh contract."[45]

While Dreyfuss was being raked over the coals and the merits of the Leach case were being discussed, Clarke attended to a little business of his own. He intended to meet in Chicago with his two pitchers who had defected to the American League. Chesbro and Tannehill were playing for the same barnstorming team managed by Joe Cantillon that Rube Waddell had performed for the previous year. Clarke hoped the meeting would succeed in bringing both pitchers back into the Pirates fold. He was left to his own devices as both Tannehill and Chesbro dodged the Pittsburgh manager. Clarke became infuriated when Chesbro later suggested that the Pirates manager did not keep the appointment. Chesbro claimed in a letter to an American League representative that Clarke was afraid to meet with the two pitchers.[46] "That is a lie," said Clarke. "I called three times at the hotel and each time was told that Chesbro was out. Then I went to a saloon kept by Joe Cantillon, the man who was managing the baseball excursion to the coast, and there I found the two players. Tannehill and Chesbro failed to mention that fact."[47]

After the 1902 season, Clarke went back to Kansas and began a project that likely would keep him occupied throughout the off-season. He planned to work night and day as he built a new seven-room house on his Winfield property.[48] Clarke was a thrifty man who had more than enough money available to take on such a venture. As Clarke began construction in Kansas, Dreyfuss hoped to do a little building of his own in Pittsburgh. In a figurative sense, Dreyfuss needed to build a bridge of unity. He had to bring the dissenting National and American Leagues together, because Dreyfuss realized that peace between the two leagues was imperative and the continued success of the Pirates depended on it.

Chapter 8

Historic Battle with an Old Friend

Barney Dreyfuss and Fred Clarke were confident that the players who defected to the American League could be easily replaced. Young Jimmy Sebring, who made a good showing by batting .325 in 19 late-season games during the 1902 season, was slated to replace Lefty Davis in right field. Eddie Phelps was also expected to succeed Jack O'Connor behind the plate. Clarke was particularly intrigued by Phelps' speed, an asset not usually contained in a catcher's body. "A fast catcher is, indeed, a rarity in these days of fast pitching," said Clarke. "I have one in young Phelps, who is an excellent base runner as well as a good catcher and batsman. We will have a team in 1903 that will be equally as strong as the Pirates of 1901 and 1902 and every man on it will be loyal to his club."[1]

Traitors such as Jesse Tannehill and Jack Chesbro still needed to be replaced. Nothing exciting happened on the pitching front during the December league meetings in New York. Victories would have to come from players already on the roster as Clarke pondered over who would replace the 48 Pittsburgh victories that Chesbro and Tannehill had accounted for in 1902.

One positive that came out of the December league meetings was the election of Harry Pulliam to the National League presidency. The three-man committee established after the 1901 season was flawed and did not work. When the time arose to elect a new president, Dreyfuss proposed the Pirates club secretary as a compromise choice. Dreyfuss sold the other league magnates on Pulliam's virtue and loyalty while with him in both Louisville and Pittsburgh. Pulliam was elected to the office unanimously by the owners.[2] Clarke took time away from his construction project to pen a letter of congratulations to Pulliam. In the letter, Clarke also made special mention about two new members of the Clarke clan. Clarke had bought two horses and named them Phil and Hans in honor of Deacon Phillippe and Honus Wagner.[3]

While Clarke continued to build his new house in Kansas, Dreyfuss began mending league fences in New York. Changes in the ownership of two franchises occurred after the conclusion of the 1902 season. Freedman sold the New York Giants to John T. Brush, who in turn allowed a group headed by August "Garry" Herrmann to purchase the Reds.[4] These changes, along with the election of Pulliam to the presidency, brought a sense of stability that had been lacking in the league for several years.

Now that the senior circuit had a secure foundation from which to build, the owners' focus turned to creating a peaceful environment between the two combating leagues. Magnates such as Frank De Hass Robison of the St. Louis Cardinals had tired of waging war against American League teams that conducted business right in their own back yard. A special committee was established at the 1902 meetings whose purpose was to draft an agreement that Ban Johnson and the American League owners found acceptable. Pulliam represented Dreyfuss' interests within a league caucus that initiated the peace process which later included American League magnates.[5]

It was first suggested that both leagues merge into a twelve-team National League, but that idea met quick rejection from Johnson.[6] The New York discussions did not bring an immediate solution, but the ideas cultivated from that dialogue led to a peace agreement being finalized at a meeting in Cincinnati on January 10, 1903. Under the terms of the agreement, the American League was recognized and accepted as an equal major league by their National League brethren.[7] Johnson was still permitted to place a team in New York for the 1903 season. Dreyfuss received a major concession when it was agreed that Detroit would not move its club to Pittsburgh. A special committee would determine the dispersal of disputed players who had signed contracts with both leagues.[8]

When the peace agreement was reached on January 10, Brush originally opposed the resolution. He wasn't happy that a competing team was being permitted to go head-to-head against him in New York. Brush felt that Dreyfuss had sold him out as protection against an American League team moving into Pittsburgh. Charles Ebbets backed Brush in this rejection because he had been hit particularly hard by player defections during the past few seasons.[9] Both men eventually relented and took up the task of passing the agreement along with their fellow magnates. On January 22, the document that bound both leagues together was ratified by the eight National League magnates.[10]

With the agreement now in effect, Pittsburgh fans began to wonder how the disputed Pirates would be dispersed. It turned out that the committee assigned Tommy Leach and Harry Smith to the Exhibit "B" list, meaning that both players would remain in Pittsburgh.[11] Wid Conroy's name was on the Exhibit "A" list which meant that he had been awarded to the American League. Jack Chesbro and Jesse Tannehill appeared on the Exhibit "A" list but were not classified as disputed players.[12] This meant that they were free to join Johnson's league without any interference from Pirates ownership. After the dust settled, Chesbro finally spoke out and explained why he jumped from Pittsburgh to New York. "I severed my connection with the Pittsburgh Club simply for business reasons," said Chesbro. "I received what I considered a very advantageous offer to play with the New York Americans. It was more that the Pittsburgh people cared to pay, so I accepted it."[13]

Even though Clarke had lost two-fifths of his starting rotation, the Pirates manager was still confident that Pittsburgh would claim its third consecutive pennant in 1903. Pitchers like Leever and Phillippe likely would be relied upon more heavily than before. Leever in particular could expect a heavier workload now that Tannehill and Chesbro were in New York. Leever, confident that he wouldn't let his manager down, also believed that Pittsburgh was the team to beat in 1903.

"I am just as confident we will win the 1903 pennant as I was that we would finish first," said Leever. "We are strong at all points and if a weakness should develop, Barney Dreyfuss will provide a player to fill the hole. No club is as well conducted as Pittsburgh, because everyone connected with it has a practical knowledge of base ball. President Dreyfuss is an expert in picking players and he treats his men so well that they give him their best services. He is not a boss over the boys; but their friend, and if there is any advantage in deals between club and players, Barney gives in. He would not have the best of it if he could get it, and when he finds that a man is playing ball that merit's a raise in salary, he boosts a man's pay. I consider myself fortunate in being in his employ and feel sure that I will retire from the game without the least cause for a kick on him."[14]

When a player praised Dreyfuss in such fashion, they certainly were not diminishing the contributions that Clarke made in his capacity as manager. Clarke was an extension of Dreyfuss. They analyzed the game in similar fashion and made decisions that were always in the best interest of the club. By 1903, Dreyfuss was giving Clarke much more freedom regarding team personnel decisions. Dreyfuss always said that it was his job to assemble the team before spring training. Once the Pirates hit the baseball field at Hot Springs, Clarke was permitted to run the team as he saw fit without interference from the owner.

Clarke made a decision regarding a new pitcher with an eye on replacing one of his star hurlers from 1902. While attending to business in Bellaire, Ohio, Clarke ran into veteran twirler Bill "Brickyard" Kennedy. Roaring Bill was trying to get his career back on track after years of partaking in the flowing bowl to excess. Kennedy told Clarke that he had been on the water wagon since last summer. Clarke believed that Kennedy's boast was legitimate, and signed Kennedy to a straight contract without the booze clause that Bill suggested should be placed in the document. Clarke trusted Kennedy and told the pitcher that his word was good enough.[15]

Kennedy was a four-time twenty-game winner with Brooklyn, having most recently achieved that mark in 1900 when he went 20–13. However, he had only appeared in 20 combined games during the 1901 and 1902 seasons. The Pirates took a chance on Kennedy feeling that the pitcher's recent sub-par performance was due to his drinking problem. Roaring Bill was a model citizen throughout the 1903 season as he kept his promise of remaining sober. Unfortunately, the best he could give the Pittsburgh team was mediocre pitching, nine wins and a 3.45 ERA.

A parade of young arms joined Pittsburgh with the hope that at least one pitcher would step forward and ease the losses of Chesbro and Tannehill. Dreyfuss' judgment was clouded because of the circumstances surrounding the exit of both players. He was confident that any pitcher scouted by Clarke or himself was better than two contract jumpers. Dreyfuss was blinded by stubborn pride which prevented him from realizing the irreplaceable talent which Chesbro and Tannehill both possessed.

Bucky Veil (5–3, 3.82 ERA), Kaiser Wilhelm (5–3, 3.24 ERA), Cy Falkenberg (1–5, 3.86 ERA) and Gus Thompson (2–2, 3.56 ERA) all paled in comparison to the former anchors of the Pittsburgh staff who were pitching for the New York Highlanders in 1903. Since none of these newcomers stepped forward and distinguished themselves, Clarke had to rely on the three pitcher aggregation of Phillippe, Leever and Doheny to win ball games.

Pittsburgh didn't bust out of the gate during the early stages of the season as they had in 1902. At the end of May, the Pirates record stood at 25–16, in third place, four games behind the league leading Chicago Cubs. Clarke's boys found the going much tougher than in previous years. Despite their struggles on the diamond, Clarke instituted a policy change that made life much easier for National League umpires. When Harry Pulliam assumed the league presidency, he stated that his first goal was to eliminate the rowdy atmosphere which prevailed in baseball. Dreyfuss and Clarke felt they could set a proper example for their old friend by eliminating kicking and general umpire abuse.

"It is true," said Clarke to a representative of the *Pittsburgh Gazette*, "that we have decided to cut out all kicking. Heretofore our policy was to obey the new rules when the umpire forced our opponents to do so. This plan got us into trouble in the Cincinnati series and as the present championship race promises to be a hot one, we will not risk having other players suspended. I realize now that President Pulliam simply did his duty when he suspended Wagner on the report of his umpires without making any further investigation. The other players agree with me and they all voted against kicking in the future. In a close game any man is likely to forget all of his good resolutions and fly off the handle, but when one of the Pirates goes wrong the others will remind him of his obligations."[16]

Pittsburgh's decision to ease up on National League umpires was made after Dreyfuss and Clarke had come to a general consensus. Dreyfuss was in total agreement with Pulliam that baseball needed to be cleaned up so that a new era of fans could be ushered in. Most rooters were not impressed by the violence that sometimes occurred on a baseball diamond. Dreyfuss was a paradigm of virtue who realized that baseball's image required a slight makeover. He convinced Clarke that behaving civilly was in the Pirates' best interest. "Harry Pulliam intends to clean up the National League," said Dreyfuss. "He's going after the roughnecks, the rowdies, the umpire baiters, and the men who swear so you can hear them all over the stands. I told him I'm all in favor of it. Now I want you to fight as hard for games as you ever did. I don't want a ball club that will let anyone push it around, but if we lay off Harry's umpires, we make it easier for him."[17]

Clarke worked diligently to stop umpire baiting on the baseball field. This new boy scout mentality didn't help Clarke off the diamond. On June 26, he was forced to defend himself before a game against the New York Giants. Frank Bowerman, a catcher who Clarke did not keep when Louisville and Pittsburgh merged in 1900, requested Clarke's presence inside a Polo Grounds box office. Once Clarke joined Frank in the club office, Bowerman began to wail away at the Pittsburgh manager with fists of fury.[18] The ticket office was small and cramped, which worked against Clarke as he attempted to mount a counterattack.

Bowerman scored a decisive victory in this short, one-round bout. Clarke was unable to defend himself adequately and didn't throw many punches of his own. Clarke finally stumbled out of the office once he was able to unlock the door. Bowerman's cowardly attack left Clarke with a black eye and various bruises on his face. Bowerman stated that he fought Clarke because the Pirates manager claimed that Frank had made derogatory comments about fellow New York catcher Jack Warner.[19] Many suspected that Bowerman also believed Clarke had told malicious stories about him when Fred and the other Louisville players came to Pittsburgh in 1900.

Since neither player was in uniform at the time and this incident occurred away from the baseball diamond, Harry Pulliam didn't suspend either player. Pulliam did fine Bowerman $100 after Dreyfuss brought the matter to his attention.[20] New York scribes backed Bowerman's behavior and John T. Brush stated that Frank would not be punished in any way by the Giants management.[21] Clarke made no statement regarding the matter and continued forward like nothing ever happened.

Games with the Giants that season were true battles as Pittsburgh split the twenty games they played against John McGraw's men. The Pirates rode the hot bats of Wagner (.355), Clarke (.351), Beaumont (.341) and Leach (.298) as they remained in contention during the season's early days. Once the summer heated up, so did the Pirates as they reeled off one of the greatest pitching performances in baseball history. From June 2 through June 8, the Pirates pitching staff recorded six straight shutouts. The streak began with Phillippe beating New York, 7–0, on June 2 and Leever returning the favor the following day by defeating McGraw's squad, 5–0. Next up was Boston. The Beaneaters were swept by Wilhelm, 5–0, on June 4, Doheny, 9–0, on June 5, and Phillippe, 4–0, on June 6. A perfect week at Exposition Park was finished by Leever when he knocked off the Philadelphia Phillies, 2–0, on June 8.

Manager Fred Clarke lost star twirlers Jack Chesbro and Jesse Tannehill to the American League after the 1902 season. After a slow start in 1903, his squad caught fire and claimed its third consecutive National League pennant. In this photograph, Clarke is sitting in the middle of the first row and owner Barney Dreyfuss is fourth from the left in the second row.

8. Historic Battle with an Old Friend

This phenomenal performance gave Pittsburgh the spark they needed. Clarke's troops rebounded from their mediocre start and posted a three-month record of 52–21 from the beginning of June through the end of August. This hot stretch enabled the Pittsburgh team to put some distance between themselves and the nearest contenders, Chicago and New York. As the team heated up, word began to surface from New York that Clark Griffith was anxious to get rid of ex–Pirates such as Davis, Conroy, Tannehill and O'Connor.[22] It seemed that Griffith wasn't happy with how some of these contract jumpers were performing.

The Pirates did not suffer at all from the losses of Davis and Conroy. Jimmy Sebring did a fine job in his rookie season patrolling right field, hitting .277 in 124 games. With Conroy out of the picture, Wagner became firmly entrenched at the shortstop position. Even though viable replacements hadn't been found for Chesbro and Tannehill, the Pirates were setting the pace in the National League thanks to the pitching trio of Phillippe, Leever and Doheny. Unfortunately, problems struck the pitching staff in early August when Doheny's effectiveness was curtailed by a minor injury. The lefty began to show signs of moodiness and irritability after a few bad outings on the mound. His mood quickly turned delusional as Doheny believed he was being followed by detectives who were hired to keep an eye on him.[23]

As was the practice of Dreyfuss at the time, certain players who were known to freely spend their salary on negative vices of the world did not receive their pay directly. For these players, Dreyfuss would send the money to their wives. Doheny was one such player and the possibility existed that this may have contributed to his paranoia. Some also believed that Doheny's sudden change in behavior could be attributed to the fact that his wife was sick. Of course, at no time was Doheny actually being followed by detectives, but he deserted the team and returned home to Andover, Massachusetts, nonetheless. It was quite possible that Doheny was cracking under the pressure of being a go-to guy on the pitching staff. With Chesbro and Tannehill gone, he was counted upon more heavily than in the past. There were also murmurings to the effect that Doheny had a drinking problem which contributed to his erratic behavior. Eddie cooled his heals in Andover for about two weeks.

When Clarke rejoined the Pirates after missing time with an injury, two letters awaited him. One was from Doheny's doctor explaining that the pitcher was suffering from nervous prostration. The second communication was from Eddie's wife stating that her husband felt much better and he was ready to report back to Pittsburgh when needed.[24] Doheny's services were certainly required, so Clarke brought the southpaw pitcher back into the fold. As writer Ralph S. Davis explained, Clarke was very understanding given his pitcher's fragile condition:

Manager Clarke telegraphed for Doheny to take a few days longer to rest and to join his comrades in the City of Churches when the Pirates reach there next Wednesday. Manager Clarke said that he was glad Doheny was improving and also glad to know that there was an excuse for his mysterious action, for, had it been discovered that Doheny had merely left the team through being miffed at anything that had occurred, he would not have been allowed to come back. As matters stand, however, he can play at any time and his return will be welcomed by his teammates, who know that Doheny is one of the most successful pitchers in the business and that he can win consistently when he is in condition. It is believed that his return will put the Pirate pitching staff in first-class condition and that from this time on the Champions will have no trouble in widening the breach that separates the Giants and the Colts from the lead.[25]

Doheny struggled in his first two starts after returning to the Pirates team on August 15. He settled down after that and put together a string of four solid performances in a row as the month of August ended. Unfortunately, a horrible start by Doheny in which Pittsburgh suffered a 13–8 defeat at the hands of Chicago on September 7 once again drove the troubled pitcher to leave the team and return home. This time Doheny did not come back to the squad; in fact, he would never appear on a baseball diamond again.

Like Doheny, Clarke had also been away from the Pittsburgh team during August for a brief period of time, suffering from a bad back and a lame shoulder. This wasn't the only reason doctors recommended that Clarke retire to his Kansas ranch for a short rest.[26] It seemed that Clarke was suffering from exhaustion. Doctors were taking precautions to insure that his nervous condition did not reach serious proportions. A little rest and relaxation was expected to rejuvenate the Pirates manager as he remained away from the stresses and worries of baseball for awhile.

It was amazing that Clarke had his team in contention considering all the injuries Pittsburgh players suffered during the season. The roll call of the walking wounded was long and lengthy: Kitty Bransfield — weak ankle, Tommy Leach — bad throwing hand, Eddie Phelps — sprained ankle, Harry Smith — weak knee and a bad hand, Deacon Phillippe — lame back, Claude Ritchey — dizzy spells (not caused by brandy), Irving Wilhelm — illness, Bucky Veil — weak and rundown from illness, Bill Kennedy — leg gashed by glass, Jimmy Sebring — lame ankle and Honus Wagner — both hands injured, one thumb dislocated.[27]

Pittsburgh's injured list got worse in early September when Wagner also wrenched the tendons in his leg. It was believed that the star Pirate would miss the remainder of the season. Honus was expected to be operated on by the famous "Bonesetter" Reese at a hospital in Youngstown, Ohio.[28] Wagner saw the bonesetter, but the operation was delayed for the time being.

8. Historic Battle with an Old Friend

Pittsburgh staggered through September, going 14–12 for the month. The Pirates limped across the finish line in first place with a record of 91–49 despite losing six of their last seven ball games. The Pirates topped second-place New York by 6½ games and third-place Chicago by eight games. Clarke's team won their third straight pennant and represented the senior circuit in a championship series against the pennant-winning Boston Americans of the American League.

When it became apparent late in the summer that Pittsburgh and Boston would likely place first in their respective leagues, Dreyfuss approached Boston owner Henry Killilea with the idea that the two teams play each other in a World Series to determine an ultimate champion between the two leagues. The details for the series were hammered out by the two owners and it was decided that the best-of-nine affair would begin in Boston on October 1. Gate receipts from the games would be divided evenly by the two owners.

Killilea ran into a problem that almost led to the cancellation of the games before they could ever begin. Boston players were only under contract through September 30, while the salaries of Dreyfuss' squad were paid through October 15. The Boston team, with manager Jimmy Collins as their spokesman, threatened to strike if all the receipts that Killilea received were not divided among the players. With the series itself hanging in the balance, Killilea agreed to pay the players a 75 percent share of the receipts while he only took 25 percent.[29]

Clarke battled against former Louisville teammate Collins as Pittsburgh and Boston represented their respective leagues in the first modern World Series. The Americans were a strong club with solid sluggers like Buck Freeman, Chick Stahl and Patsy Dougherty. The Boston hitters were supported ably by a pitching staff which included Cy Young, Bill Dinneen and Tom Hughes. Collins was also the best third baseman in either league. Clarke later took some of the credit for Collins being able to achieve such success down at the hot corner as he discussed the old days in Louisville. "Collins, of course, was one of the great third baseman," stated Clarke. "I take some credit for that, because I was the first to suggest he play third. At Louisville in 1895 or '96, we had Collins in center field. He had been bought from Boston for $1,500, but Boston had the privilege of repurchasing him for the same sum."[30]

With the series now set to go as planned, baseball fans across the country attempted to form their own opinions as they consumed all the dope being filtered about by pundits regarding the games. Pittsburgh was considered the heavy favorite by many baseball experts even though Wagner and Clarke were still suffering from injuries and the pitching staff was down to one reliable starter, Phillippe. Doheny was still at home in Andover and twenty-five game winner Leever had injured his pitching arm during a trap-shooting mishap.

Leever's arm became worse when he pitched in a late season game against Boston on a cold, raw, windy day.[31] Sam's arm went bad because he took the mound on a day when a man in his condition shouldn't have tested such elements.[32]

In spite of these setbacks Dreyfuss refused to cancel the series. He did not want to use the numerous injuries as an excuse and was still confident Pittsburgh could win. Clarke likewise believed his team was better than the Americans, but he had some reservations given his squad's injuries. Clarke also realized that his 1903 team had "gutted it out" on their way to the pennant whereas the 1902 aggregation claimed the top prize on shear talent alone.

> I may never have made the statement before, but I will say now that Pittsburgh's 1903 pitching staff is not as good or as strong as was that of last year, when we had Jesse Tannehill and Jack Chesbro. They were undoubtedly great pitchers. Had we had them again this year we would have been invincibly strong. But this season we were compelled to try out a number of young twirlers, and they did not do as well as we expected some of them. We had only three pitchers that we could depend on the season round to do good work. Otherwise our team is stronger this year than it has ever been before.
>
> Of course, the infield is practically the same, although Leach has played, if anything, better ball this year than last, with the exception of the time he was injured. The outfield was stronger this year by the addition of Sebring, who is a better player than the man he succeeded. Of course, Sebring is young yet, and he has many things to learn, but he is possessed of a good, sound head and the willingness to work. He has not yet reached the top of the ladder, and should be even better next year than this. But, after all, there is only one reason why we won the pennant this year, and that is because we had the strongest team in the league. We have demonstrated that, and there can be no dispute upon the matter.[33]

Pittsburgh looked like the strongest team in the galaxy when the World Series opened in Boston on October 1. The Pirates buried the Americans behind Phillippe, 7–3. Leach recorded the first hit and scored the first run in World Series history. Sebring's seventh-inning inside-the-park home run was also the first homer ever hit in the Fall Classic. The Pirates sent nine men to the plate in the first inning and scored four runs after Young retired Beaumont and Clarke to start the game. Pittsburgh's confidence was buoyed by the fact that they pounded out 12 hits against Boston's star pitcher. Clarke recorded two hits in the game. He singled in the second but was thrown out by Dougherty when he tried to stretch the hit into a double; he added another single in the fourth inning.

Sebring was the star of the game as he went three-for-five and drove in four runs. Clarke's team was so impressive in the first game that many believed Pittsburgh would run roughshod over Boston throughout the remainder of

8. Historic Battle with an Old Friend

the series. It was even suggested that the Pirates were so far superior that Boston would not be playing for the championship if Pittsburgh were in the American League. Most newspaper scribes believed that Pittsburgh's lineup contained too many star-caliber players for Boston to handle. Clarke and other Pirates received their due from the *New York Evening Telegraph* after the first series game: "Then comes Fred Clarke, leader of the National's champions. It's many years since Fred began playing ball, and almost from the first he was numbered among the stars. He could always hit and run bases. In covering his position in left field he is nearly always found where the ball is about to drop. In hitting this year he gained an average of .336, and in fielding made so few errors that his average in that department was .964."[34]

Many people believed that Pittsburgh was going to capture the championship with absolutely no resistance from their opponent. Everyone soon found that a nine-game series cannot necessarily be decided in just one game. Boston rebounded with a victory in Game Two as sore-armed Leever did not make it out of the first inning for Pittsburgh. The fact that Pittsburgh only lost the game 3–0 was a testament to Bucky Veil's strong seven-inning relief stint in which he allowed only one run. Clarke had one of the three Pirates hits; a single to center in the fourth inning. Clarke also received a walk in the first. Unfortunately, bad baserunning plagued Pittsburgh's manager in both instances. After the walk, Clarke was picked off first base. In the fourth inning, he was doubled off second when Wagner lined out to second baseman Hobe Ferris.

Pittsburgh extracted revenge on October 3 when Phillippe bested the Americans, 4–2, in the third game of the series. The Pirates sealed the outcome early with one run in the second inning and two runs in the third. Ritchey and Phelps each recorded two hits and drove in one run apiece. Clarke cracked a double in the third inning but eventually was forced at the plate when Ritchey grounded to Collins at third.

The Pirates headed back to Pittsburgh with the lead in the championship series. Exuberant fans awaited the squad as their train made its way back to the Smoky City. In spite of the fact that it was Sunday, 5,000 fans gathered near the Union Depot hoping to get a glimpse of their favorite Pirates player. Crowd control was a bit of a problem as police attempted to keep the cheering masses in check. When Clarke received word that a large mob was waiting for the team to pull into town, he had Phillippe smuggled off the train in East Liberty. Phillippe went home on a street car undetected.[35]

Fred Clarke didn't want any harm coming to his star pitcher. With both teams getting a two-day break in the schedule for travel purposes, Clarke intended to give Phillippe the ball once again in Game Four on October 6. After opposing Young in Game One and Hughes in Game Three, Deacon was pitted against Dinneen as the series shifted to Exposition Park. After

Phillippe made it three straight victories for himself when he nipped Boston, 5–4, Pittsburgh fans showed their appreciation for the workhorse of the series: "All did not walk, however, for Charles Deacon Phillippe, the 'steady man,' who has won all three of the games in which the Pittsburghs were victors, was simply lifted to the shoulders of a number of enthusiastic fans and escorted to the clubhouse, where for half an hour he was compelled to shake hands with his admirers."[36]

The Americans almost rallied from a 5–1 deficit with three runs in the top of the ninth inning. For the first time in the series, Boston batters were able to connect against Phillippe's deliveries. It was a foreboding sign that Phil had been knocked around in the ninth because he ran out of gas. Clarke finally scored his first run of the series after he forced Beaumont in the first inning and eventually scored on Bransfield's single to center field.

In spite of holding a three-games-to-one lead in the series, two factors began working against the Pittsburgh team. The first was a dearth of pitching. Leever gave his sore arm a try in Game Two and came out on the short end of the decision against Boston's Bill Dinneen. The result would be the same when the two locked horns again in Game Six on October 8. This, coupled with the fact that Bill Kennedy absorbed an 11–2 pasting in Game Five, now meant that the series was even at three games apiece. The momentum had dramatically shifted in Boston's favor.

The second factor that helped to sway the series in Boston's favor was the presence of a group of fanatical fans known as the "Royal Rooters" at each game. Led by longtime Boston fan Mike Regan and tavern owner Mike "Nuff Ced" McGreevey, the Royal Rooters were accompanied by a band at each and every game.[37] As the series progressed, the rooters decided they needed a song that would throw the Pirates off their game. They chose a popular song of the day called "Tessie" as their theme to achieve this end.[38] Game after game, inning after inning, the band played "Tessie" with the Royal Rooters singing verses that were altered in order to poke fun at some of the Pittsburgh players. Whether in Boston or at home in Exposition Park, the play of the Pittsburgh squad suffered dramatically as "Tessie" constantly resonated through their ears.

Clarke had dropped a fly ball off the bat of Chick Stahl in the sixth inning of Game Five which started Boston on their merry way to a six-run inning. Wagner's complicity was also apparent as he committed two errors during that stanza which led to all the runs charged to pitcher Kennedy in the sixth inning being unearned. Clarke went two-for-five at the plate in Game Six and drove in two runs for Pittsburgh as the Corsairs stranded nine runners on base.

Manager Clarke turned to Phillippe in order to stop the bleeding in Game Seven. However, Deacon was not up to the task as Boston cruised to

8. Historic Battle with an Old Friend

an easy 7–3 victory behind the pitching of Cy Young. Clarke went one-for-five and banged a triple for his squad in a losing effort. Clarke only scored one run, even though he was on base four times thanks to weak fielding by Boston. He was left stranded on base in the third and eighth innings. Clarke then left the bases loaded himself when he flied out to left field with one out in the ninth inning.

The series shifted back to Boston for Game Eight on October 13. Phillippe was called upon once again with only two days of rest to pitch for the fifth time in the series. The tired-armed pitcher of the Pirates gave a valiant effort, but it was not enough as Dinneen shut out Pittsburgh, 3–0, to claim the championship for the Boston team. Clarke had one of the four hits that Pittsburgh scratched out against Boston's star pitcher. Dinneen sealed the championship for Boston when he struck out Wagner to end the game.

Charles "Deacon" Phillippe was brilliant in defeat as writers across the nation praised the Pirates hurler for his gutsy performance. Phillippe tossed five complete games, a record that has never been approached in World Series play. Clarke realized that Phillippe had given the Pirates a fighting chance against the Boston Americans:

> If he couldn't do it, I do not know who could. That was no decision of mine, depending upon Phillippe. Sam Leever had jammed his shoulder practicing with a new shotgun. Ed Doheny had gone off the reservation. When we accepted the invitation from the Americans for the first World's Series, it was Phillippe or nobody.
>
> The Deacon did a grand job, against a team which had Cy Young (28–9), Bill Dinneen (21–13) and Long Tom Hughes (20–7) to fire at him.
>
> He won the first game from Young, 7 to 3, with six hits and ten strikeouts. He won over Hughes in the third game, with only one day's rest, 4 to 2. He beat Dinneen in the fourth game, 5 to 4, as he pitched for the third time in six days. Maybe it was too much to ask of any pitcher, but he had to go for me in the seventh game, his fourth start in ten days, and in the eighth game, his fifth start in 13 days, and he lost both, 7 to 3 and 3 to 0.[39]

Clarke's play in the 1903 World Series could best be summed up as average. He hit .265, scored three runs, had two RBIs and committed one error in the outfield. Sebring led all Pirates hitters with a .333 average, but others such as Ritchey (.148), Bransfield (.207), Phelps (.231) and Wagner (.222) failed miserably at the plate. Wagner was criticized for his poor showing and there were those who dubbed him "yellow," a term that was used in that era to describe someone who choked under pressure. Honus would carry this battle scar with him until redemption was achieved later in his career.

In spite of the anemic hitting displayed by most of the Pittsburgh squad, it was actually the ineffectiveness of Leever (0–2, 5.40 ERA) due to an injury

Charles "Deacon" Phillippe was the only reliable pitcher Manager Fred Clarke had at his disposal for the 1903 World Series. Phillippe was sensational as he pitched five complete games against Boston and secured all three Pittsburgh victories in the series.

and the absence of Doheny that doomed the Pirates to defeat. If the troubled southpaw had not deserted the Pirates a second time and participated in the series against Boston, the final outcome may have been different. As the series was winding down, Clarke and the players decided to send Doheny his jersey with the intention of cheering him up and letting the likeable player know they were thinking about him.

8. Historic Battle with an Old Friend

When Eddie Doheny received the jersey, he thought that it had been sent to him because he was being released from the Pittsburgh squad. This, coupled with the fact that Doheny was angry the Pirates were losing to Boston in the series, finally pushed the young man over the edge. On October 12, Doheny viciously attacked his nurse, faith-healer Oberlin Howarth, by striking the man over the head with a stove poker. After he felled Howarth, Doheny began to smash things throughout the home with the cast-iron weapon.[40] Mrs. Doheny rushed to her neighbors seeking help. Eddie was able to keep them and local policeman at bay for an hour. Finally he was overpowered by local law enforcement. Doctors examined Doheny and concluded that the man was insane. He was committed to an asylum in Danvers. His victim, though seriously injured, was expected to make a full recovery.[41]

Most of the Pittsburgh players weren't aware that their teammate had snapped as they prepared for what turned out to be the final game of the World Series on October 13. Many wouldn't learn of Doheny's condition until the team returned to Pittsburgh. After the final game, the downtrodden Pirates players sat in the visitors clubhouse of Boston's Huntington Avenue Baseball Grounds when owner Dreyfuss came into the locker room.

Dreyfuss was proud of his team, even in defeat. He believed they battled to the end and left everything on the field. Barney also was proud of his manager. Fred Clarke had done a masterful job of bringing the Pirates in on top after dealing with numerous injuries and the defections of players such as Chesbro and Tannehill. While Dreyfuss realized that Clarke had done his greatest job as a manager during the 1903 season, Clarke was struck by the character which Barney Dreyfuss exhibited when the little magnate came into the clubhouse after the deciding series game. "We were as low as humans could be," said Clarke. "Dreyfuss didn't have one word of criticism. He came to me and said, 'It takes a damn good man to be a good loser. Get dressed and we will have a good bottle of wine.'"[42] There was no doubt in anyone's mind that Barney Dreyfuss and Fred Clarke were both good men.

Chapter 9

Clarke Trades Proven Performers to Improve Team

After the World Series, the Pittsburgh players gathered one last time in the Smoky City before scattering about the country for the winter. The get-together was bittersweet as warriors who had battled through a very difficult year were greeted with both good and bad news. On a positive note, owner Barney Dreyfuss displayed the true scope of his generosity by placing all his monetary profit from the World Series into the players' cash pool. This meant that most of the players received a World Series share check for $1,316. The Pirates magnate also rewarded Deacon Phillippe for his great pitching accomplishment by giving the twirler a handsome bonus and ten shares of team stock.[1]

Bad news also awaited the Pittsburgh team when they returned from Boston, A letter from Mrs. Doheny was read out loud which explained the situation regarding her husband. Included with the correspondence was some money that Eddie owed a teammate. For many, this was the first time they had heard the details describing the demise of their comrade. An already reserved mood turned somber as the Pittsburgh squad tried to make sense of what had happened to their friend. Doheny wouldn't be returning to the Pirates, although there had been hope after his outburst in October 1903 that the pitcher would recover his faculties. It quickly became apparent that this wasn't going to be the case. Even though Doheny would not pitch for Pittsburgh in 1904, Dreyfuss made a bighearted gesture when he paid the twirler's salary for the entire season to Doheny's wife.[2]

Despite losing to the Boston Americans in the World Series, Dreyfuss and manager Fred Clarke still believed that they had the best team in the National League prior to the start of the 1904 season. Pittsburgh fans were confident that their beloved Pirates would win a fourth consecutive pennant and steam roll the American League representative in that season's Fall Classic. What Dreyfuss, Clarke and the Buccaneer faithful failed to realize was that both New York and Chicago had strengthened their squads to the point that they were superior to Pittsburgh. As these two teams became more powerful, Clarke's brigade took a step back as proven performers struggled and pitching concerns from the previous season continued to be an issue.

Things such as batting orders and pitching staffs were far from Clarke's mind as he spent the winter on his Winfield farm. Clarke and brother-in-law Chick Fraser were busy during the winter building a grain structure large enough to hold 5,000 bushels of wheat. Clarke was also taking time from that task to break in two ferocious broncos on his ranch.[3] Clarke sent Dreyfuss a letter which gave the Pirates owner a status report regarding his manager's physical condition during the off-season:

> "Two men, Chick and myself, are building one of the finest graineries that can be found in the State." This is the strong line in the last letter written by Manager Fred Clarke to headquarters. Then the veteran goes on to say that one would not know Fraser. He is so thin. "We feed him well, but its up at day break, put on your jumpers and then go to hustling timber or driving nails. I think that I will write Hugh Duffy that he owes me." Continues Clarke: "Things are fine out this way. Shirt sleeves outdoors, no snow, fine balmy days. Think that Barney might as well give up the lease on Whittington Park. Can bring the team here and practice on my sixty-acre patch."[4]

During the winter Clarke also planned to meet with a former Pittsburgh native named "Chauncey Bill" Stuart about oil potential in the Crowley County region of Kansas. Stuart was supposed to make the trip out to Cowley in order to meet with various farmers who owned land in nearby Akron. Chauncey Bill failed to show citing bad weather, although Clarke claimed that conditions were fine on that particular night in Winfield. Clarke wanted to look after the interests of his fellow farmers in order to prevent "gas salters" from coming to Akron and playing their con game.[5] Pitcher Deacon Phillippe figured that any man looking to swindle the Kansas farmers would rue the day he negotiated with Fred Clarke.

"Gone to see Cap to get leases!" exclaimed Phillippe. "Well. Well! I can see Cap handling that man. Any old time that Cap gives up anything to a man who comes to him the fellow is sure to know it before nightfall. He won't have to sleep over the matter in order to find out. Oil on Clarke's land? I hope that is true, but it won't do any oil smeller any good to get after the Winfield man. If there is oil there Cap is the man who will go after it. I have had some dealings with him, and he is a wonder at driving bargains. I knew that he once drove a grocery wagon, but wasn't sure of the other until I went up against him."[6]

"Cap" Clarke was so busy during the winter that he took a little more time than usual in sending his signed contract back to Dreyfuss. The little magnate finally received it in February. The deal called for Clarke to receive the second largest yearly salary in baseball behind Brooklyn manager Ned Hanlon, who supposedly pulled down $10,000 a year. Clarke's deal guaranteed that he would manage the Pirates for the next three years.[7] Clarke stated that he planned to remain a Pittsburgh Pirate for as long as Dreyfuss wanted him. When the time came that Dreyfuss no longer needed him, Clarke would then retire to his farm in Kansas.[8]

Before the Pirates left for spring training at Hot Springs, Clarke's presence was requested on the Princeton campus. He was afforded the opportunity to coach the school baseball team during early March.[9] It seemed that Clarke's success as a National League manager made him a prime candidate to convey his baseball knowledge to aspiring collegiate athletes. He taught basic baseball fundamentals on the New Jersey campus for about two weeks.[10]

When the Princeton job ended, Clarke immediately immersed himself in making preparations for the upcoming season. It seemed that many writers had written off the Pirates for the upcoming 1904 season. Most predictions and prognostications didn't seem to place Pittsburgh in their familiar position of first place. Clarke, never one to predict a pennant for his team, also didn't plan on lying down so that the rest of the league could trample his squad. "A whole lot of National League teams have won the pennant this winter," said Clarke, "but we are going to make 'em win it over again next summer or retain possession of the bunting ourselves. Yes, I believe some of the teams will be much stronger than they were last year, but this will only serve to make the race all the more interesting. I am not saying that we will again capture the flag, but we are going to make it exceedingly lively for the other fellows who think they have a chance to crowd us off the top of the perch."[11]

Positive experiences were few and far between for Clarke and his mates during the 1904 season. He did have a joyous occasion in his personal life when Annette Clarke gave birth to baby daughter Muriel Clarke on April 6, 1904. The second edition to the Clarke family was born in Philadelphia where Annette was staying with Mina and Chick Fraser.[12] While training in Hot Springs, though, Clarke had to receive treatment for his bad back at a local hospital.[13] This was an ominous sign as Pittsburgh prepared to begin the 1904 season.

The Pirates struggled during the early stages of the 1904 season and found themselves in fifth place by the end of May. Pitching was a problem once again for Clarke as men like Roscoe Miller, Watty Lee and Doc Scanlan failed miserably. The situation was so bad that Dreyfuss sent out an all-points bulletin for pitching after the team posted a 4–7 record in April. Dreyfuss was not interested in just any pitcher — he wanted stars and the magnate was willing to pay a high fee to acquire such talent. Dreyfuss had a wish list of pitchers such as Cy Young, Rube Waddell, George Mullin and Chick Fraser from which he hoped to obtain two hurlers that would solidify the Pittsburgh staff. He was willing to pay $12,500 for each pitcher and the magnate would also give a $1,000 stipend to the person who helped him land one of those coveted twirlers.[14]

Pittsburgh finally struck gold as the summer rolled around when two pitchers were brought in who solidified the pitching staff. A trade that received little fanfare when it occurred brought Patsy Flaherty to the Pirates on June 6 courtesy of the Chicago White Sox. This was the second time that Flaherty had been traded to Pittsburgh (he was part of the deal made between Louisville and the Pirates in 1899 before the Colonels fell victim to contraction). Flaherty had failed to remain with the Pittsburgh squad for the 1900 season.

Flaherty, a Carnegie native like Honus Wagner, was tremendous as he began his second stint with the Pirates. He went 19–9 and led the pitching staff with a 2.05 ERA. Flaherty started 28 games for Pittsburgh and went the distance in each outing. Quickly following Patsy into the Buccaneer fold was college wunderkind Mike Lynch of Brown College who made his major league debut on June 21. Lynch finished the season with a 15–11 record and an ERA of 2.71. Like Flaherty, Lynch completed every game that he started. Sam Leever pitched well despite lingering arm problems and gutted his way to an 18–11 record and a 2.17 ERA. Other pitchers who stabilized the pitching staff during the second half of the season were Charlie Case (10–5, 2.94 ERA) and Chick Robitaille (4–3, 1.91 ERA).

Even with the influx of solid hurlers, Pittsburgh could do no better than a fourth-place finish behind New York, Chicago and Cincinnati for the 1904 season. A composite 34–32 record against the three pace-setters proved to be the Pirates' undoing. Injuries and sub-par performances from some Pirates regulars also played a large role in Pittsburgh's disappointing season. Phelps, Phillippe and Clarke were players who spent part of the season on the disabled list.

A beaning incident limited Phelps to 94 games behind the plate. Phillippe was afflicted with an eye problem after he pitched in cool, rainy weather. Deacon wore dark goggles as he attempted to pitch through the discomfort. After Phillippe eventually consulted a specialist, the star of the 1903 World Series was ordered from the field by his physician to undergo a rigorous regimen of eye treatment.[15] Phillippe only appeared in 21 games and went an even 10–10 for the season.

Clarke suffered the most severe injury of his career when the Pirates played Philadelphia on July 15. Prior to that incident, Clarke was playing left field like a man many years his junior. Cap was sprinting to baseballs that seemed impossible to reach. Clarke also was covering more ground in the outer green pastures of Exposition Park since the early stages of his career.[16] Clarke's batting was not quite on par with his fielding, but the Pittsburgh manager's average still hovered around the .300 mark.

During the game against the Phillies, shortstop Rudy Hulswitt smacked a fly ball to shallow left field. The hit seemed destined to drop between Wagner and Clarke. Cap ran a great distance, lunged for the baseball, and secured the sphere in his glove for an improbable out. However, Clarke's momentum caused him to do a somersault after he snagged the baseball. He rose from the field holding the ball in his fist. The catch was costly as Clarke quickly realized that he had injured his leg and back.[17]

This daring play placed Fred Clarke on the injured list for the remainder of the 1904 season. The soreness in his leg became so intense that Fred needed to have a surgical procedure in August to relieve the excruciating pain.[18] Fans later learned that Clarke had experienced blood poisoning as a result of his leg injury.[19] Physicians also believed that he was suffering from a slight case of typhoid fever.[20] Because this issue also kept Clarke from his managerial duties for a brief period of time, Leach was named to replace Clarke while the veteran was on the mend.[21]

When Clarke was put out of action, the Pittsburgh team suffered doubly while Cap was unable to perform his duties. Not only did they miss his guidance and strong leadership within his capacity as team manager, the players also were forced to forge ahead without the on-field inspiration that Clarke supplied. Clarke took the team captain duties every bit as seriously as he did his managerial responsibilities. "The manager of a ball team is just like the manager of any business," said Fred. "He has full charge of everything, and he must never forget for an instant that the only way to achieve success is to conduct his business on business principles. The captain's field is considerably less wide, but not less important. He is like the superintendent of the operating department of a great industry. He must be able to carry out the manager's orders, suggest expedients, keep his men working like well-oiled pieces of machinery and take the detail work under his special personal care. It is the manager who must make up the team and see that the captain gets the work out of it that it is capable of doing."[22]

Captain Clarke didn't return to left field until Pittsburgh played Cleveland in an October post-season series. He was not in best form as the Pirates played these meaningless games against their American League counterpart. Clarke tried his best, but the injury certainly had slowed the outfielder quite a bit. Local fans were concerned that Clarke wouldn't be ready to go in 1905. Everybody knew that the Pirates currently had no one on their roster who was capable of filling the great left fielder's shoes.[23]

9. Clarke Trades Proven Performers to Improve Team

Smoky City fans expected roster changes to occur during the upcoming winter. Dreyfuss already had traded away outfielder Jimmy Sebring in August when owner and player were not in agreement regarding an injury. Sebring refused to play after injuring his ankle in a game against Cincinnati. It was Dreyfuss' opinion that the injury was not severe enough to keep Sebring off the field. Sebring was not appreciative of the fact that Pittsburgh management had doubted the extent of his injury. Sebring deserted the Pirates after he refused to go join the team during an Eastern swing.[24] Sebring insisted that he was told to go home by Dreyfuss when the two argued at the Union Station in Pittsburgh.[25] Dreyfuss wasn't swayed on this matter in any fashion when the outfielder stated that Barney had told him to quit the team. He believed Jimmy deserted the Pirates. On August 7, Sebring was traded to Cincinnati as part of a three-team deal that was made among the Pirates, Giants and Reds. Pittsburgh received outfielder Harry "Moose" McCormick, Cincinnati acquired Sebring and Mike Donlin was shipped to New York.

First baseman Kitty Bransfield was another underachieving player who had been a major disappointment in 1904. Bransfield saw his average plummet to a lackluster .223. Kitty, who was never very popular with the fans, also struggled in the field and committed 30 errors as he was relentlessly heckled throughout the summer. In fairness to Bransfield, he did suffer injuries of his own during the season. While in Philadelphia late in the season, Bransfield suffered a broken toe when he was thrown from the Pirates bus that had overturned on its way to the park.[26]

After missing time with that injury, he hurt his hand upon returning to the Pirates lineup.[27] In early June, Bransfield was benched with the suspicion being that a rift had developed between Bransfield and Clarke. "Bransfield does not want to come back again," said Clarke. "He told me so several times last year, and as he is desirous of changing scenes, I think it is best to let him go. I consider Bransfield one of the very best first basemen in the business. He can play first-class ball, but at times he did not do it last year. He was not playing his game and the action of some patrons at the park who seemed to take delight in going after him seemed to affect him. Kitty always had his ear open to the criticism. He would complain to me and I advised him to 'go after them' himself, and I would help him. Bransfield will not be given away or exchanged for any inferior player."[28]

Clarke was expected to represent the Pirates along with Dreyfuss at the December league meetings in New York. Before Clarke prepared for the trip, intending to reshape his squad for 1905, Cap decided to relax for about a month. He visited his parents in Des Moines and then returned to the "Little Pirate Ranch" in Kansas. Clarke also planned to participate in a November hunting excursion through New Mexico. As during the previous off-season, the Pirates manager once again wrote a letter to Dreyfuss which explained how he was doing:

> "Come down this way, old sport, and join us in one of the greatest hunts of the decade." This was the opening line of the letter Colonel B. received. Fred Clarke is the writer. The Premier captain writes from his farm in Akron, Cowley County, Kansas. Clarke goes on to say that "Chick" and himself have collected all the rents and plan to have great sport in a country where there is game galore. "We leave for Roswell, New Mexico, on November 3, and then hike over the prairies for sixty-five miles. Game? Why, a man cannot sleep at night, for birds, etc., keep beating up against the sides of the shack. Chick is promising wagon-loads of game to every friend hereabouts, and if he comes home without a big haul there is going to be an unwelcome citizen in Akron. By the way, how are you getting along on grand strategy? I read up on war news daily, and when the spring rolls around and there is nothing doing on the trains, I intend to get Sam Leever into an argument on the science of war and do him up. I can beat his banner story of rabbits being the tell-tale to Hooker's army when Stonewall Jackson got in his rear at Chancellorsville."[29]

Clarke broke away from his ranch work and hunting in order to represent the Pirates at the league meetings. Clarke had decided that changes in the composition of the Pittsburgh team were necessary and he planned to field trade offers from other National League teams. He had the full support of owner Dreyfuss in this matter, who didn't make the trip to New York due to illness. William Locke, Pittsburgh's team secretary, joined the Pirates manager in New York and acted as Barney's proxy vote in re-electing Harry Pulliam to the league presidency.[30] Clarke's goal was to make deals that improved the Pirates ball club. He didn't waste any time authorizing two transactions, which met strong resistance from the fans at home.

The Sporting News headline on Christmas Eve read: "Two Poor Trades Made by Pittsburgh at Recent Meeting." Clarke fired the first salvo when he shipped catcher Eddie Phelps to Cincinnati for catcher Heinie Peitz. Pittsburgh fans became further irritated when Clarke quickly followed with a deal that moved Kitty Bransfield, Harry McCormick and Otto Krueger to Philadelphia for a young unknown named Del Howard. Smoky City rooters were particularly perturbed over the Phelps deal. Clarke had traded a young, rising star for a player who was past his prime. Writer Ralph S. Davis criticized this particular deal. "Manager Clarke's first deal was to trade Catcher Eddie Phelps for Catcher 'Heinie' Peitz," said Davis, "giving a young man with a brilliant future before him for an old man whose next step is likely to be into eternity. The trade brought loud howls of indignation from the fans, and the furor created by this lop-sided deal had not yet died out. Phelps is a young man, and no more popular player ever wore a Pirate uniform. There is no denying the fact that Peitz was once a fine catcher, but he is already so old that his joints crack whenever he walks. His sprinting abilities are nil. Why, he is too slow to catch a cold. If he was on third and the next man up should triple, Peitz might get home all right."[31]

Three trends that would continue in future years developed as the Phelps and Bransfield transactions closed out the 1904 baseball season in Pittsburgh. The first was that Clarke and Dreyfuss were willing to trade away proven performers in order to shake up the roster when a pennant wasn't won. The second trend was overpaying when making a deal to secure a player that Clarke or Dreyfuss desperately wanted. Lastly, the "Bransfield First Base Jinx" would dog the Pirates for almost two decades as player after player failed when given an opportunity to guard the initial sack.

Manager Clarke believed that both deals would improve the Pittsburgh Pirates. As the Pittsburgh team prepared to convene at Hot Springs for spring training, fans and sportswriters continued to knock both deals. Many rooters thought that Del Howard was an unknown youngster whose on the job training would be a hindrance to a team with championship aspirations. Baseball pundits believed that Heinie Peitz was an over-the-hill player with nothing left in the tank. Prior to the start of the season, Sam Leever and Claude Ritchey came out in defense of Peitz and supported the trade which was made by their employer. "You can never tell what a player can do until you work on the same team with him," said Claude. "I was with Peitz at Cincinnati and know that he is a great help to a club. He is working with the pitcher all the time and makes himself particularly useful to the young twirlers, because he knows every batsmen in the league. Then he is a good fellow on the coaching lines and that is just what we need."[32]

Pittsburgh fans who criticized these two deals were also apprehensive about Clarke's ability to return as a dominant player in 1905. After the 32-year-old manager had suffered a very serious leg injury in 1904, there was great concern that Clarke would not be able to play at the same high level fans had grown accustomed to seeing. Stories that were circulated prior to the season indicated that Clarke may have doubted his present capabilities as well. "Well, I would like to make a nice big bet with some one that I retire from the game for good in two more years," said Clarke. "Mr. Dreyfuss knows my intentions, and if he is still at the head of the Pittsburgh Club at the end of the 1906 championship season — and, of course, he will unless he sells out — he knows he will have to look elsewhere for a left fielder or manager. It will be Frederick to the Kansas farm in two more years. I have made up my mind and nothing can make me change it."[33]

Before the 1904 season, Clarke had signed a three-year-contract worth $22,500.[34] Clarke believed that he was receiving fair salary for his services, so this decision to retire after the 1906 season had nothing to do with dissatisfaction over salary terms. Clarke's Kansas ranch and the many business interests connected with it had become numerous over the past few years. Clarke had also been very thrifty with his money, making wise investments in both business and real estate. Cap certainly didn't continue in baseball because he needed the money. If retirement was on Clarke's mind, it was probably the result of wanting to devote more time to his thriving interests outside of baseball.

Once the 1905 season began, Clarke was able to prove that he still could play the game of baseball. He appeared in 141 games, hit .299 for the year and scored 95 runs. His 24 stolen bases for the year showed that Cap still possessed some of the speed which made him one of the greatest players in the National League. Clarke was an iron man on the field until a ruptured blood vessel in his foot shelved the Pirates left fielder in September.[35]

Not only did Clarke quiet the skeptics who believed that he would be unable to reclaim his star status on the diamond, the Pirates manager also proved that his maneuvers at the league meetings in December had improved the Pittsburgh Pirates. Catcher Heinie Peitz only hit .223 in 88 games, but the veteran backstop stabilized the Pirate pitching staff. He also was a great aid to Clarke as a line coach who always kept the players on their toes. When young George Gibson was brought in from Montreal during the summer, Heinie imparted his wisdom upon the rookie catcher.

Peitz's presence paid immediate dividends as the 1905 pitching staff rebounded quite nicely. Deacon Phillippe was back, feeling no ill effects from the problems which plagued him the previous season. Deacon responded quite nicely in 1905, going 20–13 with a 2.19 ERA. Patsy Flaherty, the staff ace in 1904, struggled in his second season as a Pirate going an even 10–10 with an ERA of 3.50. Sam Leever (20–5, 2.70 ERA), Mike Lynch (17–8, 3.79 ERA), Charlie Case (11–11, 2.57 ERA) and Chick Robitaille (8–5, 2.92 ERA) rounded out Pittsburgh's staff. Youngster Albert "Lefty" Leifield saw action in the rotation during the last month of the season and served notice that he would be a solid performer in the future as he went 5–2 with a 2.89 ERA.

Clarke's other off-season acquisition showed strong form for the Pirates in 1905. Del Howard hit .292 for the season and placed second on the team with 63 runs batted in. Howard began the season splitting time with Otis Clymer in right field. He was later installed at first base when starter Bill Clancy suffered an injury. Howard remained at first after Dreyfuss sold Clancy to Rochester of the Eastern League in early July. Clancy angered the Pirates magnate by hanging out with a bad crowd near his lodgings in Allegheny. When Clancy broke team rules on two occasions, the first baseman became entrenched in Dreyfuss' doghouse much like Jimmy Sebring had in 1904. Clancy suffered the same fate as Jeems when he was unceremoniously cut adrift.[36]

Sam Leever was ineffective during the 1903 World Series after he injured his pitching arm in a trap shooting accident. Leever won 18 games in 1904 even though he pitched with a sore arm throughout the year. He rebounded nicely in 1905, going 20–5 with a 2.71 ERA.

Pittsburgh remained in the hunt throughout the summer as it became evident the National League battle would be waged between the Pirates and defending-champion New York Giants. Games between these two usually resembled a war rather than a sporting contest. Players like New York's Joe McGinnity and Christy Mathewson, plus Pittsburgh's Mike Lynch and Patsy Flaherty, were front and center during various altercations. The ringleader always seemed to be John McGraw when these two teams battled on the baseball diamond. Dreyfuss soon found that he wasn't exempt from harsh treatment while attending a game within McGraw's quarters.

When Pittsburgh sputtered a bit in May, many Pirates fans were expecting to read about changes to the team and trades that could possibly be made. These types of stories were not being printed in local publications. Scribes were too busy covering the events that were borne out of a verbal confrontation that occurred between Dreyfuss and McGraw when the Pirates were in New York for a late May series. Evidently, McGraw had berated the Pittsburgh magnate in some fashion while Dreyfuss was watching one of the games with some friends.[37]

Dreyfuss always believed that he conducted himself in a virtuous manner. He felt that all other men of influence in his profession should behave in a similar manner. John "Muggsy" McGraw wasn't that type of person. In 1904, McGraw stated that Pittsburgh was the team to beat and he instilled an attitude in his players that this goal needed to be achieved at all costs. If this could be done using deceitful or dirty measures, that was just fine with Muggsy. Games between the Pirates and Giants in 1904 were rowdy affairs and this atmosphere continued to prevail in 1905.

On May 19, McGraw supposedly mocked Dreyfuss and intimated that the Pittsburgh magnate had the umpires in his back pocket. The next day, Muggsy continued his verbal lambasting, accusing Barney of not fulfilling his monetary obligation to pay up after making wagers on games.[38] Dreyfuss was furious over this treatment while he was a guest of the New York Baseball Club. The Pirates owner quickly fired off a letter of complaint against McGraw to league president Harry Pulliam. During a subsequent interview, Dreyfuss also stated that McGraw should be held accountable for his actions.

> John McGraw, manager of the New York team, must answer to the directors of the National League for his unprovoked attack on me. The time has come when the leader of the Giants must be put on the rack for his conduct. He has been defiant to the rules entirely too long. It's amazing the way he runs things at the Polo Grounds. Umpires seem to be afraid of him. He browbeats them as in the old Baltimore days and gets away with the tactics. Lynch does not want to file any charges against McGraw. He takes the stand that the best way to settle with a man of his caliber is to take a punch at his frame. And

if you heard the epithets applied to Lynch you would not blame him. Michael cried through rage. It is true that Flaherty and Lynch were out hunting their tormentors. Flaherty vows that he will take a swipe at McGinnity the first chance he gets. It's pretty rough for me to stand by and take the vile sayings heaped upon them by McGraw and his band.

There must be a ruling on the habit of McGraw when ordered off the field of going into a little closet under the grand stand. It leads to a passageway to the club house. McGraw has holes cut out in the partition and can coach his team from that conning tower. Why he might as well go up into the stand and coach his men. He is clearly violating the rules and knows it. He is not off the field. I felt sorry for Umpire Johnstone Saturday. He seemed scared to death and took all kinds of things from the Giants. Klem umpired a fine game on Monday. He wasn't afraid. The National League will have to abolish such ruffians as McGraw.[39]

McGraw was incensed when Dreyfuss' complaint was printed in a number of New York newspapers. He erroneously chided Pulliam, feeling that the league president was releasing statements without hearing both sides of the story.[40] Pulliam was taking unfair heat from the New York manager. When Dreyfuss appeared at Pulliam's office to make the complaint against McGraw, he brought a newspaper reporter with him.[41] Pulliam didn't think that this paper should be permitted to scoop the other New York publications on this matter, so he released the content of Dreyfuss' grievance.

If McGraw was angry over the fact that Pulliam had made Dreyfuss' comments available for public dissection, he probably became enraged when Harry rendered a decision in the matter that wasn't favorable to New York's manager. Pulliam suspended McGraw and fined him $150 for his actions on the dates that Dreyfuss mentioned in his complaint. Even though the suspension was handed down by Pulliam, the National League Board of Directors reviewed the decision at a meeting on June 1.[42]

Dreyfuss anticipated that Pulliam's decision would be upheld when the Board of Directors convened in Boston. He was in for quite a shock when McGraw brought in one witness after another who testified at the meeting that Muggsy hadn't behaved as Dreyfuss described in his complaint. Dreyfuss didn't bring a legion of witnesses to support his claim.[43] He believed that his truthful explanation of the events described in the grievance would be ample proof for fellow magnates. This was a grievous error on Dreyfuss' part.

Much to Dreyfuss' surprise, he was censured by his fellow magnates after they heard all of the testimony.[44] They believed that Dreyfuss should have been smart enough to ignore McGraw's childish heckling. Pulliam was praised for his conviction in suspending Muggsy, even though Dreyfuss was dressed down for filing the complaint. McGraw was able to circumvent the ruling by filing an injunction in a court of law which permitted the New York manager to remain on the ball field. Everyone was a winner in this case except Dreyfuss, who was not happy the magnates deemed his behavior as dishonorable while a hoodlum like McGraw was exonerated.

In a bit of an ironic twist, Clarke and his teammates helped lead the New York Giants players out of harm's way during a fan riot on August 5 in Pittsburgh. McGraw's boys were up to their old tricks when Muggsy disputed an umpire's decision in the ninth inning of that game. With the game tied, 5–5, Pirate Claude Ritchey was called safe by umpire George Bausewine on a close play at third. When the New York players did not agree with Bausewine's decision, they began to argue with him and fellow arbiter Bob Emslie. McGraw's team then refused to continue the game.[45]

Bausewine pulled out his watch and threatened to forfeit the game in Pittsburgh's favor if New York did not resume play in one minute. McGraw waved his fist in Bausewine's face and Christy Mathewson tried to knock the watch out of his hand. After the minute passed, Bausewine declared that the game was forfeited in Pittsburgh's favor, 9–0. McGraw's players quickly surrounded the umpire. While they were doing this, a throng of about 10,000 dissatisfied fans began pouring onto the field. The Giants quickly realized that they were surrounded by an angry mob who wanted to inflict physical pain upon Pittsburgh's biggest rival.[46]

Police joined in the fray and attempted to hold the crowd back with clubs. Clarke and his men came to the aid of their adversaries. They too helped beat the crowd back with baseball bats as the New York players huddled near the bench. After fifteen minutes, New York players were escorted from the field to their carriages in groups of two. Clarke's brigade saved the New York players from harm inside Exposition Park. Unfortunately, there was no relief for McGraw's men outside the ball park as angry fans threw stones at the carriages as they made their way down Robison Street to a bridge that took them across the river.[47]

Clarke kept his troops in the race despite a rash of injuries that crippled dependable regulars. Leach hurt his ribs and Beaumont was afflicted with rheumatism in both legs. This prompted Clarke to trade infielder George McBride to St. Louis for third baseman Dave Brain. Pittsburgh did not miss a beat with Brain in the lineup. Local writers and fans alike showered the new third baseman with lavish praise. Brain played steady ball for the Pirates after his arrival from St. Louis. He only hit .257, but showed great ability in the clutch, driving in 46 runs while appearing in 85 games for Pittsburgh.

As the season entered the final weeks, Pittsburgh was seven games behind the first-place Giants. Smoky City fans wondered if the Pirates could mount a last-minute charge and overtake New York. Fred Clarke continued to boost his troop's morale even though the odds were not in their favor. "Fight it out to the end," said Clarke. "Things are terribly against us, and we may not be able to land the pennant, but whatever you do, don't quit. Play the string right out to the end, and show your friends there is nothing weak about the Pirates."[48]

Clarke kept his troops motivated as the season wound down. Pittsburgh made a much better showing than the previous year, but it wasn't enough to overcome McGraw's Men. The team's mediocre play in May, plus a combined record of 22–22 against both New York and Chicago proved the Pirates' undoing. Wagner did his usual stellar work at the plate for Pittsburgh, leading the team with a .363 average. The Flying Dutchman also paced the squad with 101 RBIs. Beaumont was able to maintain a decent average of .328 even though he was in constant pain throughout the season. Regulars such as Leach (.257) and Ritchey (.255) didn't hit with the usual luster that Pirates fans had become accustomed to.

There had been reports throughout the campaign that a division was developing between Clarke and Dreyfuss. Clarke had come out during the summer and refuted his retirement statement from spring training. Writers now claimed that Clarke was going to walk away from baseball with one year still left on his contract. Dreyfuss scoffed at these malicious tales. "We have built up our base ball reputations together," said Dreyfuss, "and we have been together in times of victory. We have a compact that when one tires of the game the other will step out at the same time. Clarke doesn't care to work for any other president and I don't care to take chances with any other manager. We'll quit together, but the quitting time hasn't come yet. It is my ambition, and Clarke's, too, to give Pittsburgh another pennant before we withdraw from the scene of action."[49]

Clarke wasn't going anywhere in 1906. After the 1905 season concluded, he left Pittsburgh for his Kansas farm, where he planned to put up four miles of fence made from Pittsburgh steel around his 1,000 acres of property.[50] After a month of hard work on the ranch in Winfield, Clarke then planned to make a trip to New York to represent the Pirates at the league meetings once again with an eye to improving his Pittsburgh squad. This time around Clarke hoped to acquire a pitcher who possessed the kind of potential that would allow the player to become his staff ace.

Chapter 10
Twenty-Nine Game Loser Becomes Staff Ace

Pittsburgh management had focused on acquiring position players when making trades during 1905. As the Pirates entered the off-season, it became apparent that manager Fred Clarke and owner Barney Dreyfuss needed to add another quality hurler to the pitching staff in order to keep pace with New York and Chicago. It was reported that Clarke had pitcher Jack Harper of the Cincinnati in his sights with the cost to acquire being Patsy Flaherty. Another story said that Pittsburgh would make a pitch for Herron Hill native Frank Smith of the Chicago White Sox.[1] A month before the league gathered at the December meetings in New York, Clarke pulled off a major coup which did not involve a pitcher. Cap was able to sign Pacific Coast League first baseman James Joseph Nealon right from under the noses of the Cincinnati Reds.[2]

Clarke left the serenity of his Kansas ranch in order to make the trip to California at Dreyfuss' request. Dreyfuss didn't want a scout or agent running the point position regarding Nealon. He wanted his must trusted envoy on the ground extolling the virtues of playing for the Pittsburgh Pirates. Clarke succeeded in inking the big first baseman after spending two days in San Francisco.[3] Pittsburgh was able to trump Cincinnati since Garry Herrmann's representative failed to show for three meetings with Nealon.

Clarke and Dreyfuss fully expected Nealon to claim the first base position in 1906, which meant that Del Howard would be on the bench as a utility player. This seemed like an unlikely scenario since Howard was too good to keep out of the starting lineup. Pundits then pondered whether it would be Howard or Otis Clymer manning right field in 1906. Scribes who believed that Howard would be traded should have been praised for their omniscient

10. Twenty-Nine Game Loser Becomes Staff Ace

powers. Manager Clarke intended to use Howard as a chip to obtain a pitcher that he highly coveted.

It would be neither Jack Harper or Frank Smith as had been speculated, but rather a veteran twirler from the Boston Beaneaters staff. On December 15, Pittsburgh sent Howard, Dave Brain and pitching prospect Vive Lindaman to Boston for pitcher Vic Willis. Clarke explained the rationale behind the acquisition of a pitcher who lost 29 games in 1905.

> If I can get one more first-class pitcher I will be happy. I made the long trip from Kansas to New York determined to land Victor Willis, the tall Boston pitcher. The owners of the Boston Club were aware of the fact that Willis expressed a desire months ago to be transferred to Pittsburgh, and I did not hide from them this hope of getting the experienced twirler. On the contrary, I hunted up W.R. Conant upon his arrival, told him frankly that I wanted Willis and asked Boston what was wanted in exchange. Conant said that owing to the failure of the Dunn deal, Boston was left without any irons in the fire for new players and said that clubs with 14 or 15 more men than they could possibly use next season should give Boston a chance to strengthen. "Tell me what your manager wants and I will help you out provided you give me Willis," I said.
>
> Conant named Brain, Howard and Lindaman, and said he would rather have these men than the $5,000 that I offered originally. As I am confident Nealon will make good at first Howard could be only a utility man next year and he is too clever a player to sit on the bench. Then, with Sheehan and Leach for third, there would not be any room for Brain, so as a matter of fact, while Pittsburgh is giving up two high class fielders, neither one would have been a regular next season if the deal had not been made. Some one tried to tell me that Willis is all in, but I retorted: "I guess you did not watch his work against the Boston Americans two months ago as closely as I did, nor bat against him as often as I did last summer."[4]

Talk of Willis being all in, the language of that era to describe a player whose career seemed to be coming to an end, did not seem to bother Clarke. Cap felt Willis would rebound to the form shown when he went 25–13 as a rookie in 1898 and 27–8 in 1899 on contending Boston teams. Willis also recorded 20-win seasons on less competitive Beaneater teams in 1901 and 1902. Clarke reasoned that poor support when Willis took the mound for Boston in 1904 and 1905 contributed to marks of 18–25 and 12–29 during those seasons. Pittsburgh fans were concerned that Willis had developed a lackadaisical attitude while pitching for those horrible Boston teams.

Reports of the Pirates' newest acquisition being all in continued to worry the rooting populace as the cold of winter settled into the Pittsburgh region. Dreyfuss and Clarke were confident that Willis would anchor the staff in 1906. The fans and press were less skeptical, feeling the 29 losses that Willis absorbed the previous season showed that the tall right-handed twirler wasn't someone who could be counted on. Willis himself tried to dispel the rumors which pointed to his imminent demise by sending Dreyfuss a letter in which Vic guaranteed a rebirth season: "Don't believe those tales you hear about me being all-in," he added. "Wait until you see me in action for your team and then form your opinion of my worth to your team. I assure you that I am delighted to be a Pirate and that I will do my best to bring another pennant to the Smoky City."[5]

While the Pittsburgh fans and scribes were once again criticizing Clarke for making a bad deal, the Pirates manager returned to his ranch after the league meetings. Cap planned on spending the rest of the off-season attending to matters on his Kansas property. Clarke took some time out from the rigors of work in order to entertain a Pittsburgh friend who spent some time on his Winfield spread. Captain John Moren, the famous Pittsburgh river man and superintendent of transportation for the River Coal Company, was a guest at Clarke's ranch for a week.[6] When Moren returned to Pittsburgh, he stopped in at Pirates headquarters and gave a glowing account of his time with Clarke in Winfield.

> I shall never forget my trip. I got into Winfield at daybreak. Knowing that Fred lived twelve miles out in the country, I decided to go to a hotel and await day dawn. I had scarcely signed the register when a man tapped me on the arm, bowed graciously and asked me if I was Captain Moren. Being answered in the affirmative, he said: "My name is Plaggmann; Harry Plaggmann. Fred Clarke told me to look out for you until he came to town." Plaggmann is the boss druggist of the place. He made me welcome until the boss farmer arrived and hauled me to his fine home near Akron. For nearly a week I lived like a king. Quail and batter cakes of some kind. Cannot just tell their make-up, but they put fat on your ribs.
>
> Mrs. Clarke is a splendid little housekeeper. She works too hard to suit me. Regular farmer's wife. Everything was fresh around there and even an invalid could eat thrice his usual capacity. Clarke has all of the horses one could want. A drive to Winfield is easy, and we had many of them. Clarke owns one of the best farms in that section. The Walnut River runs through part of it. There is a walnut tree which will yield a fortune for its owner within the next few years. Coyotes? Yes, I saw a number of them off in the distance, but could not get a shot at them. That pelt which is to be a rug for the Rueben Quinn Club is tanned and the boys can look forward with expectancy.[7]

Dreyfuss had never visited Clarke's ranch, so he relied on stories such as Moren's to stay informed about how his manager's farm was progressing. Barney enjoyed listening to these yarns and reading Clarke's letters from Winfield. Dreyfuss was never surprised when he heard accounts of Fred's escapades in the West. "Talk about a financier;" said Dreyfuss, "I don't know of a ball player or otherwise who has Clarke beaten. He has just drawn on me for

$2000. Has another farm deal on hand. Clarke knows the value of real estate in his section. He is worth — well many thousands."[8]

Moren's story also went a long way in explaining why Clarke showed up for spring training in fine condition each year. Hard work, fresh air and good food suited Clarke. He loved cultivating the soil and enjoyed every aspect of farm life, a lifestyle ingrained in him as a kid. During most of the winter, he immersed himself in his Winfield ranch. When the baseball season began, Clarke was all business as he made the transition from rancher to baseball player and manager. The Pirates manager placed lofty expectations on his team as the 1906 season kicked into high gear.

"The Pittsburgh team for the season of 1906 will be considerably stronger than it was during 1905," said the Pirates manager. "It looks as if we will have a high-class pitching staff, our men are batting well and have been during the practice games and pre-season contests and the men in the field are putting up a high-class article of base ball. In the catching department we are well fixed. Nealon, our new first baseman, is showing up in fine shape. As to the finish, we may land first and again we may be last. It is all base ball, but with a better team than last year the Pirates are sure to be heard from on the National League circuit."[9]

For the second year in a row, Clarke was vindicated as newly acquired players performed much better than his critics anticipated. Negative stories about Vic Willis continued to surface as the Pirates embarked on another season. Willis constantly protested these destructive yarns that were being written about him. Vic once again rebuked the press notion that he had been a malcontent with Boston in 1905. Willis explained that his attitude was justified, given the ineptness of the Boston team behind him. "Many a time," said he, "I have worked my rear off to win a game, and just when I thought I had things sewed up, some one would commit some error, for which there was no excuse seemingly, and things would go up in the air. With a team like the Pirates behind me, I believe that I will win the big percentage of my games. At least, I will do my best. Those stories sent out from Boston about my being all in were mere pipes, started by someone jealous of my good fortune getting away from the Hub."[10]

Playing on the same field with the likes of Wagner, Clarke and Leach must have been the proper medicine for Willis' attitude. The elongated slab artist pitched spectacularly for the Pirates in 1906. Willis made Clarke look like a genius as he sizzled for Pittsburgh, going 23–13 while posting an ERA of 1.73. The future Hall of Fame pitcher would top the twenty-win mark during each of the four seasons that he wore a Pirates uniform. He was considered the staff ace in three of those years.

Another off-season acquisition who was receiving plenty of attention from both fans and press alike was new first baseman Joe Nealon. The lad from San Francisco was penciled in to be the starter at first base. Cincinnati owner Garry Herrmann was unhappy that Nealon had slipped through his fingers and signed with Pittsburgh.[11] Once the season got underway, Nealon explained to reporters how the Pirates were able to beat out the Reds for his services. "I could have signed as willingly with Cincinnati as with Pittsburgh," said the big fellow. "I had talked with Ted Sullivan in regard to going with the Reds, and had arranged with him to meet me at a certain time to close the matter. When the specific time came, Ted did not show up. Another day passed, and still there was no Ted. And then a third day came and went; and the scout of the Cincinnati Club was still missing. It was then that I lined up with the Pittsburgh Club — and I have not regretted at any time that I did so. Had Sullivan kept his arrangement with me, I might be playing with the Reds now. As it is, I am a Pirate, and am glad now that I annexed myself to Fred Clarke's aggregation."[12]

Dreyfuss' clever subterfuge of sending Clarke to handle the Nealon recruitment personally swayed the big first baseman to come aboard the Corsair craft. Nealon rejected Cincinnati's overtures because the youngster was bitter over how he was treated by Ted Sullivan.[13] Nealon played splendid ball in his rookie campaign, appearing in all 154 games and stroking the ball at a .255 clip. He displayed a strong penchant for hitting in the clutch and led the team with 83 RBIs. Nealon showed surprising deftness around the first base bag for a big man and handled his position superbly.

Herrmann continued to stew over the Nealon situation as the season progressed. A Cincinnati newspaper had printed a false story in the spring which stated that Pirate Heinie Peitz was stabbed by a jealous woman. At the time of the supposed incident, Peitz was home in bed, suffering from pleurisy.[14] This paper ran the article despite its lack of accuracy, hoping that the scandal would also besmirch the Pirates organization. Herrmann eventually was able to extract some revenge of his own on Pittsburgh management when the Cincinnati owner pulled some funny business over the transfer of catcher Eddie Phelps from his club.[15]

Phelps was given his 10 days' release from the Reds on May 9. This meant that his notice of unconditional release would take effect on May 19 if no team put in a waiver claim for Phelps. After the ten days passed, Phelps returned to his home in Albany. Pittsburgh offered him terms on May 21. Phelps accepted, forwarded his release, and joined Pittsburgh. After this transpired, Herrmann then claimed that he had brokered a deal with the Boston Americans on May 18 in which Phelps was sold for $1,500.[16]

Phelps continued to play for Pittsburgh while the grievance was decided by the National Commission. Since it was an affair that involved both leagues,

10. Twenty-Nine Game Loser Becomes Staff Ace

presidents Johnson and Pulliam had to recuse themselves from the decision making process. This meant that Herrmann would be the sole person who would decided where Phelps played. Not surprisingly, he determined that the deal with Boston was valid.[17] This incensed Clarke who believed that Herrmann was acting in a deceitful manner. Clarke contended that Herrmann's decision was influenced by the fact that the Cincinnati owner had wagered money with New York bookies that the Pirates would not win the pennant. Fred also accused Herrmann of playing weak lineups against Chicago and New York, while a stronger team always opposed Pittsburgh.[18] "It's an outrage," said Clarke bitterly about Herrmann. "It's about the crookedest piece of work ever put through in base ball."[19]

Clarke received some verbal censure from the league for his profanity-laced tirade against the Cincinnati magnate. He wasn't suspended or fined for his actions. Pittsburgh scored a victory of sorts when Herrmann reversed his decision and allowed Phelps to remain with the Pirates.[20] Phelps split time with George Gibson and Heinie Peitz behind the plate. All three catchers did fine work handling the Pirate pitching staff. Lefty Leifield supported ace Vic Willis ably in his first full big league season. Leifield put together a mark of 18–13 supported by a stunning 1.87 ERA. Leever (22–7, 2.32 ERA) and Phillippe (15–10, 2.47 ERA) rounded out the strong pitching foursome for the Pirates.

In an ordinary season, a major contribution from a fifth starter may have made the difference between the third-place finish that Pittsburgh secured and a pennant. However, 1906 was no ordinary season. The Chicago Cubs made a farce of the pennant race, going 116–36 and finishing 20 games in front of the New York Giants, who nosed out Pittsburgh for second place.

Wagner won his fourth batting title, pacing the league with a .339 mark. Leach rebounded with an average of .286, although the veteran Pirate only drove in 39 runs. Players like Ritchey (.269), Beaumont (.265), Ganley (.258) and Sheehan (.241) assisted the Pirates attack as best they could. Nealon was the surprise of the season at the plate for the Pittsburgh Pirates, as his 83 RBIs tied Harry Steinfeldt of Chicago for top honors in the National League.

Clarke had a solid year at the plate as he finished second on the team with a .309 average. Cap scored 69 runs, smashed 14 doubles and hit 13 triples. He only appeared in 118 games for the Pirates, though as he suffered a stiff neck and shoulder when he collided with Wagner while chasing a pop fly against Philadelphia in May. Honus was none the worse for wear after the collision, but Clarke was almost knocked out by the impact's force.

After the season, Clarke and Dreyfuss had a falling out when Fred refused to join the Pirates on a barnstorming tour. The Pittsburgh magnate wanted all of his players to play exhibition games until their contracts ran out on October 15. Clarke didn't have the slightest intention of doing this.[21] He was heading home to Kansas for the winter. Fred Clarke was still unsigned and many Pittsburgh patrons believed that this little disagreement meant that he wouldn't be back in 1907.

Clarke and Dreyfuss buried the hatchet somewhat when both men attended the World Series games in Chicago. Clarke just happened to be in town since he was visiting Chick Fraser and other relatives.[22] The fears of Pittsburgh's population were quelled when Clarke and Dreyfuss met at the league meetings in New York. Clarke agreed to terms on a one-year $8,000 contract for the 1907 season. However, Cap announced that he would manage the Pirates from the bench next year, and would only take up active duty on the diamond once again if one of his regular outfielders suffered a serious injury.[23]

It wasn't surprising that retirement talk had surrounded Clarke. He certainly didn't play baseball because he needed the money. The income from his Kansas farm, a coal mine near Des Moines and other investments exceeded about $5,000 a year.[24] Cap could walk away from the game at any time and feel quite content retiring to the "Little Pirate Ranch" for his remaining days. Clarke wanted to remain in baseball because he still craved another National League pennant and hoped to reverse the negative outcome of the 1903 World Series.

While Clarke was announcing his intentions for 1907 in New York, Dreyfuss was busy making a deal that he hoped would improve the Pittsburgh Pirates. Rumors from a Philadelphia newspaper preceding the league meetings stated that an agreement on a deal between the Pirates and Phillies had already been reached. It was reported that Phillippe, Leach, Beaumont or Otis Clymer would be shipped to the City of Brotherly Love.[25] When the league meetings commenced in New York, the silence from the Philadelphia papers was deafening as this rumored transaction between the Pirates and Phillies never came to pass. Instead, Dreyfuss and Clarke swung a deal with a familiar partner on December 11 as Pittsburgh shipped Ritchey, Flaherty and a player to be named later to Boston for infielder Ed Abbaticchio.

Abbaticchio had retired from baseball in 1906 so that he could attend to business interests in his hometown of Latrobe, Pennsylvania. Abbaticchio owned a hotel which secured a liquor license in 1906, with the provision that he stay in Latrobe to monitor the business. Pittsburgh tried to acquire the infielder during the 1906 season. If they had succeeded, Clarke intended to play him only at home in Pittsburgh. A deal was squelched when Abbaticchio decided that he would appease his parents who wanted their son to remain retired permanently.[26]

Even though Abbaticchio was Boston's shortstop in 1904 and 1905, Clarke planned on using him at second base. Abbaticchio had not manned that position since 1903, but Clarke was confident the big infielder would make a smooth transition. Many patrons believed Pittsburgh was strengthening their hitting by substituting Abbaticchio for Ritchey. This opinion was a bit puzzling since both men put up similar numbers with the bat during their careers. Abbaticchio hit .279 for Boston in 1905, while Ritchey was only slightly below that for 1906 with a .269 average. Being larger in stature, Abbaticchio obviously could be expected to hit the ball with more power.

Before Dreyfuss and Clarke came on the scene after the 1899 season, most Pirates fans were satisfied when the team made a good showing in the standings. Patrons were never concerned whether the Pirates won the pennant or not. These same people became spoiled a bit after the pennant-winning years of 1901, 1902 and 1903. They began to expect first-place finishes every season. When this was not accomplished, players who were perceived as being underperformers by the faithful were subjected to the worst kind of roasting possible.

There were those who believed this type of fan abuse had played a part in the dismal season that former first baseman Kitty Bransfield suffered through in 1904. This went a long way in explaining why he was happy to be traded that winter. Dreyfuss was quick to point out that catcalls coming from a certain group of fans at Exposition Park had made life unbearable for Ritchey in 1906.[27] "All the knocking against the Pittsburgh players which is heard at Exposition Park is done by the cheap gamblers," said Dreyfuss. "They bet a few nickels on the game, then proceed to hammer the home team, the result being that visitors are given the impression that all Pittsburgh fans are disloyal. These knockers made life miserable for Claude Ritchey, than whom no more faithful player ever lived. They kept after him until he was driven to desperation and welcomed a chance to go to another club."[28]

With Ritchey being sent packing to Boston, old guard performers from Pittsburgh's glory years were quickly dwindling. Coupled with the fact that news regarding Clarke indicated that he would be managing from the bench in 1907, this now meant that half of the starting eight from the 1903 World Series team no longer represented Pittsburgh on the playing field. Beaumont was quickly added to that list of ex–Pirates when the outfielder was sent to Boston as the player to be named in the Abbaticchio deal.

Beaumont spent eight seasons in a Pittsburgh Pirates uniform. He was one of the few players that Clarke and Dreyfuss inherited when coming from Louisville who actually remained in Pittsburgh and played a key role in the team's success. Beaumont hit .332 in 1901, led the league with an average of .357 in 1902, and followed that up with marks of .341 (1903), .301 (1904) and .328 (1905). He led the league in hits three consecutive seasons from 1902 through 1904 and also topped the circuit with 137 runs scored in 1903.

Beaumont was the second outfielder who was shown the door since the

1906 season ended. Robert Ganley had been shipped to Washington over the winter. This left Pittsburgh with an outfield trio of Billy Hallman, Otis Clymer and Goat Anderson. Local rooters were buoyed a bit from a late March report which stated that Clarke was indeed participating in workouts with teammates at Hot Springs. It was not until Clymer suffered a charley horse injury that Clarke was drawn back to the left field confines which he patrolled superbly throughout his career. The city of Pittsburgh breathed a collective sigh of relief as Clarke took part in the season opener against St. Louis.

Luckily for Pittsburgh fans, Clarke remained on the field for the remainder of the season. Injuries to Leach and Nealon made it necessary for a stout player like Fred Clarke to remain in the lineup. Clarke's everyday presence was also necessitated by the anemic production that came from his original outfield trio. Hallman hit .222 in 94 games, Anderson .206 in 127 games and Clymer .227 in limited duty. Clymer also fell out of favor with manager Clarke after he refused to pinch-hit in a late June game against Chicago. Clymer wouldn't bat, claiming that he had a stomach ache.[29] Cap was enraged and reacted in a manner similar to 1901 when Ely refused to play with a cut on his finger. Clarke went to Dreyfuss and demanded swift action. "You might as well ask for waivers on that man," said an angered Clarke. "I won't put him in another game as long as I have anything to do with the Pittsburgh team."[30] Dreyfuss quickly acquiesced to Clarke's wishes and sold Clymer to Washington on June 26.

The 1907 baseball season was quite a busy one for Clarke as he battled league officials, celebrated a special anniversary one year early, fended off an attack in Philadelphia and dealt with bad actors on his squad throughout the summer. Clarke's work on the field, a .289 average, 97 runs scored, 18 doubles, 13 triples and 59 runs batted in, was phenomenal given all the administrative duties that occupied his time.

Clarke became involved in a dispute with National League officials when New York catcher Roger Bresnahan donned protective shin guards during an early May series against Pittsburgh. Since Bresnahan was the first catcher who wore such gear, Clarke believed the Giants held a wide advantage over their opponents. He was also worried about injury issues from players who slid into home plate and were blocked by Bresnahan's safety guards. Clarke immediately protested the use of such equipment and claimed that if it were permitted by the league, he would require all Pirates players to wear shin guards while out on the field.[31]

"As the matter stands at present New York has a big advantage over every other club," declared Clarke. "With Bresnahan the only catcher in the league wearing these guards, it will be next to impossible for any opposing player to touch the plate in a close play on the Polo Grounds. I am not stretching the

Fred Clarke (above) intended to manage the Pittsburgh Pirates from the bench in 1907. An injury to outfielder Otis Clymer forced Clarke back to the diamond, much to the delight of Pittsburgh baseball fans.

truth a particle when I say that those shin guards cost us Saturday's game. Bresnahan ran fully six feet to the left of the plate and braced himself on the line so that it was impossible for me to get around him in an attempt to score on the bunt. Of course, I tried to slide, but my spike caught in his shin guards and caused me to turn one of my ankles."[32]

Shin guards did seem like good protection for catchers who had to worry about players like Clarke flying at them with sharpened spikes. National League President Harry Pulliam agreed when he denied Pittsburgh's protest and permitted Bresnahan to wear his new protective equipment.[33] However, Clarke didn't outfit his whole team with shin guards as he had threatened. The sight of the brick body of Honus Wagner with further protection would have made baserunners shudder with fear. Clarke decided that only catcher George Gibson would follow Bresnahan's lead and wear protective shin guards behind the plate.

By the end of June, Pittsburgh and New York were battling for second place as the Chicago Cubs once again seemed to have a stranglehold on the 1907 National League pennant. Before the Pirates left for a swing through the East in July, Fred and Annette Clarke celebrated their ninth wedding anniversary by hosting a dinner on Friday, July 5. They entertained a large gathering of friends who then accompanied the couple to the train station in order to give them an inspiring farewell. During an off-day on Sunday, July 7, the celebration continued as Lieutenant George O'Brien hosted Fred Clarke, wife Annette, and several other Pirates players at his cottage near Atlantic City for the day.[34]

Clarke couldn't be pinned down to talk about anything which related to the parties in Pittsburgh or Atlantic City. Clarke's wedding anniversary was personal business which, as usual, he preferred to keep private. The Pirates manager never even reminisced with baseball scribes about his July wedding nine years earlier in Chicago. When the subject of Chicago in July was breached, he hearkened back to 1896 when the Louisville Colonels spent the Fourth of July in the Windy City.

"Fun," remarked Clarke, "that was one great time. Chick Fraser was overcome by the heat, though the wind was blowing a gale and it was corking cold. I recall putting a piece of ice about the size of a pigeon egg on Charles' head. Doggy Miller was with the team. My, but he hated fireworks. I watched my chance and tied a string of Jackson crackers to Miller's coat tail. The moment one exploded Miller started on a bee line for the hotel dining room. Up the stairs of the Tremont House Doggy sailed, three steps at a time. The dining room was filled. You can get that Miller made a stage star's entrance. The hotel people were going to bounce us for the affair. Louisville had Bill Hill, Bill Wilson, Elmore Cunningham and a bunch then. McGunnigle was manager. That evening Mac bought wine for Miller to cool him off."[35]

While Clarke never felt comfortable discussing his personal life, he was always willing to talk about baseball, the people who played the game, and the events surrounding his career. As manager, it was Clarke's job to instill discipline. This didn't mean that Cap wasn't one of the boys. He was a known prankster who had pulled off all kinds of stunts since his days in Louisville. No Pirates player was safe from the manager's high jinks. Teammates tried to outdo Clarke whenever they could. Even Pirates owner Dreyfuss was not excluded when a caper was perpetrated by one of his employees. "Ever hear of the put-up job Hans Wagner worked on Barney Dreyfuss?" asked Clarke. "Barney is a good marksmen and was trained as a militiaman. One day the question of shooting came up and the big German observed: 'Maybe you can shoot all right, but I'd take a chance you couldn't hit my hat.' The challenge was accepted and Hans' chapeau was hung up for a target. Barney raised his gun, blazed away and the hat was unharmed. The gang had only taken the shot out of his shell."[36]

Clarke's teammates loved the fact that their manager and captain was able to keep them loose throughout the long baseball season. They also admired Cap's win-at-all-costs mentality. Pittsburgh fans were also appreciative of Fred Clarke's hard nosed style on the baseball diamond. Opposing fans, on the other hand, were not always pleased with Clarke's methods and tactics. This was evident in Philadelphia on August 28 when the Pirates crushed the Phillies, 7–1.

Philadelphia fans became outraged when Clarke shoved Phillies catcher Charley Dooin off the basepath as he was scoring from third base following a hit. After Dooin was sent tumbling, the throw from the outfield sailed into the grandstand and allowed a second Pirate to cross the plate. Because Philadelphia rooters believed that this was cheap, dirty baseball, they let Clarke have it when he returned to his position in left field. Fans tossed pop bottles at the Pittsburgh manager. When Clarke returned to the bench after the inning was over, he was smacked in the face after an angry patron threw a cushion at him.[37] Clarke challenged his antagonist to come onto the field and fight like a man. That invitation was declined. Clarke then requested protection from Philadelphia manager Billy Murray and umpire Bill Carpenter. The umpire ignored Clarke's pleas and had police escort the manager back to his bench. Carpenter then told Clarke that it would probably be in everyone's best interest if he left the field.[38]

Clarke battled to the bitter end as the 1907 season wound down. Harry Pulliam did suspend the star outfielder for a separate umpire-baiting incident in late August.[39] Clarke had to do some suspending of his own when first baseman Nealon and pitcher Leifield were sent home for indulging in the night life to excess.[40] Nealon was the bigger perpetrator of the two. He indulged himself in such a manner that Clarke and Dreyfuss believed team rules were broken. Leifield's behavior hadn't reached the level of his friend's, but Lefty was sent home nonetheless. An anonymous Pirates player came to Nealon's defense stating that the big first baseman had been deeply affected by the constant jeers and sneers that were hurled his way by fans at Exposition Park throughout the year.[41]

Nealon's fate was a foregone conclusion in the eyes of many Pittsburgh fans. He was not expected to return. Leifield's situation was different than Nealon's. Dreyfuss believed that Leifield had shown poor judgment when he violated team rules, but he felt that Lefty's career in Pittsburgh was still salvageable. Dreyfuss had a long talk with the southpaw. Even though details of the discussion were not made known to the public, most Pittsburgh rooters figured that Dreyfuss had stressed to Leifield the importance of acting in a professional manner.

Whatever Dreyfuss said to Leifield must have sunk in. The southpaw pitcher was permitted to rejoin the Pirates in late September. As for Nealon, the man who had shown up for spring training "as big as a house" in 1907 would not be making the trip to Hot Springs in 1908. At the conclusion of the season, San Francisco newspapers reported that Nealon had decided to give up professional baseball for good in order to go into business with his millionaire father.[42]

The 1907 season proved to be a successful year for Fred Clarke's brigade. In spite of having a lighter hitting unit than usual, the Buccaneers were still able to cross the finish line in second place with a 91–63 record. They finished 17 games behind the pennant-winning Chicago Cubs. The pitching staff came together quite nicely as the season progressed. Willis once again led the way with a 21–11 record and an ERA of 2.34. Leifield (20–16, 2.33 ERA), Leever (14–9, 1.66 ERA), Phillippe (14–11, 2.61 ERA) and Camnitz (13–8, 2.15 ERA) supported Willis commendably. Camnitz was back after receiving tutelage in the minors and had the look of a future staff ace.

Two young pitchers also received late season trials for Pittsburgh. Wheeling product Nick Maddox was outstanding for Clarke throughout September. Maddox gave the Pirates strong work in six starts, all of them complete games, as he posted a 5–1 record with an ERA of 0.83. During the third outing of his career on September 20, Nick tossed a no-hitter and defeated Brooklyn, 2–1, at Exposition Park. This remarkable performance came on the heels of a strong debut in St. Louis when Maddox struck out 11 Cardinals batters. The second youngster who had a brief September trial with the team was pitcher Charles "Babe" Adams. The tall right-hander was purchased from Denver of the Western League and tossed into the fray on four occasions. However, he did little to impress Pittsburgh management. Clarke believed that a lack of speed shown by Adams on the mound made it questionable whether he had the stuff to pitch in the big leagues.

Pitching was Pittsburgh's strongpoint in 1907 as team hitting lagged behind. Wagner was his usual, solid self, winning batting crown number five with an average of .350. Newcomer Abbaticchio didn't disappoint the local fans. He gave the team timely hitting, knocking in 82 runs in spite of the fact that he only hit .262. Leach (.303), Nealon (.257), Gibson (.220) and Alan Storke (.258) rounded out Pittsburgh's hitting brigade.

After the conclusion of the season, Clarke returned to his ranch in Kansas. His main project for the coming winter was to build a motor boat that he could use while hunting on the Walnut River. The water was so shallow on his property that he had to dig a subway in the channel to create a passageway for his vessel.[43] As Clarke labored in Kansas, fans in Pittsburgh wondered if Cap would sign a contract for the 1908 season. Because Clarke's financial value had surpassed $100,000 thanks to his property in Kansas and various wise investments he made in stocks and bonds, it was questionable how much longer Clarke would stay in baseball because he didn't need the money.[44]

Concerns about baseball and work on his ranch were put on hold when Clarke was called to Des Moines to be with his seriously ill father, who had not been in the best of health for some time.[45] Clarke arrived in Des Moines and remained at his father's bedside until the esteemed gentleman began to show signs of improvement. Out of deference to Clarke, decisions that couldn't be made without Dreyfuss consulting his right-hand man were put on the back burner.[46]

When William Clarke's condition improved, Fred decided to make the trip back to Winfield. His father's improvement had been so swift that Clarke believed everything would be okay. Unfortunately, when Clarke arrived in Kansas, word awaited him that his 79-year-old father had died. William Clarke passed away on November 7, 1907, survived by his wife Lucy and six children.[47]

Because family took center stage and baseball became secondary to Clarke for the first time in many years, Pirates fans seriously wondered whether Clarke would be willing to give it another shot in 1908.

Chapter 11

Pirates Come Close During Great Race

Anxious Pittsburgh fans, concerned over the fact that Fred Clarke hadn't signed a contract for the 1908 season, worried over nothing. Before Clarke left for Des Moines to be with his sick father, the Pirates manager intended to hammer out a deal on a new contract with Barney Dreyfuss, who suspended negotiations so Clarke could take all the time he needed attending to this personal matter.

Proof that Clarke was still leading the team came from the fact that he scouted a player while in Des Moines visiting his ill father. Dreyfuss was interested in an outfielder from Texas named Owen "Chief" Wilson who split time between Little Rock and Des Moines in 1907. Clarke looked over the outfielder and gave his stamp of approval.[1] Dreyfuss took great precautions to insure that Wilson was secured by the Pirates by drafting Wilson from both minor league clubs, with the draft from Little Rock being permitted.[2] Once again, personal scouting on Clarke's part led to a new player coming aboard the Pirates craft.

Clarke didn't immediately sign his own contract after his father's funeral. The Pirates manager decided to relax and unwind by taking a hunting trip with his brother Josh in the wilds of Minnesota.[3] Clarke's younger brother was still knocking around the minor leagues playing baseball. He had a short cup of coffee with Louisville in 1898 and also appeared in 50 games with the St. Louis Cardinals in 1905. Josh Clarke finally would play a full season of baseball for Cleveland in 1908, but in 1907, he had toiled for Toledo and hit .321 in 154 games. Toledo teammate Harry Eels joined the Clarke brothers on this hunting expedition.

The hunting party left Ida Grove, Iowa, in the middle of November. A long journey eventually led the three men to Josh Clarke's property 150 miles north of Minneapolis. On Saturday, November 23, Eels was accidentally shot in both legs.[4] It was initially believed that Josh Clarke's gun had discharged by mistake. This was later proven not to be the case. Dr. J.E. Conn of Ida Grove went to the scene of the mishap and attended to Eels' injuries. It was first reported that Eels' condition was critical.[5] Eels did have some serious injuries, but he was expected to fully recover from wounds that were unintentionally self-inflicted.

With this hunting excursion not supplying the relaxation that Fred Clarke had hoped for, the Pirates manager returned to Kansas. Once back in the warm confines of the "Little Pirate Ranch," Clarke began making plans for the 1908 season. Before Clarke signed his contract, he convinced Dreyfuss to bring the Pirates to Winfield for some exhibition games during the 1908 training season. Clarke had been trying to encourage Dreyfuss to do this for years so that his teammates could see the region's beauty. It was determined that the Pirates squad would stay in Winfield on April 7 and 8 after the team played some games in Wichita.[6]

Clarke finally penned his name to a 1908 baseball contract right before the Christmas holidays. The one-year deal supposedly called for Clarke to make somewhere between $8,500 and $10,000 for the upcoming campaign.[7] Many baseball scribes believed that Fred had finally gained entry into the double-digit class of paid baseball servants. Dreyfuss, happy that his manager had signed for another year, gave some insight into why Clarke contemplated retirement the past two years. "Fred says he thinks he will try another whirl or two at the game," said Dreyfuss. "He puts it that he had a good year in the last race and will run another anyway. I never had any idea that Fred would quit. He couldn't earn half that sum of money at any other occupation and besides it's for only six months a year. He is only 35 years of age, being born in 1872, and is in prime health. It isn't so much for himself and Mrs. Clarke that he thinks over the ball-playing proposition. It is in relation to the schooling of his children. Not that there are not good schools in both sections, but the term of the children is broken and they are given one outline in this city and another in Cowley county."[8]

As Dreyfuss discussed Clarke's intention to return for another season of National League baseball, the Pirates magnate reminisced about Fred's arrival on the scene 15 years ago. Through the years, Clarke was referred to as Cap, Rough and Ready Freddie, Ferdy and Ferdinand by writers and players alike. None of these monikers were attached to Clarke when he debuted for Louisville in 1894. Dreyfuss chuckled as he relayed the story surrounding Clarke's first nickname during those early days in the Falls City. "From the first appearance of Clarke in uniform he was nicknamed by the fans and the appellation stuck to him for days," said Barney. "There was no uniform on hand to fit him and he was forced to put on spangles owned and built for Larry Twitchell, the old twirler and outfielder. The trousers were a mile too long and flopped around the ankles of the new lad. Sailor-like, Clarke had to take up a hitch in his pantaloons every other step. The gang howled in derision over the man's appearance and ere he figured in plays began to kid him. They didn't do it after the new man from Savannah had a chance to show his speed. The name was carried East and when we got to Pittsburgh and elsewhere newspaper squibs spoke of Ollie Smith and Pants Clarke as showing signs of being good enough to stick to fast company."[9]

Pants Clarke's 1908 contract called for the star left fielder to play and manage. In 1907, Clarke was only able to remain away from the game as a player through the first few weeks of spring training. Injuries and trades prevented Clarke from being a bench manager as he initially wished during the past year. In reality, Clarke quickly realized that he couldn't navigate his team from the dugout. He needed to be actively involved with any action on the baseball diamond. As long as Cap remained in the game, he intended to continue as a player-manager. "When I can't play ball any longer, I will retire to Kansas and follow the plough," remarked Clarke. "I find it the hardest job I ever undertook to sit on the bench without taking an active part in the game. None of it for me."[10]

Clarke quickly immersed himself in making preparations for the upcoming season. Some historians feel that the pennant races staged in the National and American leagues in 1908 were the most competitive in baseball history. In the American League, Detroit barely squeaked by Cleveland and Chicago when the final bell sounded at the conclusion of the season. Over in the senior circuit, Chicago, New York, and Pittsburgh staged an epic battle that wasn't decided until two combatants replayed a controversial game at season's end. The fact that Pittsburgh was involved in this titanic battle was not lost on those who could not have possibly expected such a good showing given the obstacles Clarke faced as the year began.

The first issue presented to Clarke and Dreyfuss was borne out of a Cincinnati rumor regarding a proposed trade between the Reds and Pirates in which Tommy Leach would be sent to Redland. Pittsburgh fans who believed that this was an unsubstantiated lark quickly learned that the story did have life. Cincinnati owner Garry Herrmann wanted Leach in the fold so that Tommy the Wee could manage his ball club in 1908. The Reds magnate, upset over the team's 66–87 record in 1907, fired Ned Hanlon after two uneventful seasons at the helm.

Leach was considered one of the more heady ball players in the National League. He was unofficially being groomed to succeed Clarke whenever the

Pittsburgh manager decided to walk away from the game. Herrmann pestered Dreyfuss throughout the fall and winter, but the Pirates owner refused to budge. Finally, Dreyfuss referred Herrmann to Clarke.[11] "Before I left Cincinnati," said he, "I gave Herrmann Fred Clarke's address, and told him hereafter he could deal direct with my manager. I would not think of making any deal without Fred's consent, at any rate, I told Garry that if he and Fred could arrive at terms, I will O.K. the deal, provided the players offered for Leach look good to me. The whole deal rest's on Leach's willingness to go or stay. Unless he is very eager to leave us, he will not be traded, even if the whole Red team is offered in exchange."[12]

When Herrmann and Clarke corresponded, Fred gave Garry a list of Reds which included catcher George "Admiral" Schlei, second baseman Miller Huggins, shortstop Hans Lobert and outfielder Mike Mitchell. Herrmann then talked to Leach and found that the veteran Pirate was receptive to the idea of coming aboard as Cincinnati's manager.[13] Negotiations between both teams continued with the names of Cincinnati infielder John Kane and catcher Larry McLean being added to the list as other players were removed.[14]

Even though Clarke remained the point man representing Pittsburgh's interests, Dreyfuss still held the final word regarding the culmination of any deal. Dreyfuss retained this power in spite of the fact that he had washed his hands of the whole matter. Both Clarke and Dreyfuss insisted a deal would only be made if Leach truly wanted to leave. This was a repeated mantra of Pittsburgh management even after Leach said that he would like to manage the Reds. This may have been an indication that management was actually disappointed with Leach's decision. It also meant that Leach and Herrmann would be behind the eight ball in trying to get a deal done.

The attempted deal between these two teams eventually was killed by the principle object of the trade discussions. Leach advised Herrmann to cease talks with the Pirates. He told the Cincinnati owner that Clarke and Dreyfuss' asking price was too high. If such a deal were struck, it would leave the cupboard much too bare for Leach when he assumed the managerial rein's of the Reds.[15] On January 20, 1908, Herrmann discontinued talks with Pittsburgh and named first baseman John Ganzel as Cincinnati's new manager. "The price they demanded was too high," said Herrmann. "I could not afford to give what they asked for. Then about all that I would have left would have been a manager, so I called the deal off."[16]

Leach's dream of becoming a major league manager would have to be put on hold. The fallout from this event was that Leach now felt that his value had risen, and he wanted to be compensated with a higher salary. This position could have been the result of over inflated self worth since Cincinnati wanted him as their manager or because Leach was angry at Pittsburgh management

Cincinnati owner Garry Herrmann wanted to make a deal so that Tommy Leach could come aboard to manage the Reds in 1908. Herrmann and Fred Clarke exchanged proposals, but a trade was nixed when Leach told the Cincinnati owner that Pittsburgh management was asking for too much.

for preventing this from happening. One thing was certain — an ugly holdout had occurred. When Leach came to Pittsburgh, he met with Dreyfuss and turned down an offer for a 15 percent raise over 1907 in salary.[17] "Oh," replied Leach hastily, "if that is the best you are going to offer, we might as well quit talking right away."[18]

With Leach being disagreeable toward Pittsburgh management, the local press which had commended him for his actions during the American League raids of 1902 were now condemning him. Many scribes promptly questioned his loyalty during that time. Comparing him to the likes of contract jumpers such as Jack O'Connor, Jesse Tannehill and Jack Chesbro was strong stuff. It seemed that a player could only be looked upon in a favorable light if he were loyal to the local team. In an era where ownership was in total control of an individual's fate, it didn't seem to matter when a player was possibly wronged. Clarke and Dreyfuss may not have directly interfered with Leach's transfer to Cincinnati, but they certainly had not gone out of their way to facilitate it either.

Leach and most of his brethren holdouts didn't remain unsigned for long. Leach, George Gibson and first baseman Harry Swacina all came to terms after protracted holdouts. When these three players finally came into line, this left only one Pirate still unsigned for the upcoming 1908 season. The fact that Honus Wagner was the player in question didn't go unnoticed by Pittsburgh writers and fans. They were shocked when Wagner's name was leaked out as someone who was balking at signing for the 1908 season.

It was known that Honus was told by Dreyfuss each year to write in his own salary figure on a blank contract, and that the shortstop always agreed to an amount of $10,000 a year. Wagner was happy with his berth in Pittsburgh, so it seemed surprising that a salary dispute would keep him from playing in 1908. Some scribes tossed around a malicious tale that Wagner had entered into a conspiracy with other holdouts to force Dreyfuss to pay higher salaries.[19] It was soon learned that the plain truth of the matter indicated that Wagner wanted a year off from baseball to let his body heal.[20]

There was no denying that Honus Wagner played the game of baseball to its fullest. He threw his body around the field, making plays to help the team without regard for his personal safety. The big German put it all on the line while playing. This style had taken its toll physically, mentally and emotionally. Wagner had very high self-imposed standards which would be compromised if he could not perform to the best of his ability. There were no hard feelings between Wagner and Dreyfuss. Honus sent a letter to the Pirates which explained his decision and thanked the organization for their loyalty:

> My Dear Barney—I will not be with your team this season, but wish you a pennant-winner, and will always be plugging for Cap and the boys to win.
> It is certainly hard for me to lay aside the uniform I have worn since 1897, but every dog has his day, and the sport has become too strenuous for me.
> I can look back and see that I was lucky in landing with you in Louisville, and that I made no mistake in staying with your Pittsburgh team during war times. I was offered nearly double the amount I asked from you then, but I

have been a gainer by it, as my salary has always remained the same. Besides, I have had the satisfaction of knowing that my boss appreciated the fact I always gave the club the best I had.

    I wish to thank you for your treatment of me while a member of your club, and assure you that I highly appreciate the same. Again wishing you success, I am, Very truly yours,

(Signed) John H. Wagner[21]

    Clarke had a large void to fill at shortstop during the upcoming season. Young Charlie Starr was slated to replace the brilliant Wagner. Pittsburgh's chances of contending for the pennant were reduced greatly by not having the Flying Dutchman's services. Dreyfuss believed Wagner would play baseball once again, and also felt that his star player was justified in taking a year off from the game. "Wagner has a perfect right to retire," said Dreyfuss, before he started south with the team, "and I hope that the year's rest will benefit him. Besides being a great player, he was loyal at a time when he could have gained temporary financial advancement by being disloyal. He stated in his letter to me that he did not lose anything by sticking to the Pittsburgh Club. His appreciation of this fact gives me a great deal of satisfaction."[22]

    News that hit the press prior to Opening Day painted a much different picture in respect to Wagner and Pittsburgh's adoring fans. It was reported that Honus retired because he had supposedly tired of comments from the paying public who did not seem to appreciate his play in spite of the Flying Dutchman's complete dedication to the game.[23] Once again the relentless badgering by local fans had claimed another victim. Kitty Bransfield and Claude Ritchey fell before him and now the Mighty Honus was leaving the game because he could not tolerate the stinging barbs directed toward him from the paying public. If this story were true, it didn't paint the Pittsburgh baseball fans in a very favorable light.

    Pittsburgh rooters were delighted when word came that Wagner was joining the Pittsburgh team at Clarke's ranch in Winfield. Wagner cautioned everyone by declaring that he was only participating in the exhibition game there because of an earlier promise he made to Clarke.[24] This didn't mean that Pittsburgh's star player was ready to end his retirement. No matter what the motives, Clarke was happy to see his old friend back on a baseball diamond. He was also glad that Wagner was able to join the team which was being fed and housed at Clarke's ranch during the team's stay in Winfield. Team Secretary William Locke wondered what kind of gags Clarke would pull while the team was staying on his Winfield farm.

    "If I had two guesses I think I would strike the nail on the head," said Secretary Locke. Then the local secretary mentioned the fact that Clarke planned to build a new house and turn the old one over to his farmer. "It won't be an idle day for the boys at the Little Pirate Ranch," continued Locke. "Fred does not believe in taking it easy. He will have a barn raising, a corn husking, or a foundation digging for the boys. The Pirates will have to do chores for their board. That horn will sound at day dawn. All hands out, break ice in the barrel to get wash water, a quick breakfast and then to dig. That's Clarke's game. He wants no soldiers."[25]

Pittsburgh's band of faithful rooters were ecstatic when the season started one week after the Winfield trip. Discussions about holdouts and retirement could now be replaced with conversation surrounding the events of each game and expectations for the upcoming season. Clarke showed that he meant business in 1908 by bringing his family east to Pittsburgh much earlier than usual. Annette, the two children, and Pittsburgh's skipper had descended upon the Steel City in March to set up housekeeping before Clarke left for West Baden. Usually, Clarke's wife and children didn't join him in Pittsburgh until the season was well underway.[26]

Without the services of Wagner, Pittsburgh wasn't expected to be a factor in the pennant race. The Pirates rolled into St. Louis for the opening series of the season and thumped the hometown Cardinals in a three-game sweep. As the team headed for Cincinnati for the second leg of the season-opening junket, news came that Wagner had signed a contract and was ready to play baseball. The versatile shortstop realized that he missed being on the baseball diamond and still had a burning desire to play. Clarke also had a long talk with Honus in Kansas. He told his star shortstop that the team needed him.[27] Wagner agreed and his much publicized retirement lasted a total of three games.

The performance displayed by Wagner in 1908 was nothing short of sensational as he put the Pirates team on his back in pursuit of the elusive pennant. One had to wonder what the Flying Dutchman would have accomplished if his body was not "so beat up" as had been reported. Wagner won another batting title, leading the league with a .354 average. He also topped the National League statistics in hits (201), doubles (39), triples (19), RBIs (109), OBP (.415), slugging (.542) and stolen bases (53). Wagner accomplished this in a year when hitting was down in both leagues. The nearest person to him on the Pirates was Clarke with a .265 average. If there had been an award for Most Valuable Player at the time, Wagner would have been the undeniable winner.

Solid pitching was the dominant theme in baseball throughout the 1908 season, and the Pittsburgh pitching staff did not disappoint. Rookie Nick Maddox was sensational, posting a 23–8 record with an ERA of 2.28 in his first full season. Staff ace Vic Willis was even with Maddox at 23–11 with a lower ERA of 2.07. Camnitz (16–9, 1.56 ERA), Leever (15–7, 2.10 ERA) and Leifield (15–14, 2.10 ERA) were stellar in lending support to the staff's double aces.

The fact that Pittsburgh went 22–8 in June was amazing when one took into account the maladies which plagued the pitching staff during that month. Veteran Deacon Phillippe was officially place on the injured list for the season with a fractured thumb. Phillippe had done nothing before this, making five uneventful appearances out of the bullpen. Leifield missed a few starts with what was described as strained muscles between the shoulder and elbow. Maddox labored through the month with an undisclosed illness.[28] In spite of these injuries, Pittsburgh ended the month in first place, one full game ahead of Chicago and three in front of New York.

Clarke was able to keep his team in the hunt despite the fact that he wasn't getting much production from the first base and center field positions. Clarke rectified this situation when he purchased veteran outfielder Roy Thomas from the Philadelphia Phillies on June 1. Clarke intended to place Thomas in center field and bat the newest member of the Pirates in the leadoff spot. This allowed the Pirates manager to move rookie Owen Wilson to right field as a replacement for Danny Moeller who only batted .193 in 1908. Wilson had struggled in the early going, but the move to right seemed to ease the burden on the rookie outfielder.

Roy Thomas came to Pittsburgh with a solid resume. The veteran outfielder had been a consistent performer with the Philadelphia Phillies for almost a decade, topping the .300 mark in 1899 (.325), 1900 (.316), 1901 (.309), 1903 (.327) and 1905 (.317). The fact that Thomas had gotten off to a sluggish start for the Phillies didn't concern Clarke or Dreyfuss. They felt that Thomas would feel rejuvenated having the opportunity to play for a contender like Pittsburgh. He played solid ball for the Pirates, hitting .256 and receiving accolades for his immediate impact on the squad.

The first base position was solidified when Alan Storke returned to the Pirates after the academic year at Harvard was over in June. Storke batted .252 in 64 games and fielded the position with a smoothness that hadn't been seen since Kitty Bransfield manned the initial sack.

Harry Swacina and Jimmy Kane both failed to impress when Clarke gave each player early season trials at first base. Clarke even attempted to pry prospect Bill Abstein from the Providence team in the Eastern League early so that he could improve the weak first base slot. Providence refused to do so until their season was over. This left Storke as the guy in Pittsburgh for the campaign's duration.

As the Pirates caught fire in June, their manager also was doing sensational work on the baseball diamond. It seemed that Clarke had drunk from the fountain of youth as the star left fielder played the best baseball of his career. Cap was hitting with a purpose and pulling off amazing plays in the field, which left fans gasping for breath. For the most part, Clarke was leading by example as he drove the Pittsburgh players to perform to the best of their ability.[29] He was called out on one occasion when he used profane language during a June game. Clarke questioned umpire Bill Klem after the arbiter called a strike on him. He wasn't censured for verbally challenging the umpire. Clarke was criticized because the whole grandstand could hear him when Cap yelled the vulgarity.[30]

Clarke's strong play didn't go unnoticed in opposing cities. After the Pirates won three out of four games against the Giants on June 9 through June 12, New York newspapers praised both Clarke and shortstop Wagner. The Big Apple scribes acknowledged that these players were National League stars. Dreyfuss found it fascinating that New York writers needed so much time to realize what Pittsburgh fans always knew—Fred Clarke and Honus Wagner were two of the greatest players in baseball history.

"I note that the metropolitan papers have finally made the discovery that Wagner is a great ball player," commented Dreyfuss. "After many days it has come. They would not acknowledge it until this trip. Now the papers teem with the play of the big fellow and he lands all sorts of plaudits. Clarke is also credited with being a star. They say that Fred was most active in the series, playing wonderful base ball. He was here, there, and everywhere. His feat of scoring from second base on what should have been an out was heralded as a fine piece of work. I don't think that Fred is as fast as he was once, but he can go some still. I mean that he doesn't get down to first base with old time fleet footedness. When making a long hit, however, you would not think that he had lost any of his speed, for he can go some on the bags, once under way."[31]

As Clarke continued to terrorize opposing pitchers, the Pirates manager was also keeping a close eye on construction that was occurring on his property back in Kansas. Through letter correspondence, Clarke was staying informed about progress that was being made on the erection of a water plant at his "Little Pirate Ranch." The construction project took a large step toward modernizing his Winfield home. When the new plant was completed, it would then be possible to pump water to the top floor of the Clarke residence without any trouble.[32]

Clarke didn't let this construction at his home in Kansas interfere with the challenging National League pennant race. The standings were still tight in late July when Pittsburgh made another move to fortify their roster. Dreyfuss and Clarke claimed local boy Spike Shannon off waivers from the New York Giants. Shannon was an outfielder by trade who led the National League with 104 runs scored in 1907. Reduced to a utility role in New York and bitter over the fact that John McGraw had cut him loose, Shannon did little to justify his acquisition once in Pittsburgh. Spike hit a less than robust .197 while scoring only 10 runs in part-time duty with the Pirates.

Despite a 16–12 record by the team in July, Pittsburgh still clung to first place. They were leading Chicago by half a game and New York by two as the month concluded. As the Giants continued to make it a three-team race, they were also a part of the news in Pittsburgh for various reasons. They were hanging tough, even though most scribes believed that Chicago and Pittsburgh would slug it out for the pennant. The Shannon acquisition had made the Giants and McGraw interesting copy in Pittsburgh newspapers. All of this paled in comparison when New York second-string catcher Tom Needham made a bold statement that shook the very foundation of the Pirates nation. He claimed that Honus Wagner planned to retire after the shortstop was honored at Exposition Park during a game against Boston.[33]

"I had a long talk with Wagner," Needham said, "and he told me positively that after the game on Friday, he would quit the Pirates and leave ball for good. I thought he was joking at first, but he assured me that he was in dead earnest. He is completely disgusted with the way he has been treated by the Pittsburgh fans. During the past ten days he has been playing with a sore hand that would have put most players out of the business. Yet, because he slipped up on a few difficult chances, he was roasted unmercifully."[34]

Statements which suggested that Wagner was still contemplating retirement had to be disturbing to both Pirates fans and management. The fact that Needham touched upon Wagner's disappointment over Exposition Park fans who roasted him could mean two things. Needham was either rehashing old information and giving out an inaccurate quote, or Wagner had really confided in the New York catcher, upset that he was being subjected to the fans' venom in spite of having a phenomenal year.

Authentic Pittsburgh fans paid homage to the Pirates star during "Honus Wagner Day" on July 17. Wagner was honored and received various gifts from fans and Pittsburgh management.[35] After the game, there was no retirement announcement. Wagner closed the door on this subject for good the next day. "I never told Needham nor any other person anything of the kind," said Honus. "When I signed my contract in the spring, it was for the season of 1908, and I intend to live up to my contract and give the Pittsburgh team my best services as long as I play ball. I will probably be in harness again next season, too. My health is better now than it has been for a long time and I do not feel like giving up the game. I love baseball more than anything else on earth."[36] This statement from Wagner put an end once and for all to retirement talk for the 1908 season.

The Pirates limped through August, going 14–11, and slipped down two notches in the standings to third place. The Cubs and Giants were in a virtual tie with Pittsburgh, trailing by half a game. As Pittsburgh prepared for the stretch run, Clarke benched himself for a few games because of a batting slump and placed Spike Shannon in left field.[37] The Pirates play in September became as hot as the molten steel produced in the Pittsburgh mills. They tore through the league at a 25–8 clip. When fans viewed the National League standings on October 1, New York was on top with a record of 93–53 and Pittsburgh was second at 95–55. Mere percentage points separated the two teams, with Chicago a distant third, half a game behind the rival Giants.

For Clarke's boys, the whole season came down to their final game against the Cubs in Chicago on October 4. A Pittsburgh victory would bring the pennant to the Smoky City, regardless of the outcome of New York's last three games against Boston. Vic Willis took the mound against Pirate killer Mordecai "Three Finger" Brown. Pirates fans crowded downtown Pittsburgh streets in order to receive updates that were reported by telegraph. The faithful were sent away disappointed as Brown and the Cubs stifled the Pirates, 5–2.

Pittsburgh finished the season with a 98–56 record and Chicago stood at 98–55. The Pirates' slim pennant hopes hinged on Boston defeating New York in one of the three games they had left and the Giants then beating Chicago in a make-up game. If this were to occur, all three teams would be tied for first place. Boston failed in its effort to assist the Pirates as New York steamrolled through them in three games. In spite of the heartbreaking loss in the finale against Chicago, Dreyfuss commended his team for their pluck and grit.

"Only one team could win," said Dreyfuss, "and it wasn't ours. It was too bad. Willis was in grand form and the other members of the team played the game of their lives, but against Brown and the support given him by the Cubs chances were indeed slim for the Pirates taking the crucial game. If it develops that New York and Chicago must meet in three games to decide the supremacy in the National League, I hope the series can be staged in Pittsburgh. The Cubs should duplicate their feat of last year in the coming series with the American League leaders, for I believe Chicago is going to nose out New York."[38]

There would be no three-game series between New York and Chicago, just a make-up game to determine the league champion. The Giants would have already won the pennant if a game played between the two teams on September 23 hadn't been declared a suspended tie. An apparent New York win was nullified when Fred Merkle, subbing for Fred Tenney at first base that day, failed to touch second base as the winning run scored in the ninth inning.[39]

As was the practice at that time, Merkle headed straight for the clubhouse to avoid the rush of fans storming the Polo Grounds field. Second baseman Johnny Evers was able to retrieve a baseball from the flowing masses and umpire Hank O'Day called Merkle out as Evers completed the force play at second base to end the inning. The game could not be resumed because the field was littered with fans.[40] National League president Harry Pulliam eventually decided that the game would be replayed if it had any bearing on the final standings. Chicago claimed the pennant when Jack "The Giant Killer" Pfeister defeated Christy Mathewson, 4–2, in the make-up game on October 8.

Even though Pittsburgh lost the pennant in heartbreaking fashion, Clarke's boys had competed with passion throughout the season. Their record against the Chicago Cubs (12–10) and New York Giants (11–11) showed just how tight the race was. A surprising statistic was that Pittsburgh played far better on the road (56–21) than at home (42–35). Even more glaring was the run differential for the season. The Pirates scored 227 runs at home, while allowing 255. They put up far better numbers on the road, scoring 358 runs and allowing only 213. To the casual observer, this seemed odd since contending teams usually performed better with the backing of the home crowd. It didn't seem strange, however, to anyone that had been around the team for a whole season. While Clarke had bitten his tongue as the 1908 campaign unfolded, he finally spoke his mind at the conclusion of the home slate.

Honus Wagner retired for a total of three games during the 1908 season. When he returned, the Flying Dutchman carried the Pittsburgh Pirates on his back in an effort to claim the National League pennant. Those pennant hopes were dashed when Chicago defeated Pittsburgh in the Pirates' season finale.

We have made a good fight, and there is nothing in our record about which we have any right to feel ashamed. But, I must say it, the fans of Pittsburgh have not supported us as they might have done, and any glory that may accrue to the city from the way we finish the season belongs to the players and not to the people. Had we been compelled to depend on the encouragement we got at Exposition Park for our inspiration, I fear very much we would have landed in the second division, instead of being up there fighting for the lead all season long.

But the boys did not depend on the plaudits of the multitude, and, they paid little attention to the sneers and criticisms that were hurled at them. They are the gamest lot of fighters it has been my good fortune to command, and I am proud of the way they have acquitted themselves. Sometimes, it is true, they have made mistakes. That was to be expected. And once or twice mistakes were bunched, so that some of us did look amateurish, but the best evidence that we were out there doing our best all the time is found in our present standing, for in a race like that in the National League this year, no team of quitters could have stood the pace as we did.

Ball players are not angels. They are not expected to be, but I believe they will measure up well alongside of men in any other calling when it comes to the matter of sobriety, morality and honor.

One or two members of the Pittsburgh team have been accused of being drunkards and bums. The accusations have been basely false. "Lefty" Leifield has, for some reason or other, come in for more censure from the fans than any other member of the team, but I am as positive as I am of anything that the St. Louis boy has not touched a drop of intoxicating liquor since last June. He never did use it to excess, but when he saw that his taking a drink of beer was starting ugly stories about his habits, he cut it out altogether. I never demand that my players be teetotalers — never did demand it. All that I ask is that they keep themselves in condition to play ball. There never was a more earnest ball player than Leifield, and I am at a loss to understand why the fans should have seen fit to roast him as they have done. He is always willing to work. If I needed a man for some extra task, I always called on Lefty because I knew that I would not be turned down.

There are a few other players who have not been given the credit due them, for some reason or another. However, I know very well that every man has done his best, and that satisfies me. They cannot all be Wagners. If they were, no other team would ever have a look-in. But they can all play ball, and they have all done their full duty this season.[41]

It seemed that the second player who may have been perceived as a boozer in the eyes of heckling fans was pitcher Howard Camnitz. After the season concluded, Camnitz was spotted in some of the more popular gin joints throughout the city upon returning to Pittsburgh from Kentucky for a few days. The local press quickly caught wind of this and published a story.[42] The angry pitcher issued a terse denial, although in later years many would wonder if he had told the truth in this instance when the connection between Camnitz and drinking arose again.

While Clarke defended his players to the press, the Pittsburgh manager also explained how he had recently made a foray into the world of invention and innovation. He came up with a scheme to produce canvas coverings which covered ballpark diamonds when it rained. Pittsburgh used the device at Exposition Park in 1908 and Clarke claimed his invention helped save three games from being postponed. The contraption paid for itself since these games would have been rescheduled as doubleheaders later in the season. Clarke anticipated other big league clubs purchasing the covering for their fields in 1909.[43]

Clarke wasn't the only Pirate giving interviews after the heartbreaking 1908 season ended. Honus Wagner was still irritated over the fact that a pennant had slipped right through Pittsburgh's fingers. "Bosh! With those hits and all that stuff," snapped Wagner, "what does it all amount to when we didn't win that game at Chicago? I would have gladly given every world's record I have had or ever hope to have if we could only have pulled that game out of the fire on Sunday.... I'm awful sorry for Clarke. If ever there was a man who deserved to win it was Fred. That fellow has things awful hard at times, but he never lost heart and he kept us going all the time. The ground rule hurt at Chicago — hurt us more than it did Chicago. There were four balls dropped in the crowd right back of Fred Clarke each going for two bases, when he would have eaten them up. It's awful. I'm going to kill 10,000 birds this winter to forget it."[44]

Leisure time for players like Wagner and Clarke during the off-season would be spent hunting as usual. For Clarke, it was weeks of camping out in the open during November and December. After the expedition, Cap had two big wagons of game which included raccoons, quail and live coyotes.[45] Clarke's time in the wild gave the Pirates manager a chance to unwind after a long, arduous season. Time away from the pressures of baseball allowed Clarke to recharge his batteries. Although Pittsburgh came close to winning the pennant in 1908, Clarke believed that he had his team positioned to make a run at the National League banner in 1909.

Chapter 12

Championship Glory

Pittsburgh's strong showing during the 1908 campaign galvanized a section of the fan base who believed a pennant-winning season was within the team's grasp. While there were many rooters who seemed to revel in knocking and hissing when in attendance at Exposition Park, the majority of the fans were diehards. These passionate Pittsburgh baseball fans would be rooting for their favorite team in new stomping grounds during the 1909 season, as in October 1908, Barney Dreyfuss announced that the Pirates would have a new ballpark to be built near the entrance of Schenley Park in the Oakland section of the city. The land, bought by Dreyfuss from the Schenley Estate, was currently being leased to the Carnegie Technical Schools. Dreyfuss hoped to begin construction on this state-of-the-art facility when the lease expired on December 1. Dreyfuss anticipated that the new park would be ready in June 1909.[1]

Dreyfuss had decided on a new park since permanent improvements could never be made at Exposition Park because he was unable to acquire a long-term lease from the Baltimore and Ohio Railroad Company that owned it. The railroad told Dreyfuss on several occasions that it was going to use the land where the park was for yard purposes.[2] Dreyfuss also realized that he needed a new ballpark that could cater to higher class patrons whom the Pirate owner felt would want to see the game of baseball as it grew in popularity. Exposition Park was located in a poorer section of town where affluent fans, especially women, detested the idea of attending a game there. The new ballpark would be located in a nice area of the city where people from all walks of life could attend games without concern for their well being.

Construction on the actual ballpark wasn't expected to begin until March 1909.[3] Nothing could be erected until manager Fred Clarke decided how he wanted the diamond at the new field to be laid out. Clarke had to make determinations as to what direction the sun should hit his new playing grounds, give advice on dimensions and counseled contractors about infield grading. Once Clarke finalized these plans, architects could then worry about things such as stands and walls.[4] He also believed that Dreyfuss' investment in the Pirates' new playground would turn out to be a prudent business decision. "It looks like a big sum of money to lay out at one time," wrote Clarke to his employer, "but I do not need to tell you that base ball is not only a big business, but a growing and prosperous institution, and that you will reap handsomely in the future. With such a plant, you ought to be able to make money, even with a second-rate team. We were right in the fight last season, and I am confident that with one or two changes, we will have a team that will stay in the running all summer."[5]

Manager Clarke had no intention of expecting his group of players to be second-rate in 1909. He was just making a point to Dreyfuss that the new ballpark would probably draw fans even if Pittsburgh wasn't contending for the pennant. Clarke believed his squad would battle for the National League championship once again in 1909. National League president and friend, Harry Pulliam, praised the Pirates manager for his work in 1908 and likewise anticipated great things for 1909. "I consider the Pittsburgh team a good aggregation," said Pulliam, "and Fred Clarke a magnificent leader. Considering everything that he and his team have had to contend against this season, I would consider it a miracle if they won the fight. But, no matter whether they win or lose, they have well represented Pittsburgh in the National League race. Manager Clarke started the season with only one regular outfielder, and it was a long time before he landed a man who would make a good showing. He also tried four first basemen during the season. Yet, despite this great handicap, the Pirates battled gamely throughout the season. With Wagner in the game at the start of next season and the team going nicely, the Pirates will be right in the 1909 race."[6]

Having Honus Wagner on hand when spring training commenced was a strong positive in Clarke's mind as he prepared for the 1909 season. As Clarke prepared to make the trip east, word leaked out of Kansas that Clarke's land likely contained rich and fertile oil. To the south of his property in Oklahoma, the 101 Ranch owned by Clarke's friend, George L. Miller, was producing gas and oil. East of him in the Osage Nation, there were 2,000 wells and to the west in Blackwell there likewise was a bounty of riches. Miller contended that Clarke's property probably contained black gold since he was surrounded on all sides by oil-producing land.[7] Oil drilling didn't concern Clarke, however, as he prepared for the 1909 baseball season.

As most of the Pirates players were preparing to trek to Hot Springs, all had signed a contract except for Vic Willis. Word had reached Pirates headquarters that Willis was going to walk away from the game in order to pursue business interests at home.⁸ Replacing a man who had won 67 games during the past three seasons would not be an easy task. While some in Pittsburgh had feelings of anxiety and apprehension when they heard this news, Dreyfuss was not one of them. "I can't prevent Willis or any other player from retiring if he wants to," said Dreyfuss. "Willis had decided to quit in the fall of 1907, but he didn't. Club-owners all have to stand for this sort of talk in the winter time. Frankly, I don't think Willis means it, though he has not yet signed a contract."⁹

Dreyfuss saw this action on Willis' part as posturing, pure and simple, in an attempt to receive a salary increase from the Pittsburgh team. The threat of retirement as a ploy in contract negotiations was really the only recourse a player in that era had, other than demanding a trade to another team. Dreyfuss' strategy was to say nothing and make Willis sweat it out for awhile. It was reported by Pittsburgh papers that Dreyfuss was willing to pay Willis $4,100 for the 1909 season; Willis supposedly was holding out for $5,000.¹⁰ One month went by before Dreyfuss finally commented on the Willis situation. An agitated Dreyfuss fired back with guns blazing when it became apparent to the little magnate that Vic's holdout had gone on too long. "I presume Newark, Del., is as cheap a place to spend the summer as anywhere else, so you may as well remain there," was Barney's ultimatum.¹¹

Willis finally decided that his only option was to come in line and sign at the team's figure if he wanted to play baseball in 1909. His hesitance at reaching an agreement in a timely fashion ended up costing the star pitcher financially. When it became apparent in Dreyfuss' mind that Willis' haggling had gone too far, the Pirates owner rolled back the right-handed pitcher's salary to its 1908 level of $3,500.¹²

The Pirates were lucky that Willis' pitching ability was not on par with his negotiating savvy. Clarke still anticipated big things from his star right-hander. Clarke didn't expect the protracted holdout to affect Willis' mental approach to the game. With everyone on the squad present and ready to play ball, the Pirates could now concentrate on the season ahead. It didn't seem as if the team was very focused through April as the Pirates stumbled out of the gate with a 5–6 record. In spite of this rough start, there was praise galore being heaped upon a handful of Pittsburgh rookies.

Youngsters Jap Barbeau and Bill Abstein ably manned the corner positions for Clarke's squad through the spring of 1909. Barbeau was installed at third when Tommy Leach was moved to the outfield after Ward Miller failed in center field. Abstein claimed the first base job during spring training and quickly served notice that the first base jinx was dead in Pittsburgh.

Abstein was solid for the Pirates during his rookie campaign. He hit .260 for the season and drove in 70 runs while appearing in 137 games. While not quite as deft around the bag as Kitty Bransfield, Abstein was a substantial upgrade over the likes of Del Howard, Joe Nealon and Harry Swacina. With Abstein, Wagner and Barbeau all off to a strong start for the team, Pittsburgh just needed Ed Abbaticchio to break free from his shaky play. If Abby could hit his stride, the Pirates would then possess the strongest infield quartet in the National League. Abbaticchio never got a chance to break out of his slump. Clarke benched him and gave rookie Jack "Dots" Miller a shot at second base.

Miller had received a tryout at Exposition Park the previous summer. Clarke liked what he saw from Miller, but the Pirates manager was reluctant to break up his current starting combination. Miller was farmed out to McKeesport of the Ohio-Pennsylvania League for more seasoning.[13] Clarke was impressed by the young man's confidence when he talked to Miller for the first time that hot, summer day. Miller possessed the kind of spunk that reminded Clarke of when he was a rookie back in Louisville. "What position do you play?" asked the Pirates boss. "I play wherever I am put," responded Miller.[14]

Miller's confidence in his own ability was definitely not misguided. The New Jersey lad had the type of rookie season that would probably have netted him the award for best first-year player if one existed at that time. Miller hit .279 and knocked in 87 runs while batting behind Wagner for most of the season. Even though Miller was described as big and awkward, he covered enough ground to lead National League second basemen in putouts and fielding percentage during his inaugural season. Wagner took a quick liking to the youngster. The two players formed a cohesive combo on the field and were inseparable off the field as well. Miller certainly made the most of his opportunity after Clarke plugged him into the lineup. "If I ever get on that team, they'll never get me off," said Miller to a friend before the season opened.[15]

With Miller now rounding out the starting unit, the team began to hit stride in May and waltzed through the opposition on their way to a 20–6 record for the month. One of the things that worked in Pittsburgh's favor was the fact that Clarke was able to put the same starting eight on the diamond each day. Wagner and Abstein were the only players who missed any time with minor injuries. When St. Louis rolled into town during the middle of May, stories bubbled to the surface indicating that a change was coming to that Pittsburgh group of regulars. Writers speculated that Clarke was interested in acquiring Cardinals third baseman Bobby Byrne. When St. Louis left Pittsburgh, Byrne was still a member of the Cardinals squad. It had been rumored prior to the season that Byrne would be a Pirate in 1909, but once again a trade between the two teams didn't transpire.

The Corsairs followed up their strong showing during the month of May with a stellar record of 19–3 in June. As the team took control of the National

12. Championship Glory

League race, anticipation grew throughout the city of Pittsburgh as the christening date for the Pirates' new ballpark drew near. Dreyfuss had conducted a contest for fans to determine the name of his new baseball palace. It was decided that the ballpark would be named Forbes Field, in honor of General John Forbes, a hero from the French and Indian War who had captured Fort Duquesne from the French in 1758 and renamed it Fort Pitt.[16] The three-tier steel and concrete park was designed for Dreyfuss by architect Charles Leavitt, Jr. Leavitt had designed both the Saratoga and Belmont racetracks, but Forbes Field would be the only ballpark blueprints which bore his name.[17]

The Nicola Building Company erected the structure in a mere 122 days. The estimated cost to build Forbes Field was somewhere in the range of $1 million to $2 million.[18] With 1,500 tons of steel used to construct Dreyfuss' state of the art facility, the new ballpark contained a host of amenities which would bring pleasure and enjoyment to potential patrons.[19] Forbes Field also included one of Clarke's patented roll-up tarps to keep the field dry during bad weather.[20]

As Pittsburgh prepared to make the transition from Exposition Park to Forbes Field, two stories began making the rounds which indicated that Clarke wouldn't be playing many games at the new baseball palace. The first report stated that Clarke faced a possible suspension and fine after the Pirates manager claimed that some of the National League magnates were not as honest as they should be.[21] Clarke made this statement after Pittsburgh received an adverse decision over a protested April game against Cincinnati which Pittsburgh originally won. Clarke criticized some magnates and the National Commission after this unfavorable verdict was rendered.[22]

Cincinnati owner Garry Herrmann was once again front and center in a dispute with the Pirates manager. As a key member of the National Commission, Herrmann would have a hand in deciding if Clarke deserved a suspension. National League by-laws stated that a player or manager could be suspended for the season and fined $200 if they engaged in scandalous conduct on or off the field.[23] Before Herrmann could render judgment, he needed to know if Clarke had been correctly quoted as making such malicious statements. Herrmann sent Clarke a letter asking the Pirates manager to issue an apology.[24] Clarke declined to oblige Herrmann with written correspondence feeling that handling the matter in that fashion could come back to haunt him.

"I'm not going to answer that letter," said Clarke. "When one goes writing letters the other fellow usually gets something on you. I'll wait until I get to Cincinnati and then I'll tell it to Mr. Herrmann, and right. But as to writing it, no, not Freddie. I guess that Mr. Herrmann would like to get something on me."[25]

Clarke was not brought before the National League Board of Directors as Herrmann had hoped. Herrmann did not receive a letter of explanation from Clarke, but Fred had no qualms about sending one to acting league president John Heydler. Clarke's claim that he acted unwisely during a time of heated passion and made derogatory remarks which were unintended satisfied the league president. Heydler considered the case closed as he ruled on June 28 that Clarke wouldn't be fined or suspended.[26]

While Heydler was determining Clarke's fate, a second report surfaced which indicated that 1909 quite possibly could be the Pirates manager's last year in baseball. During the past few seasons, Clarke had contemplated retirement on several occasions. Precedent usually dictated that these stories were either verified or denied by Dreyfuss or Clarke himself. On this occasion, a surprising third party was the source of a statement which led fans to believe that Clarke was hanging up the spikes. His wife Annette, someone normally never quoted in print, was the person responsible for the latest comment regarding Fred's desire to leave baseball and permanently retire to his Kansas ranch.

"Fred will retire," said Mrs. Clarke. "He has had his innings and his departure will mean an opportunity for some other player. While we are attracted to the Smoky City, there is a great big ranch in Kansas that needs his attention, and after this year it is the ranch life for both of us. It is not generally known that Fred did not hanker after playing this year and did not actually decide to play until he went to Hot Springs to join the team. Then he decided to try for just one more pennant, but this is his last try."[27]

Clarke corroborated his wife's story when approached by baseball writers.[28] If this was truly going to be Clarke's last season, he certainly intended to go out in style. His Pittsburgh Pirates were setting the National League pace as Dreyfuss prepared to open his new baseball palace. The last game at Exposition Park was played on June 29, 1909, as Lefty Leifield and the Pirates shellacked the Chicago Cubs, 8–1. Excited fans who had tickets to the inaugural game at Forbes Field saw that the Pirates were atop the standings of the National League, 7½ games ahead of the second-place Cubs, when they opened their newspapers on the morning of June 30.

The scheduled time for the great event at the new ballpark between these two rivals was at 3:30 P.M., but fans began flocking to the gates right before noon. The seating capacity of the Pirates' new home of 23,000 was stretched to the limits as 30,388 paying customers attended the festive event.[29] Much of the overflow crowd took up residence in roped off areas of the outfield. Local and national dignitaries occupied seating located much closer to the action on the diamond. Mayor W.A. Magee threw out the first pitch to Public Safety Director John M. Morin and the game commenced.[30]

Willis was pitted against Ed Reulbach of the Cubs in this much anticipated contest at Forbes Field. Willis, possibly feeling a tad nervous given the situation, was a bit wild at the start as he plunked leadoff batter Johnny Evers. Evers came around to score the first run at the ballpark when Frank Chance recorded the first hit in Forbes Field history. Neither club did much hitting on that day as the Cubs ruined the gala event by defeating the Pirates, 3–2. Clarke went hitless in four trips at the plate, but the star left fielder did score one run on a Miller double in the eighth inning.

In spite of the loss, Dreyfuss was ecstatic over the praise his new ballpark was receiving. Initially referred to as "Dreyfuss' Folly" by some baseball writers, Forbes Field quickly assumed the title of best ballpark in the business. One of the dignitaries who had been in attendance at Forbes Field's opening was Clarke and Dreyfuss' good friend Harry Pulliam. The president of the National League had just returned to his post on June 28 after a brief sabbatical in which Pulliam traveled throughout the United States.

Life for Harry Pulliam had been very stressful over the past year. The root of his aggravation were the two leaders of the New York Giants, John T. Brush and John McGraw, who launched one diatribe after another toward Pulliam in protest of the league president's decision regarding the "Merkle Incident" from the previous season. New York management believed Pulliam had erred in declaring the game on September 23, 1908, against the Cubs a suspended tie. If the original score of 2–1 favoring the Giants had been permitted to stand, there would have been no replayed game on October 8 and New York would have won the pennant.

McGraw and Brush were relentless as they bombarded Pulliam with complaints and accusations day after day throughout the winter. This, coupled with some other issues that were placing a strain on the president, began to wear on Pulliam's psyche. People close to him began to detect a change in his personality. He seemed to be moody and detached. There were some within Pulliam's inner circle who felt he was headed for a nervous breakdown. The president subsequently took his self-imposed vacation in order to recuperate from exhaustion. Secretary John A. Heydler was named to replace Pulliam on a temporary basis.[31]

When Pulliam returned to his job, the league president still seemed to be suffering from nervousness. As Pulliam immersed himself in his work just the same, friends and colleagues were concerned that the president was still suffering from depression. Steel City associates close to the league president were not surprised when his behavior escalated in a tragic manner. While attending the inaugural game at Forbes Field, Pulliam talked to one local dignitary like it would be the last time the two men would ever see each other.[32] On the night of July 28, 1909, Harry Pulliam shot himself with a revolver through the right temple in his third-floor room at the New York Athletic Club at about 9:30 P.M. The head wound was so bad that doctors couldn't move Pulliam to a hospital and had to attend to him there.[33] Pulliam died the following morning.

Pulliam was laid to rest at Cave Hill Cemetery in his hometown of Louisville on August 2. Play was suspended on that day in both leagues out of respect for the former president. Luminaries such as Ban Johnson, Charles Murphy, Charles Ebbets and John Heydler were in attendance.[34] Representing the Pittsburgh Pirates at the service were Barney Dreyfuss, William Locke, Fred Clarke, Sam Leever and Lefty Leifield. Honus Wagner was devastated when he couldn't attend the funeral after doctors said the Carnegie native's current injury made travel too dangerous.[35] As the National League got back to business after the memorial service, league magnates decided that Heydler would finish out Pulliam's term as president for the remainder of the year.

Dreyfuss was devastated over the death of his friend. Clarke was likewise saddened, but the Pirates manager had to concentrate on the task at hand. Clarke needed to focus on suppressing the surging Chicago Cubs and holding on to win the team's first pennant since 1903. The Pirates made a good showing in July with a 20–10 record and followed that up even stronger in August at a 22–7 pace. The problem was that the Cubs weren't going away, as they played equal or better ball than the Pirates during that time period.

Compelling the crisis from Pittsburgh's standpoint was the fact that Wagner missed time with an injury during the month of August and was replaced by the less than effective Abbaticchio for a few games. Just when it looked as if the Pirates ship was listing and beginning to take water, Clarke added the final piece of the puzzle when the long anticipated trade for Bobby Byrne of St. Louis was finally consummated. On August 19, Byrne was acquired from the Cardinals for Jap Barbeau and Alan Storke. Clarke's only comment after the deal was that Byrne was just the player he needed to balance Pittsburgh's team.[36] Dreyfuss was a bit more effusive in his praise of the third baseman as Pittsburgh's baseball magnate backed Fred Clarke's decision. "Fred Clarke made the trade. He tells me that he has strengthened the team, and I believe him," Dreyfuss said. "Will Byrne bat? Watch him. You will see that he is a pretty fair man with the club. Any player can work with him. That's a fine point. As a defensive man he needs no recommendation. He is steady and sure. You must have every spot well cared for in a team that is seeking for the highest honors."[37]

Pittsburgh fans were upset over the fact that Clarke acquired a player who had only hit .214 for the Cardinals in 1909. Jap Barbeau had posted a slightly better average of .220 in 91 games for Pittsburgh. On paper this deal seemed to favor the Cardinals, but the value of trades cannot always be measured by statistics. Byrne possessed the pep and ginger that separated those who would do whatever it took to win from the ballplayer who just plodded along wishing to pick up a paycheck. In regards to the effect this acquisition had on the team's play, only the Willis trade a few years earlier could be looked upon as a more significant deal made during the Dreyfuss-Clarke tenure so far. After a few weeks in Pittsburgh, Byrne was gushing with enthusiasm over his new berth. "They said several times in St. Louis that I did not give the Cardinals my best services," said Bobby. "That was false. I always tried my hardest, but it was mighty difficult, at times, to do the right thing. However, I like the Pirates and the boys are treating me fine. You can bet that I intend to do my best for them."[38]

Byrne gave Pittsburgh his best during the stretch run, hitting .256 and hustling his way to 31 runs scored in 46 games. Byrne was also rock-solid in the field, committing only two errors as a member of the Pirates. His ambition of joining a championship team also became a reality as the Pirates held off the Chicago Cubs to win the 1909 National League pennant. They needed every one of their franchise-record 110 wins as the Cubs finished the season with a total of 104 victories. In almost any other season, Chicago's victory total would have been good enough to win the championship. The series versus New York (11–11) and Chicago (13–9) were competitive ventures, but the Pirates feasted on the remainder of the league, losing only 22 games to the other five teams.

The Pirates boasted the best infield in the league as the work of Abstein, Miller, Byrne and Wagner outclassed all National League quartets. Wagner secured his seventh batting title with an average of .339. Clarke (.287), Wilson (.272) and Leach (.261) formed the most solid hitting Pittsburgh outfield in many years. Clarke, Miller and catcher George Gibson all led the league in fielding at their respective positions and George had his best season to date at the plate as he stroked the ball at a .265 clip.

Phenomenal pitching by the Pittsburgh staff gave the Pirates the final ingredient in their pennant-winning recipe. Howard Camnitz had a career year, and tied the great Christy Mathewson for top honors in the National League with a 25–6 record and a minuscule ERA of 1.62. Support for the staff hammer came from Willis (22–11, 2.24 ERA), Leifield (19–8, 2.37 ERA) and Maddox (13–8, 2.21 ERA) who all hurled over 200 innings for the pennant winners. Veterans Phillippe (8–3, 2.32 ERA) and Leever (8–1, 2.83 ERA), plus rookie pitcher Charles "Babe" Adams (12–3, 1.11 ERA) rounded out the best pitching unit seen in Pittsburgh since the pennant-winning seasons at the beginning of the decade.

The month of September wasn't without incident as the Pirates wrapped up their fourth pennant of the decade. On September 8, Clarke was arrested on a charge of assault and battery after he attacked a brick manufacturer from

Manager Fred Clarke added the final piece of the puzzle to his 1909 pennant-winning team when he acquired peppery third baseman Bobby Byrne on August 19 from the St. Louis Cardinals for Jap Barbeau and Alan Storke.

Bridgeville named Casper P. Mayer. Clarke pushed Mayer down a flight of stairs at Forbes Field on Labor Day after he objected to the Bridgeville man invading Pittsburgh's dugout. Casper refused to leave the area so Clarke used force to remove the intruder.[39] Although Mayer eventually sued Clarke for assault, the case was settled before it went to trial.[40]

12. Championship Glory

On a more positive note, Pittsburgh fans celebrated Fred Clarke Day on September 28 at Forbes Field after Captain John Moren suggested the city honor its great baseball manager. A fund of $600 was raised and this gift of gold cash was presented to Clarke at a ceremony during the game against New York. Speeches were given as Mayor Magee proudly gave Clarke his bullion bounty.[41] Clarke was touched by this honor. "I intend to purchase something with this money," stated Fred, "which I can always keep and look back upon after I have quit the game, with kind remembrances for the many friends I have in Pittsburgh. I have had many pleasant years here, and I hope to return next spring to spend another happy summer with you."[42]

This particular statement contradicted something Clarke had said only a few weeks earlier. In early September, Clarke stated that he was still in agreement with the comments his wife made in June. Rumors stated that he was retiring out of respect for Annette Clarke since she supposedly didn't really like the eastern life and preferred the tranquility of their Kansas farm.[43] It was believed that Clarke would be walking away from a yearly salary of $12,500 if he retired.[44] However, money was not the point. "There's more in this world than money, for me at least," responded Clarke. "I would sooner make only half the amount I am receiving now and be with my family and in my home. I simply will not stand for the long separation that a season of base ball means—an entire spring and summer apart from the ones you love, traveling on the road or playing in a city that is not one's home. This is the finish for me."[45]

Clarke seemed to be torn between continuing his career and retiring. Whatever clash Clarke was having internally, the Pirates manager knew that he couldn't let this become a distraction during the World Series. Pittsburgh's opponent in the Fall Classic was Hughie Jennings' Detroit Tigers, led by a young keg of dynamite named Ty Cobb who was considered the best player in the American League after only four seasons. For the first time ever, the two batting champions of each league met head to head in the World Series. Cobb had claimed top honors in the American League with a hardy .377 average. Comparisons between Wagner and Cobb were made in publications throughout the country. These scribes should have been comparing Clarke and Cobb, since both players played the game of baseball with a similar, fiery style. When it was reported that star pitcher Howard Camnitz had taken ill with quinsy on the eve of the series, manager Clarke wrestled with the decision on who to choose as his starting pitcher for the first game of the World Series on October 8 at Forbes Field. There were some who felt the Pirates skipper would select Phillippe, the sentimental choice because of his valiant work on the mound against Boston in the 1903 series. Others figured that Camnitz would be sent to the hill in spite of being weakened by his supposed illness.

Many rooters were surprised when the Pittsburgh manager tapped the shoulder of rookie Babe Adams to make him the opening-game starter.

The cool youngster didn't disappoint as he shut down the vaunted Tigers attack in front of a hometown crowd that could only be described as electric. Adams pitched a masterpiece as he tossed a complete game and bested George Mullin, 4–1, in the series opener. Adams was shaky at first, but he settled down after Detroit scored their lone run in the first inning. Clarke was a hero in the first game when he hit a home run in the fourth inning which knotted the score at one apiece. Pittsburgh then scored two runs in the fifth and one in the sixth inning to secure a victory. Cobb had a chance to bring his team back in the seventh inning, but the star Tiger flied out to Leach in center with two men on base. Clarke later explained the psychology he used in order to prepare rookie pitcher Adams for that opening game.

> Pitching Adams was a decision a fellow makes once in a lifetime, when he follows a hunch, and feels he is right, but cannot convince anybody else he is not crazy.
>
> Howie Camnitz was our best. It would have been easy to pitch Howie. But I knew Adams had the kind of curve ball which had bothered Detroit all season. If he could throw it, I knew he had a chance.
>
> My job was to make sure Adams pitched his game, because you never know how a young pitcher will do in a big spot. We had Charlie with us two years before for a look, but this was his first full season in the big leagues.
>
> I could only figure on making Adams mad. For the week before the opener, I refused to name my starter, which drew criticism, and I needled Adams. I called him names; I got him fighting mad. He was ready to pop when he went out to the mound to face Detroit.
>
> He was jumpy. For the first three innings, I called him a yellow stiff when he came back to the bench. After that he settled down and was just what I thought he would be.
>
> In the clubhouse, I went to him and complimented him for his wonderful game. He had held Cobb hitless, and I asked him how he felt when he faced the terrific hitter.
>
> Adams snapped back: "I was thinking what a dirty stiff you were, and how I would like to knock your block off." I did all I could to keep him thinking that way.[46]

Game Two of the World Series did not go so well for the Pirates on Saturday, October 9. Camnitz was knocked out of the box in the third inning and Wild Bill Donovan and the Tigers cruised to an easy 7–2 victory. Clarke went hitless at the plate as Pittsburgh never mounted a serious challenge. One of the highlights from the game was when Ty Cobb greeted relief-pitcher Willis by promptly stealing home in the third inning. During his first four years in baseball, Cobb was perceived by many to be an ornery, ill-tempered man with a nasty disposition. Cobb showed surprising charm and humbleness when scribes started making comparisons between him and Wagner. "Oh, you mustn't compare us," replied Ty, "he is a baseball veteran, and I am only a youngster. He has had years of experience, and is up in all the tricks of the trade. I have never seen him play, but from what I have heard of him, he must be a wonder. I don't know whether I will make a single hit in the series, but I don't care if Wagner bats .400 and I only bat .100, if the Tigers win out."[47]

Before the two teams prepared to do battle in Game One, Cobb and Wagner had posed for the cameras, showing each other their batting stances. The two talked of doing some hunting together after the series and wished each other luck. There was an admiration on the part of Cobb toward Wagner that the Georgia Peach was not always inclined to show against star opponents from the American League. Fans realized that Wagner also respected Cobb's ability. Many expected the battle between these two teams represented by the best players in each league to go down to the wire.

The series resumed in Detroit on Monday, October 11, at Bennett Park with Nick Maddox opposing Ed Summers of the Tigers. Pittsburgh jumped out to a quick 5–0 lead in the first inning, knocking the Detroit starter out of the game. The Tigers showed resilience and battled back. Pittsburgh hung on for an 8–6 victory. Clarke went hitless for the second game in a row, but the Pirates manager scored a run in the first inning and drove in Bobby Byrne with a sacrifice fly in the ninth. The Tigers rebounded the next day as George Mullin whitewashed Lefty Leifield and the Pirates, 5–0. Clarke's struggles at the plate continued as he went hitless for the third straight game and struck out twice.

Babe Adams took the mound once again as the series shifted back to Pittsburgh for Game Five on October 13. Adams and the Pirates were in for more of a battle this time around as the Tigers erased a 3–1 Pittsburgh lead with two runs in the top of the sixth inning. Luckily for the Pittsburgh faithful, Detroit starter Ed Summers imploded in the seventh and four Buccaneers crossed the plate to seal the deal in an 8–4 complete game victory for Adams. Clarke finally broke out of his slump at the plate, recording two hits, scoring two runs, walking once and driving home three runs. Clarke provided a clutch hit during the pivotal seventh inning when his bounce home run scored Byrne and Leach ahead of him.

Willis was called upon for Game Six in Detroit on October 14. When the Pirates scored three runs in the top of the first off Mullin, it looked as if Pittsburgh would be champions of the baseball world. Detroit hung in there, though as they scored five unanswered runs and held on for a 5–4 victory as a single tally crossed the plate for the Pirates in the ninth inning. Clarke went one-for-three in the game, scored one run and recorded one run batted in.

For the first time in history, the World Series went the full limit of seven games. New territory was ventured into, as a coin toss was used to determine the city to host the seventh game. Pittsburgh won the toss. In a surprising move, Clarke deferred much like a football coach and decided that Detroit should host the deciding game.[48] Fans in Pittsburgh probably assumed that Detroit had won the coin toss when it was announced the final game would be at Bennett Park. Had they known Clarke acquiesced, there probably would have been an uprising in the Smoky City. Clarke, of course, had something up his sleeve.

> When I won the toss of the coin, I knew if I chose Pittsburgh we would have everybody pulling for us and sympathizing with us. If we were in Detroit, we would get a riding, and that would rile us, and that's when my club was best. They had to have somebody on 'em to live up to their top game.
>
> I had no doubt we would get the best from them in Detroit, but what I wanted to do was take the edge off them before they played. One of the big secrets in any sport is to know how to take the tension off athletes. When any competitor is nerve-tight, he cannot play his game.
>
> I knew only one way. The night before the game I called the boys into my sitting room. I had a big table full of sandwiches in the middle of the floor, and tubs of beer and pop around it. We ate and drank, told stories, and got up a good barber shop quartette. I brought Barney in and got him a beer. At 10 o'clock I sent them to bed with this message: "If we do we do, and if we don't we don't, and to hell with it. Just have a good night's sleep."
>
> They did. I don't think anybody ever had a better club for natural, reckless spirit which put all of the pressure on the other side.[49]

The pitching match up for the final game on October 16 pitted Adams against Donovan. The fact that it was a raw, cold, windy day didn't bode well for Tigers fans since Donovan was a power pitcher who needed to be loose in order to throw the speed pitch. Conditions wouldn't affect Adams, who relied more on his curve and change of pace pitches. Those who expected a tightly contested affair were disappointed as Game Seven ended up being the most lopsided of the series. Pittsburgh scored two in the second, two in the fourth and three in the sixth as they blitzed Detroit, 8–0. Clarke displayed consummate teamwork during the deciding game as he didn't record an official at-bat. Clarke walked four times, scored twice, drove in one run, sacrificed a runner to third and handled four chances flawlessly in left field.

The Pirates were world champions. Babe Adams was the toast of the town as he single-handedly shut down the Tiger juggernaut. Adams posted a 3–0 record with a 1.33 ERA as the vaunted big three of Camnitz, Willis and Leifield choked mightily under the post-season pressure. Neither team hit the ball well. Pittsburgh only struck the ball at a .224 clip with Detroit being only slightly better at putting the ball in play with a .241 average. Wagner outplayed his star counterpart from the Tigers in every facet of the game and out hit Cobb, .333 to .231. For Wagner, this performance was sweet vindication for the man who had been labeled as "yellow" after the 1903 World Series.

While Clarke only hit .211 in the 1909 series, he still utilized his plate appearances to their fullest as he reached the pinnacle of his career as both a player and manager. Clarke scored seven runs, drove in seven, smacked two home runs, walked five times, sacrificed runners four times and made only one error in left field. He believed that this was only the beginning for his Pittsburgh Pirates. "I am too happy to say much," said Clarke. "This is the first time I have had the honor of being the manager of a world's championship team, and I will tell you I am proud of it. The Tigers gave us an awful battle, but I was sure we would pull out ahead. I would have liked to seen these games from the stand, for I am sure

Fred Clarke in 1915, his last season as major league manager. He would return to the Pirates in 1925 and 1926 at the request of Dreyfuss, to assist skipper Bill McKechnie, but that second stint would end in what became known as the "ABC Affair."

they were interesting enough even if not so well played. Too much credit cannot be given to Adams for his three great victories. He is nothing but a kid and we are fortunate in having him. I expect to see Pittsburgh win again next season."[50]

Smoky City fans were absolutely giddy over the fact that the Pittsburgh Pirates were baseball's current champions and likewise thought that more titles were in the team's future. Baseball-crazy rooters honored their team upon its return to Pittsburgh with a parade, followed by a ceremony at Forbes Field in which each player came up on stage and received their monetary share of the series proceeds. Each player was cheered wildly as his name was announced.[51] These same patrons became ecstatic days later when Dreyfuss announced that Clarke had confided to him, before his departure to Kansas, that he probably would be back in 1910.[52] Cap still had a thirst for more baseball pennants.

Chapter 13

Clarke Betrayed by Pittsburgh Fans

While Barney Dreyfuss said that Fred Clarke probably was returning as both player and manager in 1910, Clarke still needed to sign a contract. During the December league meetings, various New York publications reported that Clarke had done just that.[1] When Clarke visited Pittsburgh to perfect his baseball diamond covering patents, local writers began questioning him about the veracity of those New York articles.[2] "But I haven't signed yet," laughingly commented Clarke. "Have agreed to sign. That's as good as my signature."[3]

While Clarke explained to the Pittsburgh scribes that signing a contract for the 1910 season was a foregone conclusion, he also began to reminisce about his long relationship with Pirates owner Barney Dreyfuss. Clarke and Dreyfuss had been together for many years, but Barney wasn't Fred's boss during the early days in Louisville. Dr. Stucky and other Falls City dignitaries were his employers when Fred Clarke broke into the league 16 years ago. Dreyfuss was only the team treasurer at that time, whose main responsibility was to make sure the Louisville players were paid their salaries. "Whenever we wanted our checks in Louisville days, even as far back as I can recall, we hurried to the big whisky warehouse and laid for Barney," Clarke recalled. "Many an hour did I hover in that section, keeping a weather eye for the little fellow who doled out the papers. This will be the seventeenth year Barney and myself have been in base ball. Long time, but I know that it has been a pleasurable and profitable period for me."[4]

When Clarke reflected upon these bygone days, he also talked about another dear friend from those Louisville years. With all of the pressure and excitement that came from winning both the National League pennant and baseball's World Series, Clarke didn't have an opportunity to reflect back on

13. Clarke Betrayed by Pittsburgh Fans

Harry Pulliam's life in proper fashion. The mourning period had taken place for Clarke after Pulliam's death, but the Pirates manager hadn't gotten a chance to talk much about his former management partner in both Louisville and Pittsburgh. Clarke remedied this by relaying a tale about one particular celebratory team dinner thrown by the Louisville Colonels board of directors. "There were lots of directors in those times," said Cap. "One in particular do I remember. He was a Scotchman with a burr on his tongue that beat chestnuts on Phil's farm. Sandy, they called him. One season the club showed well and a banquet was the result. Sandy took a seat on my right and Harry Pulliam on my left. Harry was then a mirthful, happy fellow. Full of jokes, he suggested to Sandy that he could improve his oysters by a liberal dose of Tabasco sauce. The director fell for the suggestion, fairly smothered his bivalves with the peppery juice, not knowing its fiery stings. Harry and myself waited for the results. To our amusement Sandy downed that decoction without even watering an eye. Gamest man I ever ran across."[5]

Most of the baseball fans in Pittsburgh believed that there was never a gamer man who played baseball than Fred Clarke. He was revered by the rooting populace for his hustling style, positive attitude and strong dedication to the game. Cap was a fan favorite because he played the game without reservation. Clarke did whatever it took to win, and he always expected his troops to follow their manager's lead.

Pittsburgh rooters were ecstatic when they learned that Fred Clarke signed a two-year contract to play and manage through 1911. Terms of the deal were not released, but many baseball pundits believed that Clarke was now making $15,000 a year. Clarke's change of heart regarding retirement was a direct result of Pittsburgh defeating Detroit in the World Series. Clarke believed that this team had a chance to become a dynasty like his teams of 1901, 1902 and 1903.

Clarke showed everyone in Smoketown that he meant business. Clarke decided to rent out his Kansas ranch for two years and spend the whole time in Pittsburgh. Cap figured he could better devote his time to baseball if the Clarke family was living in Pittsburgh during the spring, summer, autumn and winter.[6] He believed that by fully concentrating on baseball for 12 months, he increased Pittsburgh's chances of repeating as champions. Dreyfuss was a bit surprised when he heard that Clarke was temporarily giving up life on the farm so that he could properly defend Pittsburgh's title. "I think Fred would be foolish to cut away from farm life altogether," said Dreyfuss. "He has a magnificent place out there and loves the life, but the country has proved a disadvantage in educating his children. I do not know his plans, but I predict in three years he will return to the life of an agriculturist. There is one thing certain, working on a farm has never impaired his value as a ball player."[7]

Not only was Clarke leasing his farm for two or three years, he also sold off some of his assets during a public auction on February 1, 1910. Items that Clarke put up for sale included 12 mules, 11 horses, six head of cattle, 500 bushels of corn, 15 tons of alfalfa, a Jackson runabout, cultivators, binders, hay loaders, hay rakes, mowers, plows, drills, grain wagons, buggies, harness, and a boat.[8] The auction did quite well as Clarke received $100 for the mule named Honus.[9] This decision was bittersweet for Clarke. He was torn between his two loves, baseball and farm life. Clarke was committed to bringing more pennants to Pittsburgh, but he also was an important figure around Winfield.

> I was a kind of sheriff around my diggings in Kansas. You know, they don't allow the sale of liquor in Kansas, but some fellows sell it anyway. One of these fellows got hold of an old farmer and promised him a bottle for a dollar. He took the old fellow back into his barn and as he produced the bottle the old man produced a roll of big bills big enough to choke any cow in the State. As the salesman saw the roll, he picked up a club and hit the farmer over the head and, grabbing the money, ran. The farmer was not quite unconscious and he let out one big yell. I happened to be passing at the time with my bulldog. I "sicked" the dog after the salesman and he grabbed the fellow by the seat of the trousers and held him till I came up. The farmer got his money back and the whisky salesman is still in jail. Guess I wouldn't make quite a sheriff, eh?[10]

Clarke was trading in his temporary law enforcement duties in Kansas to be Pittsburgh's baseball sheriff for at least two more seasons. Clarke was only confronted with one issue during the winter of 1910 which once again involved his jinxed first base position. Even though Pittsburgh won the championship in 1909, there were those who felt the title would have been sewn up sooner if not for the boneheaded play of first baseman Bill Abstein throughout the World Series. Abstein wore the classic "goat horns" during the series as he killed numerous rallies courtesy of baserunning gaffes and nine strikeouts at the plate. On the field, Abstein committed five errors and threw to the wrong base on so many occasions that the Pirates fandom couldn't keep count. It was reported that Dreyfuss was very dissatisfied with Abstein's play. After a regular season game when Abstein struggled mightily at first, Clarke supposedly told Barney to release Bill immediately.[11]

Abstein was abjectly deficient at first when a play was in front of him. He could handle throws to the bag from other fielders. Unfortunately, when Abstein had to make a snap decision, he usually panicked. It was obvious to local fans that Abstein had a glaring weakness when making mental assessments as game situations dictated. Dreyfuss purchased first baseman Jack Flynn from St. Paul for $4,000 on December 14, 1909. Clarke shipped Abstein to the St. Louis Browns on January 6, 1910, as former contract jumper Jack O'Connor secured the maligned first baseman for his American League team.

13. Clarke Betrayed by Pittsburgh Fans

Baseball pundits were in agreement that Pittsburgh was the best team in the National League in 1910 with resistance coming from the usual antagonists in Chicago and New York. Scribes felt that the team would perform even better than they did in the championship season of 1909. The Pirates would benefit from having Bobby Byrne in the lineup the whole season. Babe Adams' addition to the starting rotation full time also gave the staff a strong fifth twirler it could depend on. The team's only glaring weakness was at first base, but management believed that Flynn would be an adequate replacement for Abstein. Another pennant in Pittsburgh looked like a sure thing to both writers and Smoky City fans.

As it turned out, 1910 wasn't the glorious season that everyone expected. Years later, Dreyfuss would refer to this season as being one of the biggest disappointments during his time in baseball. Never before had he seen such a great team fold so quickly. Throughout the season, players, management, writers and fans alike searched for answers to explain the team's sudden decline. Many patrons were shocked prior to the season when the perfect five man rotation became unhinged before any games were played.

The first man to be eliminated from the pitching staff was Vic Willis when Clarke sold him to the Cardinals on February 15. Pittsburgh released the veteran pitcher because management believed that his drinking during the 1909 season violated team policy established by Clarke during spring training in Hot Springs.[12] The Pirates skipper also felt that Willis' behavior was not setting a proper example for Pittsburgh's young twirlers. The team released a player who had won 89 games for them during his four seasons in Pittsburgh because Clarke wasn't a person who compromised where discipline was concerned.

Clarke had so little confidence in Willis during the 1909 World Series that the star twirler wasn't given a start until the sixth game. Willis had also claimed to his teammates after Babe Adams won the first game of the series against Detroit that the Tigers would be easy pickings when he took the mound. Willis stated that if he didn't beat Detroit, he would eat his uniform. It was reported that several of his teammates reminded him of that boast after Game Six and demanded the pitcher to chow down on his jersey.[13] Willis' 1910 season in St. Louis would be a farewell tour as the tall right-hander posted a less than impressive 9–12 record in his final season of big league baseball.

A second player who supposedly drew the fury of manager Clarke was pitcher Howard Camnitz. As was suggested in the story of a local newspaper after the 1908 season, Camnitz liked to burn the candle at both ends. A rumor also began circulating to the effect that Camnitz didn't suffer from a bout of quinsy prior to the start of the World Series the previous October as was reported. He actually had been feeling the ill effects of partaking in the flowing bowl to excess. Clarke was willing to give Camnitz a second chance if he agreed to adhere to established team rules. After a protracted holdout on Camnitz's part, Clarke personally worked out a deal which brought Pittsburgh's star pitcher into the fold prior to the season opener.[14]

Jack Flynn was anointed as the starting first baseman when he beat out Bud Sharpe during spring training in Hot Springs. Fans believed Sharpe would be farmed out so he could receive more playing time. Instead, he was packaged with pitcher Sam Frock and dealt to the Boston Doves for pitcher Kirby White. As a rookie in 1909, White had posted a record of 6–13 with an ERA of 3.22 for the Doves. The Pirates believed White would add solid depth to the Pittsburgh pitching staff. Management was hoping to catch lightening in a bottle once again with a Boston reclamation project. White was an unspectacular 10–9 in 1910 with an unusually high 3.46 ERA for that time period. If the prevailing feeling was that White would replace Willis, the Pirates brass had to be sadly disappointed.

Another Pittsburgh youngster faired quite nicely in his rookie season. Vanderbilt University product Vin Campbell sparkled for Pittsburgh in limited action. The outfielder got his chance early on when Chief Wilson was sidelined for a few games and impressed Clarke with his play. The Vanderbilt lad was a solid hitter who stroked the ball at a .326 clip while appearing in 97 games during the 1910 season. Campbell's only glaring deficiency was in the field. Clarke tutored him everyday, leading fans to believe that the manager had taken a special interest in the lad because he was grooming Campbell to take over in left field.[15]

As Campbell was working with Clarke to improve his fielding deficiencies, Pittsburgh broke out of the gate in strong fashion and sported a 7–2 record for the month of April. Fred Clarke knew that his team would contend once again in 1910 if they approached this season in a manner similar to the previous year. This meant that every Pittsburgh player needed to be on their toes, willing to give their very best each and every game. Clarke cautioned his team not to become complacent. He knew that the other seven National League teams would be gunning for Pittsburgh since they won the title in 1909. "There is one thing I want to impress upon you all," said Clarke, "and that is that there are no easy games in base ball. Reputed tail-enders are often just as dangerous as world's champions, and you can't tell in advance when they are going to rise up and swat you. So if you fellows want to earn my approbation, you will let out every kink of speed and energy you've got in every game. That's the way we won last year, and it's the only course to pursue if we expect to win this year."[16]

Pittsburgh certainly didn't seem to have any easy games as the 1910 season moved into May. Their excellent start was followed by a perplexing slump as the team played unsteady baseball throughout the month. The Pirates recorded a horrible mark of 11–13 during May. Pittsburgh didn't fare much better in June as the team was only able to reverse the two numbers from the previous month by posting a 13–11 record. The Pirates were mediocre through the season's first three months as they languished in third place behind both Chicago and New York, with a record of 31–26. Clarke quickly intimated that bad luck contributed tremendously to Pittsburgh's early season woes. "Our team is in far worse condition now than it was the first week of the season," said Clarke. "We were all in high spirits when the campaign started, but we have not had a single ideal base ball day since then. We have encountered nothing but cold weather, rain, snow and wet grounds. We have been going back instead of advancing. We have not had a single morning's practice since we left the South except on last Friday and then the boys had to work in heavy sweaters. I am free to confess that this is the most backward spring I have known since entering base ball."[17]

Reasons for Pittsburgh's poor play were tossed about by disappointed fans and criticizing scribes. One theory was that the team was feeling a figurative hangover after the tough battle from 1909 and couldn't get on track. Another explanation was the bad weather in Pittsburgh that spring, which caused games to be postponed and prevented the team from getting a chance to practice mornings or off days because of the rain.[18] This lack of work made the team stale and prevented them from staying sharp. A third guess was that some members of the team had seen their play suffer because of an infatuation with a new gizmo called the automobile. One local auto enthusiast claimed that players ruined their batting eye when they rode in an automobile. Wagner, Miller and Clarke were all auto aficionados. Wagner in particular loved getting as much horsepower and speed out of his cars as was humanly possible. This recklessness behind the wheel had resulted in many accidents where Honus walked away unharmed.[19]

Batting slumps occurring because the eyes became impaired when driving an automobile made for an interesting premise. The car was a relatively new novelty. Research into how the human body reacted when driving around at high speeds hadn't yet been documented. It was possible that the batting eyes of Wagner, Clarke and Miller were affected because of their newfound passion for driving. The part of this theory that didn't pass the litmus test was that many Pittsburgh players who never drove cars were also suffering from batting slumps. For now, the only conclusion that could be drawn from the players and their automobiles was that the health of any Pirate driving in a car with Honus Wagner was at risk.

When a team is going bad, the jackals are usually not far behind waiting to tear away at anything they can sink their teeth into. As parties with hidden agendas become involved in the hunt, the fine line between fact and faction becomes more clouded. One publication that had an ax to grind with Dreyfuss printed false stories about team dissension and fights which involved Flynn, Miller, Wagner, Gibson, Clarke and Dreyfuss himself.[20]

A game against the Philadelphia Phillies on August 23 lent further proof that 1910 was a star-crossed season for the Pittsburgh Pirates. Clarke tied a major league fielding record when he threw out four base runners in one game.[21] Amazingly, Pittsburgh still lost the game to Philadelphia by a 6–2 score. Clarke threw out two runners at second base, one at third and one at home as he became the first outfielder to record four assists in a game since old Louisville teammate Ducky Holmes turned the trick in 1903.[22] Pittsburgh's manager drew little solace from the fact that his work in left field only prevented a rout that late summer day.

When the month of August ended, Pittsburgh found themselves in second place, 10 games behind the league-leading Chicago Cubs. Frustration abounded from many sources as the hopes of a second consecutive pennant made a hard landing. Pittsburgh fans always expected baseball pennants each a year, and when this was not accomplished, the local rooters sometimes turned ugly. On August 29, the unthinkable happened when Pittsburgh's paying public at Forbes Field unmercifully roasted Clarke during a doubleheader sweep by New York.[23]

The Pittsburgh faithful had reached a breaking point, and they decided to vent their frustration on the Pirates manager. Fans heckled and hissed Clarke throughout both games. The crowd became obnoxious in the ninth inning of the second game when they demanded that Clarke let Ham Hyatt pinch-hit for him. The Pirates left fielder responded to the knockers by cracking out a double, but the pain and humiliation inflicted a deep wound in Clarke. He announced the following day that Vin Campbell would replace him in left field for the remainder of the season.[24] Clarke refused to comment on the matter any further.

Longtime nemesis John McGraw wasn't quite as restrained when he took aim at criticizing the Pittsburgh fans who betrayed a baseball icon. "Never, never in my connection with base ball, extending over a period of 21 years," said McGraw, "did anything ever transpire to hurt me so much as did the demonstration against Fred Clarke in the second game of yesterday's doubleheader. How the people of Pittsburgh, for years renowned as game base ball fans, would hiss and jeer at the man who brought the city of smoke its first pennant and first world's championship, is beyond my comprehension."[25]

Some national baseball publications criticized Clarke for his decision to remain on the bench because of the incident.[26] What these writers didn't understand was that Clarke had given up everything in order to concentrate totally on baseball in 1910. Pittsburgh fans rewarded this sacrifice by heckling and jeering the man who had delivered four baseball pennants to this city in ten years. Clarke always gave his best on the baseball diamond, but this didn't seem to be enough for heartless Pittsburgh fans any longer.

The 1910 Buccaneers limped home in third place with an 86–67 record, 17½ games behind the pennant-winning Cubs. Many Pirates struggled at the plate as Miller, Gibson and even Wagner slugged below expectations. Byrne was phenomenal in his first full season as a Pirate, hitting .296, scoring 101 runs and stealing 36 bases. He also led the National League in hits (178) and doubles (43). Clarke (.263) and Leach (.270) chipped in where they could.

It cannot be understated how much worse the Pirates would have been in 1910 if not for the work of Deacon Phillippe. The veteran pitcher gave a commanding twilight-of-the-career performance, fashioning a 14–2 record with a 2.29 ERA as he split time between the roles of starter and reliever. While Sam Leever was not as spectacular at 6–5 with an ERA of 2.76, "The Goshen Schoolmaster" did admirable work for the team. Babe Adams pulled himself together after a rough start, finishing with an 18–9 record and an ERA of 2.24. The rest of the staff generally disappointed as Howard Camnitz (12–13, 3.22 ERA), Lefty Leifield (15–13, 2.64 ERA), Bill Powell (4–6, 2.40 ERA) and Nick Maddox (2–3, 3.40 ERA) all pitched below expectations. Nick's career in Pittsburgh ended when Dreyfuss sold him to Kansas City on September 22.

Camnitz was a colossal failure in 1910 as his win total from 1909 was cut in half and his ERA ballooned from 1.62 to 3.22. After the season, a sensational story, the likes of which hadn't been seen in this city for years, bobbed to the surface. While in Pittsburgh with an illness as the team was on their last swing in the West, Camnitz abruptly packed his things and left for his home in Kentucky. Before Camnitz left, he gave a statement to the local press claiming that he was through in Pittsburgh. It was his contention that the team owed him $1,200 in back salary. Pirates management claimed that the money in question was a bonus that Camnitz hadn't earned.[27] Dreyfuss claimed that the $1,200 was a temperance bonus to be paid only if Camnitz stayed sober throughout the season.

"But it is not true that it was part of Camnitz's regular salary," Dreyfuss explained. "He was paid his salary in full up to October 13, the last day of a playing contract in the National League, and the $1200 I withheld was in the nature of a bonus which I am not convinced he has earned. He was to have received that sum in addition to his regular salary, if he fulfilled a temperance clause in his contract. That contract was entered into between Camnitz and Manager Clarke and I asked the pitcher to wait until Saturday, when Clarke returned from Chicago. I told him that if the manager decided that Camnitz had lived up to his contract, I would gladly pay over the money."[28]

Pitcher Howard Camnitz starred for Pittsburgh in 1909, going 25–6 with a 1.62 ERA. Camnitz struggled mightily in 1910 amid suspicions that he was not abiding by a temperance clause in his contract, which would have paid him a $1,200 bonus.

Dreyfuss then produced Howard's contract and showed the clause which stipulated that Camnitz was entitled to a bonus of $1,200 if he refrained from indulging in intoxicating liquors altogether during the period of this contract.[29]

"I simply asked him to wait two days until Clarke came home," Dreyfuss continued. "I made no charges against him. I merely said I was not satisfied that he had lived up to his contract, which, by the way, was made against my wishes by Clarke. If he is so certain he has not taken a drink all summer, I can't understand why he should refuse to wait two days for Clarke to come home. Clarke can settle the matter. If he says Camnitz has walked the straight and narrow path, then I'll pay the bonus. Otherwise, he will never get the money."[30]

It was unlikely that Dreyfuss didn't already have information in his possession that invalidated Camnitz's bonus when the mogul met with Howard and his father. Even the casual observer of the game had to know something was up given the dreadful numbers posted by Camnitz during the season. Clarke usually updated his boss about issues with the team. If Clarke hadn't caught Camnitz drinking at some point during the season, he was either stupid or naïve. Dreyfuss probably was leaving the matter to his manager because it was Clarke who agreed to such an foolish clause in the first place.

When Clarke returned to Pittsburgh from Chicago, he met with Dreyfuss to discuss the state of affairs in respect to Camnitz. The Pirates skipper did have evidence which verified that Camnitz hadn't lived up to the conditions of his contract. A new policy for the 1911 season also came out of this meeting between Pittsburgh's hierarchy. Clarke and Dreyfuss decided that all player contracts for 1911 would include a temperance clause.[31] "The day of the boozer is over, so far as the Pittsburgh Base Ball Club is concerned," Dreyfuss announced. "I have stood for a lot from ball players, but I am done being a good fellow. Next year every man who signs a Pittsburgh contract will have to first sign the pledge. There will be a total abstinence clause in every document handed out by the club to the players. If the men do not want to subscribe to the temperance clause, they can not sign a contract, and we'll get somebody to take the places of those who do not care to pledge themselves to give the club what is coming to it. We are done with the careless fellows, the men who do not appreciate a large salary."[32]

Clarke was among a group of Pittsburgh players that scattered for the winter after the season. While Pittsburgh's manager originally intended on living in the Smoky City during the off-season, he changed his mind after the ungrateful display by Pirates fans in September. Clarke and his family left their Neville Street residence in order to spend the winter in Kansas. There would be no leasing of the property for two years as planned. Thanks to Pittsburgh Pirates patrons, Clarke couldn't wait to spend time at his ranch.[33]

Even though the baseball season was a major disappointment, Clarke did thrive from a business standpoint. The New York Giants purchased one of his patent diamond covers for the Polo Grounds. Clarke believed that he could make $100,000 in four years if he were to devote all his time to this invention.[34] He also tinkered with another innovation during the season which would aid outfielders against the sun's rays. Clarke was working on a sun field cap that would help shield players' eyes from the sun.[35]

Clarke continued on an inventor's roll in early 1911 when two other items were favorably accepted by the Federal Patent Office. The first item which passed muster in February was a property trunk that could be used by baseball clubs when they traveled. Clarke's new invention would end the custom of packing uniforms in canvas rolls and clothes in suitcases. Clarke's trunk would allow players to pack their clothes in separate compartments with the chest then accompanying the team to their next destination. This made it possible for the players to receive their clothing without actually having to transport the garments themselves.[36]

Clarke's second invention gained prominence in May. Clarke created a rubber device that was placed in front of the regulation pitching slab which prevented hurlers from digging large holes on the mound with their spikes.[37] In a short period of time, Clarke had devised four different ways to improve baseball with practical inventions. This Thomas Edison side of the Pittsburgh manager didn't mean he wouldn't return as a player and manager for the 1911 season.

While Clarke was wintering in Kansas, rumors from papers in Chicago, Cincinnati and New York indicated that he planned to dismantle the 1910 team. According to these stories, Camnitz, Leever, Phillippe, Simon, White, Leifield, Flynn, Miller, McKechnie, Leach and several others were expected to go. The ridiculous rumor that Honus Wagner was to be sold to the highest bidder at the winter meetings in New York surprised many local fans.[38] Pittsburgh's manager quickly dispelled this outlandish suggestion. "If Hans Wagner plays ball next year Pittsburgh will have him," declared Clarke. "I never said he was on the market, because I haven't gone crazy. But I've got some other men I am willing to trade if I can see my way clear."[39]

All of the wheeling and dealing that was expected once Clarke and Dreyfuss hit New York never materialized. The meetings were surprisingly quiet for Pittsburgh as no deals were brokered. Clarke did offer Camnitz to John McGraw for pitcher Otis Crandall and outfielder Al Bridwell, but the New York manager quickly rejected that idea. Clarke and Dreyfuss came home with no new items for the cupboard. Expected changes to the roster were placed on the back burner for now.

Clarke faced a dilemma as Pittsburgh geared up for the 1911 season. Camnitz didn't want to play in Pittsburgh and Dreyfuss also preferred that his former star pitcher play for another team. If Camnitz was to be moved, Clarke would bear the responsibility of getting the deal done. As had happened in the past, Dreyfuss washed his hands of the whole affair and laid the task of handling the Camnitz fiasco at Clarke's feet. It was Dreyfuss' belief that a trade was the best thing for everyone involved. He also felt that if Clarke still wanted Camnitz on the team in 1911, then the Pirates manager was entitled to have the final say in this matter.

The main problem confronting Clarke in his attempts at trading Camnitz was that possible partners weren't willing to give equal value in return. Some teams were legitimately concerned about receiving a player whose drinking problem would then become their headache. Others were looking to fleece the Pirates, who were not in a strong position from which to bargain because of Camnitz's behavior in 1910. As time went by and no deals to Clarke's liking were presented, the Pirates skipper finally decided that he would keep Camnitz for the 1911 season.[40]

Clarke was willing to gamble that Camnitz could return to the pitching form he showed during the 1909 season. In Clarke's eyes, Camnitz was a twenty-game winner rather than the broken down version that exhibited limited ability during the liquor-laden season of 1910. If Camnitz were to return in 1911, it would be at the terms dictated by Pittsburgh management. This meant that he would have to sign the pledge, just as any other player who wore a Pirates uniform for the upcoming season. Clarke was taking a risk, but he really had no choice. For the Pirates to be competitive during the upcoming season, Cap needed Camnitz.

Camnitz wasn't the only player who needed to change his ways in 1911. After a sensational rookie campaign in 1909, Jack Miller was inadequate in performing all facets of the game during his second season. Pirates management felt that this drop off in Miller's play was the result of the young second baseman not taking care of himself.[41] If Miller was willing to change his ways, Clarke and Dreyfuss believed this problem could be corrected.

Miller also had a partner in crime when showing questionable judgment and making bad decisions in 1910. Wagner didn't conduct himself in the manner that Pittsburgh management had become accustomed to. Honus always enjoyed relaxing at one of the local taverns and quaffing a few beers. In 1910, Wagner's drinking habits became a little excessive. Wagner and Miller were almost inseparable from the time Jack came on the scene in 1909. The two hit the night life with an extra zest and zeal after the World Series victory, which did not endear them to club management.

After the 1910 campaign, Clarke gave Wagner an ultimatum which indicated that both he and Dreyfuss were tired of the Dutchman's shenanigans. Clarke had a talk with Wagner and told him, flat out, it was either no booze or no baseball. Honus took this suggestion to heart and promised Clarke that he would truly reform.[42] Miller and Wagner quickly agreed to terms as Dreyfuss had little trouble in signing up his players. Each player accepted the requirement in their contract of taking the pledge without much protest. Even the leader of the booze brigade was quick to sign after he lost his claim before the National Commission to a $1,200 bonus from the previous season.[43]

There was some question as to whether Clarke would play left field in 1911. Various rumors stated that he would only manage from the bench. Those who were concerned that Clarke's active playing career was over shouldn't have been worried. Mrs. Clarke stated that Fred loved playing the game too much to lurk in the shadows as he directed his men. She said that the tension of watching without participating caused Clarke severe headaches.[44] Clarke quashed these rumors at Hot Springs when the Pirates manager stated he would play in 1911. Before the Pirates left the Valley of Vapors to begin another season, Clarke handed out his rules of conduct, which each player was expected to follow without hesitation:

> Following are the rules laid down by Manager Fred Clarke for the Pittsburgh team, of the National League:
> 1. The use of intoxicating drinks of any kind is absolutely prohibited.
> 2. When the team is at home, every player must report at Forbes Field, in uniform, not later than 10:30 A.M., each day; and must be on the field at least one hour before game time, at home or abroad.
> 3. All players must be in their rooms for the night not later than midnight, and should arise not later than 8 A.M.
> 4. The smoking of cigarettes is absolutely prohibited.
>
> The penalty for violation of any of the following rules will be a fine or suspension, or both, according to the offense.[45]

With stringent team rules now in place, many wondered if this new atmosphere would propel Pittsburgh back to the top of the mountain or if the players were likely to rebel as the season progressed. Players like Camnitz, Wagner and Miller would need to rebound from horrible years if Pittsburgh were to be crowned National League champions once again. The 1911 season would prove to be interesting, as one young phenom arrived from St. Paul and a veteran star finally decided to hang up his spikes forever.

Chapter 14

Marty O'Toole's Three-Ring Circus

In the opening game of the 1911 season, it certainly looked as if Fred Clarke's brigade was focused on avenging its poor showing the previous season. Babe Adams tossed a complete game shutout in a 14–0 victory over the Cincinnati Reds. The Pirates banged out 16 hits with leadoff hitter Bobby Byrne going a perfect five-for-five at the plate. In spite of rumors that Alex McCarthy would supplant Jack Miller as the starting second baseman, Dots was at his customary position on opening day. The starting lineup for that game was stocked with veteran players. The only newcomer to wedge his way in was first baseman Newt Hunter. One noticeably absent Pirate as the season began was veteran pitcher Sam Leever.

Leever and Pittsburgh management never came to an agreement on a contract for the 1911 season. It was believed that the document sent to Sam over the winter called for a pay cut of $1,500.[1] Leever technically was not considered a holdout because most people believed that Barney Dreyfuss intended to sell the former twenty-game winner to a minor league team. As a matter of pride, it was Leever's preference to work out his own deal. In early May, Dreyfuss gave Leever his unconditional release so that the Goshen Schoolmaster could offer his services to interested suitors throughout the minor league circuit.[2]

Now that Leever was moving on, this left only Fred Clarke, Honus Wagner, Tommy Leach and Deacon Phillippe as the remaining Pirates who had played in the 1903 World Series. Leever's work in that battle against the Boston Americans was shoddy because of an arm injury, but this failing on his part couldn't diminish an overall great career. Sam Leever pitched for the Buccaneers from 1898 until 1910, going 194–100 while posting a 2.47 ERA. Leever had risen to the top of his profession and was considered one of the premier right-handed pitchers in the National League during the previous decade. Father Time began to creep up on Leever in 1909 and the veteran filled the role of second line pitcher during his last two years in Pittsburgh. Given the chance to find a new baseball home of his own, Leever joined old teammate Rube Waddell in Minneapolis and helped the Millers win the 1911 American Association title.

The Pirates navigated through the early part of the season without any incidents or complaints from either players or management. As the month of May concluded, Pittsburgh stood in fourth place, three games behind the first-place New York Giants. It looked as if the National League race was destined to be a four-team battle between the Pirates, Giants, Cubs and Phillies. It seemed as if the whole Pittsburgh team was following the rules of conduct established by Clarke before the season, with Pittsburgh's manager setting his customary, proper example. "I never drank anything but an occasional glass of beer," said Clarke, "but I know it would not be right for me to indulge even to that extent, and at the same time forbid my men to touch it, so I have cut it out. There will be no boozers on our club this year."[3]

Clarke's tone of obedience off the field wasn't his only exemplary contribution to Pittsburgh's cause as the baseball season moved into June. Clarke accomplished another record-breaking feat on the diamond when he recorded 10 putouts in left field against St. Louis on April 25. Cap was the first major league outfielder in history to flag down this many balls in a game.[4] The 38-year-old outfielder showed speed and grace usually seen in players many years younger. This, coupled with the fact that Clarke was batting around .400 through early May, indicated that he was still a force to be reckoned with.

A majority of the Pittsburgh team continued to play effective ball as the season entered the month of June, when Pittsburgh posted a 15–10 record. This left them in the same position of fourth place, 3½ games behind the leading Giants. A change in the Pirate lineup was made by manager Clarke as summer moved into the city when Tommy Leach was benched in favor of rookie Max Carey. It was evident to local scribes that a rift had developed between Pittsburgh's skipper and Leach. Rumors were flying about stating that Leach had bashed Dreyfuss. It seemed that waivers were asked on the veteran player and Leach roasted Dreyfuss for not dealing with him properly.[5] This story brought a response from Fred Clarke who chastised Leach for airing his dirty laundry in the local newspapers. "In the story that appeared in the Chicago papers were several statements that were true," stated Clarke, "but which were known only to two persons—myself and Leach. I know that I never gave them out to any newspaper man, and Leach says he didn't. So there you are. I am now conducting an investigation, and when it is finished, I will know all about it, and whether Leach has been deceiving me."[6]

14. Marty O'Toole's Three-Ring Circus

It was surprising to many that a division had developed between Leach and Pittsburgh management. Leach had attempted a jump to the American League in 1902, but for the most part, he was the consummate professional throughout his career. Clarke and Dreyfuss had been less than cooperative when Cincinnati wanted Leach to manage the Reds in 1908. Although he was disappointed when this didn't happen, Leach continued to give his best effort on the baseball diamond. For whatever reason, Leach's performance at the beginning of 1911 was below expectations.

The local fandom roasted Leach for his tepid hitting and overall laissez-faire attitude toward his trade. As had happened in the past, Pittsburgh rooters were quick to turn on a revered champion when his skills began to show signs of erosion. News came to the forefront that quickly humbled these fans and Pittsburgh management as well. Tommy Leach's second wife passed away in June after a month-long illness.[7] For Leach, this was the second time such tragedy had struck. His first wife died from pneumonia in 1908.[8] The fact that Leach had continued to play during his wife's illness, in spite of the hardship, was quite amazing and went a long way in explaining his behavior.

As Leach dealt with his loss, it was business as usual for the Pirates. Clarke was still searching for the perfect winning combination. Believing the team needed to upgrade its defense, Clarke set his sights on Charley Herzog of the Boston Rustlers. Herzog was a third baseman by trade, but he could also play second base and shortstop as well. Fans debated over which players were offered to Boston. Whatever Clarke had in mind became irrelevant as the Rustlers opted to trade Herzog to New York instead.

As Clarke continued to look for ways to improve the Pittsburgh team, Dreyfuss was busy finalizing a deal of his own that would put Pittsburgh in baseball's spotlight. He had been scouting a spitball pitcher in the American Association who was gaining national attention for his twirling feats. Dreyfuss beat all suitors to the punch when he purchased pitcher Marty O'Toole from St. Paul for $22,500.[9]

Dreyfuss began receiving criticism for this acquisition before the ink on the check for $22,500 had dried. This was an unheard of amount to shell out at that time and was double what New York had paid for Rube Marquard in 1908. Marquard's slow start at the big league level had gained him the moniker of "The $11,000 Lemon" early in his career.[10] In 1911, Marquard hit his stride by winning 24 games and leading the Giants to the National League pennant. Dreyfuss was confident that O'Toole would develop in like fashion and handle all of the pressure that came his way.

O'Toole was purchased by the Pirates on July 22. One week later on July 27, Dreyfuss also bought catcher Billy Kelly from the St. Paul team. Dreyfuss felt that since O'Toole was a spitball pitcher, it wouldn't be a bad idea to have a catcher he was comfortable with join him in Pittsburgh. It was reported that Dreyfuss paid in the neighborhood of $6,500 to $12,000 for Kelly.[11] When local pundits quickly knocked Dreyfuss for both purchases, he responded swiftly to the criticism in an effort to sooth the paying public.

> O'Toole can pitch for my money any day of the week. He certainly looked like the best pitcher I had ever seen in the minors when I looked him over. When I first heard of him and his great work for St. Paul, I sent Billy Murray, the old Quaker manager, to look him over. Billy told me to buy him. "He is the best pitcher in the minors today," was Murray's report.
>
> I have a lot of faith in Billy's judgment, but in this case I decided to take a first-hand peep at the man. So I went to St. Paul. I saw O'Toole against Minneapolis, and I was pleasantly surprised. I had expected to see a fairly good pitcher, but I had not counted on watching a man who appeared to have everything, and of whom the hard-hitting Minneapolis batsmen seemed mortally afraid. The Millers have some sluggers on the roster, and yet every man on the team pulled away from the plate when O'Toole shot his benders over.
>
> That settled it. I wanted O'Toole more than ever — and I got him, even if I did have to pay a record price for him I understand that the deal is questioned in certain quarters, and that there are intimations that the price given is not bonafide. That sort of talk doesn't bother me a bit. I know I paid $22,500 for the man, and I think it was money well spent.
>
> Everybody will want to see the "$22,500 beauty," the "highest-priced player in the business." The curiosity of the fans will help to pay for him, and I am confident that when he reports, his good work will drive the lovers of the game to the park.
>
> I bought the man because I figured that the Pirates needed one more winning pitcher to give them the pennant. Camnitz, Adams and Leifield have been bearing the brunt of the burden all season and have done yeoman work, but they have been unable to win quite enough games to put us on top. O'Toole will help them out, and if we win the pennant, I think the public will then agree that no price was too high to pay for him.[12]

Once again, Dreyfuss proved that he was an owner who always thought outside of the box. For him, Marty O'Toole was more than a pitcher. O'Toole was a drawing card who likely would spike attendance both at home and on the road when he pitched. Dreyfuss believed the payoff on the $22,500 price tag would be twofold. He was adding a quality starter to his staff whose high price tag would also cause curious fans to flock to the ballpark in droves.

The "Marty O'Toole Circus" would have a slight delay in launching. After the Pirates purchased the spitball pitcher, St. Paul management had O'Toole take the mound for a game in a driving rainstorm. As luck would have it, O'Toole developed a sore arm.[13] When he arrived in Pittsburgh, O'Toole was in no shape to pitch. The long awaited debut of the "$22,500

Beauty" was put on hold. As the pennant race rocked through the dog days of August, O'Toole had to be content with picking up pointers from the bench. Surprisingly, an unexpected member of the team was pondering a switch to the splinter board from the outfield's green pastures. Once again, Fred Clarke seriously contemplated retiring as an active player for good.

> Fred had been resting and allowing young Carey to cavort in left field. But when the Giants came along last week, one of the scribes said to Clarke, "I suppose you will be in the game today."
>
> "Why should I be?" he queried in reply. "Isn't Carey doing all right?"
>
> "Yes," the scribe agreed, "Max has been playing good ball against Brooklyn and Boston, but in a hard series the fans would like to see you in there. They figure that, even aside from your playing ability, your presence inspires the other men and makes them play better ball."
>
> "Well, I'll tell you," said Fred. "I figure differently. I think the boys play better ball when I am not in there. On the bench I have better opportunity to watch everything that goes on, and I am in close touch with the infielders. They know I am watching them closely and they are on their toes all the time. Moreover, I believe the pitching is better when I am on the bench. I can watch the twirlers every minute, and can see just what is going on.
>
> "This young Carey is a great ball player and he is getting better every day. I need not worry about a man to fill my place in left field as long as he is on the roster. When Max came to us, with scarcely any minor league experience behind him, he had a lot to learn about inside base ball. When he broke into the game he was a right-handed hitter. Now he is batting left-handed, and he is a good hitter. He has hit safely in every one of the games he has been in since our last Eastern trip, and I believe he will continue to clout close to the .300 mark. He is ambitious and is learning something every day. And with a thing once learned, he never forgets it.
>
> "So with him on the team and other good outfielders to fall back upon, I feel safe in staying out of the games, and directing the team from the bench, and I think in the end my plan will have proved itself a good one."[14]

Clarke's decision to remain on the bench for the remainder of the 1911 season surprised many Pittsburgh fans. Clarke posted his best average in years as he smacked the sphere for an average of .324 in 110 games. Clarke wasn't wrong when he stated that the team had other good outfielders to fall back on. Chief Wilson had his finest season to date, hitting an even .300 while slugging 12 home runs and knocking in a team high 107 runs. Tommy Leach returned to the team after his wife's burial. Although he only hit .238 for the year, the veteran showed unexpected spunk and grit given the circumstances.

Many fans were of the opinion that the Pittsburgh aggregation would be better with Clarke playing rather than Leach. Max Carey was the new darling of the city. He performed quite admirably in his rookie season, hitting .258 with 77 runs scored and 27 stolen bases. Pittsburgh rooters believed that

Late during the 1911 season, Fred Clarke decided he would no longer be a full-time player. The rapid development of outfielder Max Carey allowed Clarke to hold himself out of the lineup, except on rare occasions, and focus on his job as Pirates bench manager.

Carey should move to center field so that Clarke could return to left. Dreyfuss even asked Clarke why he was walking away from active duty when it was apparent that Cap could still play the game. Clarke explained to Dreyfuss that his legs were the culprit. They just couldn't take his body around the bases as in his younger days. "When I came up to the majors and hit the ball to third on a couple bounces," stated Fred, "I beat it out easily; as time went on that kind of hit made me hustle just to get a debatable decision. Now, I am out by a step on that kind of hit, and when I have slowed down that much, I am not going to help the club, but hurt it, no matter what I hit."[15]

Pittsburgh was still in the thick of the pennant race when Clarke announced his intention to be a bench manager for the season's duration. The Pirates went 15–12 for the month of August, leaving them in third place on September 1 with a 70–49 record. They trailed the league-leading Giants by 3½ games. The fact that New York had so many games in hand on Pittsburgh meant that the Corsairs would need to play flawless baseball for the rest of the season. As August ended, Marty O'Toole's much anticipated debut finally became a reality when he took the slab against Boston on August 30.

O'Toole gave a gutsy performance at the South End Grounds, defeating the Rustlers, 6–4. O'Toole was not at his best. Marty worked out of many jams as he went the distance in his inaugural game. He allowed two earned runs, while walking 10 batters and striking out nine. O'Toole continued his mastery of the league, starting at 3–0 before a classic matchup against New York on September 16. As would happen many times in O'Toole's big league career, he was pitted against one of the opposing team's top pitchers. This time it was Rube Marquard who got the best of O'Toole in a 6–2 New York victory. O'Toole lost his last outing against Philadelphia to finish the season 3–2 with an ERA of 2.37.

Pittsburgh pitching overall had only been average at best throughout the season. Clarke had three pitchers that he relied on heavily. He could never cultivate that fourth or fifth twirler to round out the staff. Adams was the ace, posting a 22–12 record with an ERA of 2.33. Camnitz bounced back from his abysmal 1910 season, going 20–15 with a 3.13 ERA. Camnitz didn't touch a drop of liquor the whole season. This change in behavior was attributed to his marriage in February. Leifield rounded out the upper tier of Pittsburgh pitchers with an even 16–16 mark and an ERA of 2.63 achieved in a team-high 318 innings.

Young slab artists were given every chance to show their stuff, but few impressed Clarke. Claude Hendrix (4–6, 2.73 ERA), Jack Ferry (6–4, 3.15 ERA) and Elmer Steele (9–9, 2.60 ERA) were brought along slowly. Of the three, Hendrix seemed to have the proper temperament needed to succeed in the big leagues. Even though Steele had the second-lowest ERA on the staff after Adams, he was sold to Brooklyn on September 16. If the Pirates made it to the World Series, O'Toole would need to become the fourth starter that Clarke had searched for all season.

A total collapse in the month of September guaranteed that Pittsburgh would not be representing the National League in the 1911 Fall Classic. They did some of their worst work of the season as they secured a third-place finish for the second year in a row with a 14–17 record for the month. Pittsburgh's play was particularly rancid against pennant-winning New York as the Corsairs went an unimpressive 6–16 against McGraw's Men for the year. Players such as Bobby Byrne and George Gibson slumped horribly at the plate. On a positive note, Honus Wagner and Jack Miller did rebound with strong performances in 1911. The Flying Dutchman won his eighth and final batting crown by topping the circuit with a mark of .334. Miller only hit .268, but he regained his touch in the clutch, knocking in 78 runs while participating in 137 games.

Pittsburgh fans didn't seem to care at whose feet individual blame for the bad showing in September should fall. The local rooters felt the Pirates had given less than adequate effort and the whole team was dubbed as quitters. There were even those who believed that the fix was in with it being predetermined that New York be crowned National League champions.[16] It always seemed that Pittsburgh's spoiled fandom was never happy when the Pirates crumbled under the pressure of a pennant race.

The 1911 baseball season couldn't end soon enough for Clarke. Things got so bad for the Pirates manager in July that he actually was able to peruse his own obituary in a Cleveland newspaper. It seemed that the overly fervent publication wanted to scoop other papers in the country by reporting that Clarke had died after being hit in the head by a pitched ball. Clarke had indeed been hit in the head, but a wire service erroneously reported that he died.[17]

Frustration finally got the best of Clarke as the season wound down in September when he lashed out at umpire Bill Klem during a game against Chicago at Forbes Field. Johnny Evers had been ejected from the game after arguing a decision, but the Cubs second baseman stood in an open doorway behind his team's bench rather than head to the clubhouse. Klem asked Clarke to close the door. Clarke refused and then he ran onto the field and began to berate Klem. He basically told the umpire that if he wanted the door closed, then he should take care of it himself. Klem then asked Clarke to have a policeman close the door and Cap responded by telling Bill that he wasn't there for the purpose of doing the umpires' bidding.[18]

After the season concluded in Pittsburgh, Clarke packed up his family and took them on the final trip to Chicago. While finishing up in Chicago, the Clarkes planned to visit Chick and Mina Fraser.[19] After the Pirates lost their finale to the Cubs on October 9, Clarke reiterated that he would only be back as a bench manager in 1912. He certainly didn't need to continue playing baseball in order to earn a salary, since the Kansas entrepreneur was now worth in the neighborhood of $250,000 through investments in real estate and stock securities.[20] Clarke figured that it was time to hang up his spikes because he was getting too old to play the game. "I find it too difficult to keep in training," said the veteran leader. "It is too much of a strain, at my age, to go through as a regular player after this season."[21]

After Clarke and his family visited the Frasers in Chicago, they headed back to the "Little Pirate Ranch" in Winfield. Fred and Annette Clarke didn't stay there long. They left on November 4 to join a big hunting excursion which included baseball players such as Josh Clarke, Buster Brown, Rube Geyer, Peaches Graham and Claude Hendrix. Josh and Rube's wives were also there, and Lucy Clarke visited her two sons during this expedition near Ulora, Minnesota. Fred Clarke chronicled his week long trip for *Baseball Magazine*.[22] "Although the excursion was a most pleasant one and amusing to those who took part in it or their friends, I had hardly thought it important enough to be of general interest. However, I am assured that anything a professional ball player may do is of interest, and as the entire party was made up of ball players and their wives and immediate friends I shall be glad to tell all about it."[23]

Fred Clarke wrote an eloquent narrative for baseball fans across America. He described the trip in full detail and touched upon the camaraderie which existed between this group of men. Clarke possibly felt comfortable discussing this subject since it paralleled baseball in some ways. Cap considered each to be a sport. He also felt that men were able to bond together when they hunted or played baseball. The hunting trip was a rousing success as the group was able to bag a large number of grouse, rabbits and eight deer.[24] Josh Clarke secured the biggest prize when brother Fred gave him his 33 Winchester which the younger brother had admired throughout the expedition.[25]

While Clarke was writing his piece for *Baseball Magazine*, New York pitcher Christy Mathewson continued to do a syndicated article of his own. Within one of these morsels of written prose, the great pitcher addressed the spiking incidents that involved Philadelphia Athletics third baseman Frank Baker. Mathewson defended both Ty Cobb and teammate Fred Snodgrass who spiked Baker during the 1909 regular season and 1911 World Series, respectively. Matty then claimed that if Baker had ever played against Clarke, he would have been cut to ribbons by the spikes of the competitive Pirate.[26]

After the hunting excursion ended, Clarke looked into some business matters which required his attention over the winter. In February, Clarke talked of the modifications that he was making on his special sun field cap. The prototype from the previous year had failed after numerous tests. Clarke modified the apparatus and believed it would now work properly. His invention called for an aluminum visor with a slot in it, fixed for the glasses. There was a spring attached and when it was pressed, the glasses dropped down before the fielder's eyes. It wouldn't be necessary to press the spring on ground balls, but a fielder could effortlessly drop the glasses on a fly ball.[27]

Clarke's entrepreneurial appetite was further satisfied when it was reported in early March that he purchased a half-interest in the J.P. Baden mill in Winfield. The mill was considered one of the largest in Southern Kansas. Clarke's cost to invest was unknown, but many experts believed the mill was worth $50,000. This little venture was expected to add thousands of dollars to Clarke's bank account each year.[28]

Clarke's business interests were placed on hold when the time came once again to make the trek to Hot Springs for spring training. He was sticking by his guns and still intended to manage Pittsburgh from the bench in 1912. This meant that Cap wouldn't be playing baseball for the first time since he was a child. Clarke still was bubbling with enthusiasm as always when writers questioned him about the upcoming season. He believed the team would contend even if the manager had to replace a star left fielder in the lineup.

"I am very well satisfied with our club and the prospects for the coming season," said the veteran manager. "I will not claim any pennant, but will say that the Pittsburgh Club, as at present constituted, is much stronger than it was during the 1911 season. I expected to witness a great improvement when I came South and there has been no disappointment. You can say for me that we are much better — much stronger than we were last season."[29]

Clarke revamped his lineup for the 1912 season. Max Carey and Chief Wilson would be joined in the outfield by veteran Mike "Turkey" Donlin, who was acquired in a February trade which saw Vin Campbell shipped off to Boston. Clarke planned on circumventing the first base jinx by moving Jack Miller to the initial sack. Young Alex McCarthy was slated to replace Miller at second and Bobby Byrne would man third. George Gibson was expected to split time with Mike Simon and Billy Kelly behind the plate. Honus Wagner once again held down the shortstop position. Clarke also named Wagner to replace him as the field captain. "Wagner has had a world of experience," explained Clarke, "and he was named because he thoroughly understands my system and consequently there will be no change in the team's style of play by my dropping out of the game."[30]

For the first time in many years, Pittsburgh was considered a long-shot choice to win the National League pennant in 1912. They had performed below expectations in both 1910 and 1911 and were no longer deemed as a threat to the championship aspirations of New York and Chicago. The team was expected to garner plenty of attention thanks to Marty O'Toole. The "$22,500 Beauty" was able to tease fans with his capabilities late in 1911 before being roughed up by New York and Philadelphia in his final two outings. For Pittsburgh to contend in 1912, O'Toole would have to perform as advertised the previous summer when Dreyfuss purchased him from St. Paul.

There was some concern that the sore arm O'Toole was nursing when he arrived in Pittsburgh still ailed him. Reports throughout the winter indicated that O'Toole wouldn't be ready when spring training began. Dreyfuss wasn't even worried when O'Toole reportedly was unable to get his work in during the training season. Dreyfuss scoffed at these rumors. "There is absolutely nothing the matter with O'Toole's salary wing," said Dreyfuss. "I see that the calamity howlers have been sending out fake reports about it, but let them howl. We are satisfied, and so is Marty with his condition. The whole truth of the matter with O'Toole is that he is weakened because Clarke made him take a full course of baths at Hot Springs, with the water at a temperature of 110, about 12 to 14 degrees over the usual tonic bath. Two of Marty's brothers have rheumatism, and Fred thought there might be a touch of it in his system, so he insisted on the hot baths. Of course, they weakened him so that he was unable to put anything on the ball, but now that he is away from Hot Springs, he should regain his strength very rapidly, and he himself believes he will be in tip top trim when the season opens."[31]

Before the 1912 season opened, another Pirate great quietly slipped into retirement without much notice. Deacon Phillippe called it a career after he only appeared in three games of mop-up duty during an injury-laden 1911 season.[32] He left the ranks of baseball with a lifetime record of 189–109 and an ERA of 2.59. Deacon spent all but one season in Pittsburgh, coming over to the Pirates as part of the Louisville consolidation after the 1899 season. Phillippe was a twenty-game winner in each of his first five seasons in the National League. He was the hero of the 1903 World Series in a losing effort. His control was impeccable throughout his career. Deacon Phillippe was one of the most dependable pitchers of that era and one of the greatest hurlers in Pirates history.

All the worry about new pitching sensation Marty O'Toole's arm was for naught. Once the regular season began, O'Toole was ready to go and took the hill against Cincinnati on April 16. The "$22,500 Beauty" halted a season-opening four-game losing streak by defeating the Reds, 8–2. The rough start played a big part in Pittsburgh finishing the month of April with a 5–7 record. Claude Hendrix was another spitball pitcher on the staff who was impressive during spring training. It was hoped that both of theses hurlers would supply a solid one-two punch.

It was possible that Hendrix eventually would be the wonder of the present campaign. The title of early season sensation belonged to second baseman Alex McCarthy. McCarthy won the starting job from Jimmy Viox after Jack Miller was anointed as the new starting first baseman. McCarthy came out of the gate strong, striking the ball at a .450 clip during the first ten games. His blistering start gave Pirates fans hope that the infield aggregation of Jack Miller, Alex McCarthy, Honus Wagner and Bobby Byrne would be the best since the pennant-winning season of 1909.

McCarthy didn't hit over .400 for the whole season, but he was a smashing success during his first year as a starter. He appeared in 111 games and stroked the ball at a .277 clip. All four members of the Pirates infield performed admirably, just as Pittsburgh fans envisioned. Jack Miller was stellar at first base, hitting .275 and driving in 87 runs. He learned the nuances involving the position rather quickly and served notice that the old first base bugaboo was now history. Honus Wagner and Bobby Byrne rounded out a group that was the best infield unit in Pittsburgh since 1909. Wagner hit .324 and led the team in RBI's with 102. Byrne was the top fielder in the league at third base and chipped in with a .288 average and 99 runs scored.

Pittsburgh's trio of starting outfielders also turned in a great season at the plate. Chief Wilson hit an even .300, pounded 11 home runs and drove in 95 runs. Wilson also established in 1912 the single-season record of 36 triples, which still stands today. Max Carey hit .302, led the team in runs scored with 114 and stole 45 bases. Mike Donlin showed that he could still hit, posting a .316 average in 77 games. Donlin's problem was that injuries limited his ability to stay on the baseball field. Tommy Leach did solid work as the utility outfielder when called upon.

Pittsburgh, as a team, hit .284 for the season and led the National League in hits. This was the best hitting unit that Clarke had put together in years. Despite all of the solid stick work, the local baseball media's focus was on Pittsburgh's pitching. As the season entered May, the "Marty O'Toole Circus" had hit full stride. Stories about the right-hander were published in every baseball city across America. The Pirates went 13–10 in May, leaving them in fourth place at month's end. Even though the team was only one game above .500, opposing players like Joe Tinker were quickly jumping aboard the O'Toole bandwagon.

"O'Toole is the best looking young pitcher I have seen in years," said the Chicago shortstop. "He will certainly make good. I believe the free swingers like Schulte, Mitchell and others of that class, will have unlimited trouble in making base hits off his delivery. The only man looks to me to have a chance to hit him safely is the one who chokes his bat and chops at the ball. Why? Because Marty's shoots have such a sharp break that the man who starts a free swing is likely to find his bat going inches under or over the ball as it crosses the plate."[33]

As O'Toole impressed opposing players throughout the National League, Pittsburgh continued to struggle collectively. The Pirates' uneven play during the first two months of the season was something that both Clarke and Dreyfuss needed to address. A step toward accomplishing this was made when the Pirates orchestrated a deal with Chicago which rattled the organization to the core. On May 30, Leach and Leifield were sent to the Cubs in exchange for pitcher King Cole and outfielder Art "Solly" Hofman. Dreyfuss rid himself of a problem player in Leifield, who had been used sparingly by Clarke. Underlying issues existed in Leach's dismissal as well.

Pittsburgh picked up two players from the Cubs who had shown great ability in the past. Leonard "King" Cole was the National League's top pitcher in 1910, going 20–4 with a circuit leading ERA of 1.80. He slipped slightly in 1911 with a record of 18–7 supported by a 3.13 ERA. Arthur "Solly" Hofman actually appeared in a few games for the 1903 Pirates squad, but he eventually made a name for himself with Chicago. He was solid for three seasons prior to the trade, hitting .285 (1909), .325 (1910) and .252 (1911). Both Cole and Hofman had gotten off to rough starts in 1912. This left one question looming in the minds of Pittsburgh fans. Could these two players rekindle their past glory?

The decision to move Leifield wasn't surprising since the pitcher had burned his bridges with management during contract negotiations for the 1912 season.[34] Leach's transfer was bittersweet. The veteran player was still well liked throughout the city even though his skills were deteriorating because of advancing age. After the deal was made, Dreyfuss even wrote Leach a letter thanking him for his years of service and wishing the player good luck. Leach never received the correspondence. He slighted Dreyfuss, never stopping at team headquarters to say thank you to the man who treated him like family.[35] No response was uttered as Leach went on his way to the Windy City. A month after the deal, information arose indicating Leach had soured toward the organization during the past year.[36]

No one quite knew why Leach's attitude changed. Many fans wondered if the veteran performer was unhappy with his new role as a utility player. Others took into consideration the effect of his wife's death on Leach's emotional condition. Whatever the explanation, it was now an issue for the Chicago Cubs. Pittsburgh was having enough problems on their end of the deal. It quickly became apparent that the Pirates received damaged goods from Chicago when an injured Hofman remained in Akron, Ohio, with his family.[37] He was acquired on Decoration Day, but was still sitting at home when Independence Day rolled around. Hofman didn't put on a Pirates uniform until he finally joined the team in late August.

Pittsburgh fans probably wished that Cole was injured much like Hofman, since his work for the team was disappointing in 1912. The former twenty-game winner saw action in 12 games, going 2–2 with an inflated ERA of 6.43. Despite seeing no immediate return on this deal with the Cubs, Pittsburgh played quite well on the baseball field after the trade, going 19–8 for the month of June. This left the Pirates in second place, 13½ games behind league-leading New York. With Hofman out of commission, Clarke even contemplated a return to left field. This became a moot point when Clarke fractured his finger during a June morning practice before an afternoon game against Boston.[38]

The Pirates went 15–12 in July. They gained no ground on the Giants and dropped to third place in the standings. Pittsburgh sizzled during the last two months of the season. They posted a 41–21 record over that time period, but this wasn't good enough to make up the necessary ground as Pittsburgh finished in second place behind New York with a 93–58 record.

Pittsburgh was one of the best hitting teams in the National League. It was their pitching that deserted them at times and prevented the Corsairs from meeting Boston for the championship in a World Series rematch from nine years ago. Claude Hendrix (24–9, 2.59 ERA) and Howard Camnitz (22–12, 2.83 ERA) did yeoman's work on the mound for Clarke in 1912. Rookie southpaw Hank "Rube" Robinson was a pleasant surprise as he debuted with a 12–7 record and a 2.26 ERA. Staff ace Babe Adams was a major disappointment and appeared in only 28 games. He was relatively ineffective en route to an 11–8 record and a 2.91 ERA.

When discussing the 1912 Pittsburgh Pirates pitching staff, all talk among fans and the media began and ended with Marty O'Toole. Dreyfuss and Clarke considered the rookie season of the high-priced pitcher a success even if the numbers didn't bear that out. O'Toole finished below the .500 mark, going 15–17. He did have some hard luck as was evident by his 2.71 ERA. O'Toole showed wildness on the hill as he led the league in walks with 159. After the season, David J. Davies of the *Pittsburgh Dispatch* sat down and talked with O'Toole about his first season in the Smoky City.

"As the season progressed, the one thing which bothered me mostly was my lack of control. I tried my hardest to pitch winning ball, and I guess I tried too hard. You know when a fellow is expected to pitch $22,500 ball he wants to come across with the best he has in him: and in my case it was too much effort," O'Toole remarked. "Some time ago I reached the conclusion that if I took matters easier — if I depended more upon the men behind me — I would succeed better. I did this, and the results are known to everyone who reads base ball. At first I tried for strikeouts. Later on I realized that an out via the fly ball route or at first base counted just as much for the pitcher as a strikeout. Manager Clarke helped me to reach this conclusion, and I have profited mightily by his advice."[39]

O'Toole finished the interview by stating that he hoped to be accepted as just an ordinary ball player in 1913.[40] O'Toole was probably being naïve in thinking that he could assume the identity of a common performer. Until he showed grand form, the $22,500 price tag would continue to haunt him. In fairness to O'Toole, anything short of a thirty-win season in 1912 would have

Barney Dreyfuss purchased pitcher Marty O'Toole from St. Paul in 1911 for the record price of $22,500. Reviews regarding O'Toole's performance in 1912 were mixed as the pitcher posted a 15–17 record with an ERA of 2.71.

been looked upon as a failure by Pittsburgh fans. As Dreyfuss prepared for the upcoming season, he had no choice but to hope that O'Toole wouldn't sink under the weight of the pressure placed upon him.

Dreyfuss also knew that Clarke would be back to nurture him along. One week after the 1912 season ended, Clarke quickly confirmed that he planned to manage the Pittsburgh Pirates in 1913. "I have signed a contract for 1913," stated Fred, "because I am perfectly satisfied with conditions here, and because I would rather work for Barney Dreyfuss than for any other employer. We have never had a serious difference during all of our associations, and I have been most liberally treated."[41]

Chapter 15

A Great Career Winds Down

"I am glad to sign my twentieth contract with Barney and it surely pleases me to know that our close relations, both business and social, are as firm as ever," remarked Fred C. Clarke. "We may have differed on some matters, but that is liable to happen in the best of regulated families. Had the Pirates any kind of luck I imagine you would have seen them higher up in the struggle, but enough of that. We didn't get there, that's all."[1]

Fred Clarke was coming back in 1913 with one goal in mind. He planned on going after the National League flag once again. The Pittsburgh manager decided that he wanted to put 1912 behind him and not even think about it as he rested during the off-season. The strain of not playing baseball any longer had worked wonders for Clarke after he received a less than exemplary bill of health following the 1912 season.[2] Clarke's health had improved substantially in the past year. This positive report from his doctor played a significant role in Clarke's decision to return as Pittsburgh's manager in 1913.

"My physician gave me a good going over yesterday and then said that my health was 40, if not 60 per cent better than at this time last Autumn," said Clarke. "Winding up 1911, he examined me and expressed disappointment over the discovery that my blood pressure was some above normal, a fact undoubtedly due to the rigors of a hard campaign, both on and off the field. The condition has altered itself, in fact it no longer exists. I feel a heap better than I did when it came close to the last going for 1911."[3]

Clarke quickly showed the rest of the National League that he meant business in respect to the 1913 season. During the December 1912 league meetings in New York, Pittsburgh's manager proposed a trade with the St. Louis Cardinals that would have brought star first baseman Ed Konetchy to Pittsburgh. Clarke and Dreyfuss had been trying to acquire Konetchy since 1908. Year after year, St. Louis manager Roger Bresnahan rejected the overtures of

Pittsburgh management. Events after the 1912 season seemed to work in Clarke's favor as Bresnahan was fired from his managerial post.

Bresnahan's release from St. Louis afforded Clarke the opportunity to strike while the iron was hot, since he had a new trading partner in Miller Huggins. It was believed that Clarke offered Jack Miller, Howard Camnitz, Alex McCarthy and George Gibson to the Cardinals. In return, Pittsburgh would receive Konetchy and outfielder Rebel Oakes.[4] After much discussion, a consensus was eventually reached by the respective managers. Clarke thought he had a deal worked out between the two clubs until St. Louis ownership intervened and quashed the proposal. After the deal fell through, St. Louis newspapers reported that Pittsburgh management placed the blame at the feet of Cardinals owner Helen Hathaway Robison Britton.[5]

Huggins quickly admonished the Pirates for insinuating that Mrs. Britton was at fault.[6] In reality, it was Huggins who walked away from the deal after he received unsolicited advice from New York's John McGraw and Chicago's Charles Murphy.[7] One week after Mrs. Britton was accused of sabotaging the Konetchy deal, Pittsburgh management denied that they were complicit in any of the accusations being made. Dreyfuss reacted to this situation in a different manner than usual. Rather than have Clarke or himself make a statement professing innocence, Secretary William Locke addressed the media and denied all the charges surrounding the affair. "Please make it strong that no one connected with the Pittsburgh Club ever accused Mrs. Britton of 'butting in' on the Konetchy deal, and spoiling it," stated Locke. "We never made any such charge, and we had no idea until now that a story to that effect had been sent out of New York."[8]

While negotiations with first-time manager Miller Huggins hadn't gone quite as expected, Pittsburgh management believed that Huggins would be more receptive while considering a deal than was his predecessor Roger Bresnahan. Since this was Huggins' baptismal foray into the peddling of baseball flesh, baseball enthusiasts believed that experienced Pittsburgh management would have the upper hand in any discussions. The Pirates were not trying to take advantage of Huggins. They felt a fair deal could be hammered out which would benefit both teams. While this deal was being discussed, the Pirates were also one of the teams who had the inside track on gaining the services of free-agent Roger Bresnahan. Pittsburgh eventually lost out on signing the catcher when Bresnahan hooked up with the Chicago Cubs.[9]

After the disappointing meetings in New York, Clarke returned to Kansas for the winter. Clarke quickly added to his small empire in Winfield when he purchased the famous Gold Ore farm, located a few miles south of Udall. The farm, which consisted of 320 acres of land, was purchased by Clarke for $14,000. It had been owned by a brewer from New York named J.V. Ruppert.

15. A Great Career Winds Down

At one time, this property was the town of Gold Ore during a prospecting boom that occurred in 1877. Claims that were staked in the area didn't bear fruit as the place had been "salted" to give the impression that gold was there. Eventually, the town became abandoned.[10]

Clarke also dealt with some off-season baseball matters during the winter of 1913. Three key players were holding out. Bobby Byrne and Jack Miller eventually were brought into line by Dreyfuss, but Clarke had to take care of negotiations with star pitcher Claude Hendrix. Discussions between Dreyfuss and Hendrix became so acrimonious that the Pirates magnate refused to iron out their differences.[11] Clarke came riding in like a white knight and took control of the negotiations with his pitcher. The Pittsburgh manager visited Hendrix at his Kansas home and quickly brokered a deal that was satisfactory to both sides.

With all players now under contract, Clarke began focusing on the task of preparing his team for the upcoming season. A little twist was added to break the monotony of spring training at Hot Springs. Clarke arranged for an exhibition series against the World Champion Boston Red Sox. Ten years after both teams played in the first World Series, the two would get together to play a slate of highly publicized games. Even though these games were only exhibitions, Clarke felt they would provide a good test for his team.

Once the competitive series began, the Pirates manager probably had second thoughts as one Pittsburgh player after another was struck down on the baseball diamond. Bobby Byrne was hit in the head by a blazing offering from Smoky Joe Wood in one of the games. It was feared that Byrne's skull was fractured as he experienced torturous pain that evening. An examination the next day showed there was no fracture, but Byrne missed some time due to the injury. Later in the game in which Byrne was beaned, Alex McCarthy was injured when he was spiked by Tris Speaker at third base. Artie Butler also participated in a game while he was afflicted with ptomaine poisoning.[12]

Clarke wasn't exempt from health issues during the 1913 spring training season. Because it seemed that Clarke was headed for a breakdown, Clarke's physician advised him to rest for a few days. On April 1, Clarke left Hot Springs with wife Annette at his side and returned to Winfield in order to relax and recover his strength. Clarke planned on rejoining his team in time for the season opener on April 10. While Fred Clarke was mending at home, Honus Wagner assumed the mantle of acting manager.[13]

Clarke probably should have remained in Winfield throughout the summer. The 1913 Pittsburgh Pirates weren't a team that was good enough to contend for the National League pennant. Clarke's troops played lackluster baseball throughout the season's early months. When June ended, Pittsburgh was holding down the unfamiliar spot of fifth place with a mediocre 30–35 record. Since Clarke and Dreyfuss came to Pittsburgh in 1899, no Pirates team had ever finished in the National League's second division. Cap was facing the strong possibility of having this negative stigma attached to him for the first time since he came to Pittsburgh.

Pittsburgh's poor play was rooted in the disappointing seasons of two twirlers who were expected to anchor the 1913 pitching staff. Star hurler Claude Hendrix had a horrendous season, going 14–15 with an ERA of 2.84. At one point, Hendrix was so undependable as a starter that Clarke used him in relief on 17 occasions in 1913. Marty O'Toole had another disappointing season, although it was shortened when he underwent an operation after being stricken with an appendicitis attack in July.[14] Before that, O'Toole could muster nothing better than a 6–8 record with a 3.30 ERA, leading to whispers among the press and fans that Marty was in fact the "$22,500 Lemon" rather than the "$22,500 Beauty."

Things had gotten so bad for the Pirates that rumors began flying around to the effect that Clarke planned on making a triumphant return to left field.[15] These rumors were substantiated when Clarke did indeed return to the diamond on Friday, June 13. He played left field and batted seventh in the batting order during a 3–2 loss to New York. Clarke appeared in nine games that season and recorded one hit in 13 trips to the plate.

Clarke and Dreyfuss brought in new blood in an effort to shake the team out of their funk. Veteran pitcher George McQuillan was rescued from the minor league scrap heap on July 7 and outfielder Mike Mitchell came to Pittsburgh via waivers from the Chicago Cubs on July 29. These moves only improved Pittsburgh's standing slightly as the Pirates stood in fourth place on August 1. They were one game above .500 and trailed the first place New York Giants by 17½ games.

With an eye to the 1914 season, Clarke made a trade in August which proved to be disastrous from both a baseball and public relations standpoint. On August 20, Clarke shipped Bobby Byrne and Howard Camnitz to the Phillies for infielder Albert "Cozy" Dolan. Pittsburgh fans were not disappointed that Camnitz had been cut loose, since he was horrible for the Pirates in 1913, going 6–17 with a 3.74 ERA. Local rooters were chaffing over the fact that Clarke had traded the ever popular Bobby Byrne. Reports that this deal was supposedly in the works for months did little to console the Pittsburgh faithful. Most of the rooting populace didn't see how this transaction aided the rebuilding process, no matter how positively it was spun by team management.

The deal that secured Dolan from Philadelphia for Byrne and Camnitz probably was the worst player exchange to date during the Dreyfuss-Clarke regime. Pittsburgh had traded a sparkplug in Byrne. In return, they received a player who had only been successful at the minor league level. Clarke initially was not the object of the fans' venom. The rooting populace attacked Dolan daily with vicious barbs and epithets in the manner that an angry asp strikes at an enemy.[16] Poor statistics did little to change Pittsburgh's opinion of the new third baseman as he hit a less than inspiring .203 in 35 games.

Pittsburgh fans passed judgment on Dolan just as quickly as they threw in the towel for the 1913 season. The Pirates never figured in the race as New York captured the National League flag. A strong 17–10 record during August made up for a mediocre September (14–13) and helped the team secure a first-division, fourth-place finish. Babe Adams (21–10, 2.15 ERA) and Hank Robinson (14–9, 2.38 ERA) performed admirably for the club in direct contrast to struggling pitchers like Hendrix and O'Toole. Youngster Wilbur Cooper was used in spot duty and went 5–3 with a 3.29 ERA in 93 innings pitched. The love-hate relationship with Jack Miller continued. Management loved his stick work, a .272 average supported by seven home runs and 90 RBIs. They hated his mechanical approach on the field and wished that Dots would let his natural ability take over when laboring at the initial sack.

The 1913 season was a disappointment in many respects. Better things were expected from the team after their surprising performance in 1912. Clarke received his fair share of criticism for the team's fourth-place finish. At the conclusion of the season, Clarke spoke out in defense of third baseman Cozy Dolan. "He is a pretty fair ball player," said Fred, in discussing his case. "I am sure that he is capable of better things than he has yet shown here. He has not hit a lick since he joined us, but he never hit at a ball in Philadelphia like he has done since he joined the Pirates. He has been hitting up at the ball and under it with us, but I think that is simply since he is off his stride. I believe that if he had got a good start here he would have been all right. He is certainly one of the best base runners I ever saw, and he is as game as a pebble. If he were not, the abuse that he was forced to stand for here would gave driven him away."[17]

Clarke's unwavering confidence in Dolan's ability was admirable. Dolan was probably the happiest person in Pittsburgh when it was announced that Clarke had signed to manage the Pirates in 1914 as he agreed to terms offered by Dreyfuss.[18] Although the 1913 season had left a bad taste in the mouth of the Pittsburgh manager, Clarke still believed he had championship-caliber personnel and the Corsair manager wanted to give it another whirl in 1914. "I have decided to come back and try to redeem myself," stated Clarke in a written letter to Dreyfuss. "I realize that I didn't win any laurels last season, but our team is capable of much better things, and I am coming back to try to prove it."[19]

In order to prove that Pittsburgh could rise back to the top, Clarke knew that changes to the team's roster were necessary. One half of the St. Paul battery was sent packing when Dreyfuss sold Billy Kelly to Toronto. Kelly's sale to Toronto was child's play considering what Clarke and Dreyfuss had up their sleeves for the trip to New York in December. Joe Tinker of the Cincinnati Reds had been dismissed from his managerial post after one season on the job. As was the custom during that time, player-managers usually were not kept around after such a firing so that the authority of a new man in charge would not be compromised in any way. Garry Herrmann intended to move Tinker at the league meetings and Clarke planned on making a pitch to secure the veteran shortstop.

When the time came for Herrmann and Clarke to exchange proposals in New York, it was evident from the start that the two were not on the same page in regards to who should be shipped to Cincinnati for Tinker. Garry wanted Jimmy Viox, a second baseman who led the 1913 Pirates in hitting with a .317 average, and Max Carey to be included in any deal for Tinker. Clarke supposedly offered the Reds owner a choice of Art Butler or Alex McCarthy plus either Hank Robinson or Wilbur Cooper.[20] This quickly brought an end to the Tinker negotiations from the Pirates' perspective. As it turned out, Pittsburgh never had what Herrmann wanted, which was money. Brooklyn won the Tinker sweepstakes as Charles Ebbets purchased him for $15,000 from Cincinnati. Ebbets then promised Tinker a $10,000 signing bonus when the shortstop signed a Brooklyn contract for 1914.[21]

Brooklyn's ability to secure Tinker was disappointing to both Clarke and Dreyfuss. This frustration was quickly replaced by elation courtesy of the other team in New York City. John McGraw had interfered with the attempted transfer of first baseman Ed Konetchy to Pittsburgh the previous off-season by putting a bug in Miller Huggins' ear to the effect that Clarke was trying to rip off St. Louis. The sole purpose for McGraw doing this was that the Giants manager wanted Konetchy for himself. Secretary Foster of the New York Club was sent to the 1913 league meetings with explicit instructions. Make a deal that would bring Koney into the Giants' fold.[22]

Foster made an offer to Huggins in which outfielder Fred Snodgrass, first baseman Fred Merkle and catcher Art Wilson would be sent to St. Louis in exchange for Konetchy. Miller wanted another player. Foster countered by including third baseman Buck Herzog in the package if Huggins was willing to part with pitcher Bob Harmon. This wasn't acceptable to the St. Louis manager who still wanted another player in return.[23]

With the deal between the two teams dying, Huggins looked up Clarke to see if he still had any interest in acquiring Konetchy. The two talked and a deal was quickly hammered out. On December 12, Pittsburgh shipped Art Butler, Jack Miller, Cozy Dolan, Chief Wilson and Hank Robinson to the

15. A Great Career Winds Down

Cardinals for Ed Konetchy, Bob Harmon and third baseman Mike Mowrey.[24] Clarke and Dreyfuss finally had the first baseman they coveted since 1908. The player who manned that position for the last two years in Pittsburgh was philosophical when he learned that a deal including him had been struck. "I guess I am just another victim of the first base jinx in Pittsburgh," said Jack Miller. "Anyway, I held the job longer than anybody since Bransfield, and that is something."[25]

Pirate fans were on cloud nine after hearing the news of a trade between Pittsburgh and St. Louis in December. Many in the world of baseball believed that the additions of Konetchy, Mowrey and Harmon to the Pirates team guaranteed a pennant flag would fly in Pittsburgh after the 1914 season. Even if the deal between the two teams eventually played out to be an even one, rooters

Jack "Dots" Miller was part of the blockbuster deal made on December 12, 1913, which saw Fred Clarke acquire Ed Konetchy, Mike Mowrey and Bob Harmon from the St. Louis Cardinals. After the trade, Miller intimated that he was just another victim of the fabled first base jinx in Pittsburgh.

could take solace in the fact that Cozy Dolan had been sent packing. Fans were excited about the upcoming season and couldn't wait for spring training to arrive. Sadly, Pittsburghers were jolted back to reality when it was reported that a new renegade league had its sights set on stealing players from the Pirates roster.

A new third league wanted to become a major player in direct opposition to Organized Baseball in 1914. The Federal League was borne out of the Columbia League which had been established as an independent minor league in 1912. Unlike the United States League which had failed, the Columbia League persevered and changed its name to the Federal League before the 1913 season.[26] The six-team aggregation that was still considered an outlaw league didn't pose any threat to Organized Baseball during that season. When James A. Gilmore took control of the league halfway through the year, the Feds' philosophy toward Organized Baseball changed somewhat. Gilmore decided that he wanted to take on both the National and American leagues in 1914.²⁷

The Federal League expanded from six to eight teams for the 1914 season. Four cities that had established major league teams comprised the league along with Baltimore, Buffalo, Indianapolis and Kansas City. The invaded territories were Chicago, St. Louis, Brooklyn and Pittsburgh.²⁸ Dreyfuss would have an outlaw entry competing against him in his own back yard. The Feds entry in Pittsburgh was slated to play their games at old Exposition Park. They hoped to fill their roster by signing players away from Dreyfuss' team.

There was concern in Pittsburgh when it was reported that Ed Konetchy and Mike Mowrey were listening to Federal League overtures. This anxiety wasn't quelled until both players inked their signatures to 1914 Pirates contracts. Clarke wasn't so lucky with two of his other players. Catcher Mike Simon and pitcher Claude Hendrix quickly signed contracts to play in the new league. Hendrix once again held a rancorous holdout when he didn't like the terms being offered by Dreyfuss. Clarke went to Kansas City in an effort to bridge the gap between the club's offer of $3,600 a year and Hendrix' demand for $6,000 a year. This time, talks between Hendrix and Clarke didn't go well. Clarke left the meeting enraged and claimed that Hendrix would only play for Pittsburgh if Dreyfuss did the signing himself.²⁹

Hendrix signed with the Feds after these contract negotiations broke down. Simon supposedly had reached a verbal agreement to sign a Pittsburgh contract, but he too cast his lot with the outlaw league. As Clarke began to map out plans for the spring training trip to Hot Springs in March, it was reported that Simon and Hendrix were considering a return to the Pirates. Clarke quickly responded to this notion by stating that both men would not be welcomed back under any circumstances. "When a man throws the hooks into me, I seldom rest until I have paid him back in his coin," said Fred. "I do not want either of these men on my team, but I do hope the time will come when I can pay them back for the manner in which they have acted with me."³⁰

These were the only two players that Pittsburgh lost to the renegade league. Others such as Babe Adams, George McQuillan and Jimmy Viox were targeted in spring training by former Pirate Howard Camnitz, who was acting as an emissary for the Feds. Camnitz's treachery was circumvented when Dreyfuss filed a court injunction which prevented Howard from approaching his players in Hot Springs.³¹ Camnitz wouldn't be heard from again, but Federal League agents continued to make life difficult for both Dreyfuss and Clarke throughout the summer of 1914.

As Pittsburgh Pirates were being courted by the new league, Dreyfuss had his sights set on acquiring another veteran National League player who was for sale. Johnny Evers had been fired as manager of the Chicago Cubs and team owner Charles Murphy planned on selling him to the highest bidder. Dreyfuss was definitely interested, but the Pirates owner was unable to communicate this desire to Clarke in a timely fashion. Unfortunately, Pittsburgh was left out in the cold again as Evers signed with Boston.[32] On a positive note of some degree, Clarke's brother-in-law Chick Fraser was added to the Pirates staff as a scout and pitching instructor.[33]

Thoughts about the new Federal League and court injunctions were placed on the back burner when the Pirates opened with a 2–1 loss against St. Louis on April 14. Pittsburgh's season-opening result turned out to be an anomaly as the team tore through April with a 10–2 record. Pundits who believed that Pittsburgh would cruise to the National League pennant were given further justification when the Corsairs raised that mark to 15–2 in early May. Clarke loved the fighting spirit and aggressive attitude that his troops displayed during this spectacular, early season, run. "I am claiming no pennant," said Clarke, "but I will say that I never commanded a better bunch of fighters and hard workers than I have this year. Every man on my team is in dead earnest about his work, and I know the boys possess ability. If we are able to avoid accidents and injuries, I am confident that we will be able to make a lot of trouble for somebody before the season is over."[34]

As the season progressed, the only trouble this team caused was for its manager. Unfortunately, the strong play shown by Pittsburgh in April and early May didn't continue. National League opponents began turning the tables on the Corsairs in quick fashion, leading to an 11–12 record in May for the hometown team. This left the Pirates in third place, 1½ games behind the league-leading New York Giants. Many fans felt this slump was just a small bump in the road from which Pittsburgh would eventually recover.

The Pirates didn't rebound in June as had been hoped. Pittsburgh remained in a frustrating slump that saw the team tumble down the standings ladder. Local fans couldn't understand how a team that had dominated during the early stages of the season was so horrible now. The pitching, which hadn't been that bad, received no support whatsoever from hitting and fielding that bordered on criminal at times. Early season enthusiasm on the part of fans was being replaced by feelings of disenchantment as Pittsburgh sunk to depths that hadn't been seen there for years.

Clarke was receiving much of the blame for Pittsburgh's shortcomings. In this case, Clarke did deserve his share of criticism. He adopted a new system in which players were given instructions on exactly what type of pitch to hit at the plate.[35] The Pittsburgh Pirates were no longer an aggressive team thanks to Clarke's micro-managing methods. When batting at the plate, players needed to react instinctively to pitchers rather than waiting for instruction from the bench. The Pittsburgh manager was taking the term "small ball" to a dangerous extreme that compromised team performance. Clarke also was criticized on a daily basis when Ed Konetchy, Mike Mowrey and Bob Harmon were all very short of spectacular. The rooting populace was disgusted, the players' confidence was shattered and the season quickly slipped away.

Clarke was blasted throughout the summer as his much publicized trade with St. Louis the previous December turned out to be a colossal failure. Harmon was the only member of the trio who did viable work. The right-handed pitcher posted a misleading 13–17 record, with an ERA of 2.53. Runs were hard to come by for the anemic 1914 Pirates hitting squad, and Harmon suffered in this respect along with fellow hurlers Babe Adams and Wilbur Cooper. Third baseman Mike Mowrey gave little to no effort during his abbreviated season in Pittsburgh. Mowrey batted .254 in 79 games before being cast adrift in August.

Konetchy, the main piece of this package of players acquired from St. Louis, was the most disappointing of the three. Clarke and Dreyfuss expected clutch hitting and stellar fielding from the star first baseman. What they received instead was a player who loafed around the first base bag as the season progressed and hit only .249 at the plate to boot. The problem with Konetchy was that he was a primadonna. While in St. Louis, Konetchy had always been treated like royalty by St. Louis fans and management. There was no chance of this happening in Pittsburgh, and Koney began to sulk and mope as a result.[36]

Not only did Clarke have to deal with quitters like Mowrey and Konetchy, he also finally tired of Marty O'Toole and his inconsistent pitching. O'Toole was of little use to Clarke once again as the pitcher posted a 1–8 record with an unsightly ERA of 4.68. The Marty O'Toole era in Pittsburgh officially ended when the right-hander was sold to New York on August 14. O'Toole so little impressed John McGraw that he was returned to Pittsburgh after the 1914 season. The second-rate investment then passed from the majors for good when he was sold to Columbus in 1915.

Clarke relinquished the managerial reins for a few games in August after he was afflicted with ptomaine poisoning in Philadelphia.[37] It may have been the atrocious play of the Pittsburgh players that actually made Clarke sick to his stomach. A seventh-place finish was guaranteed after the team posted records of 13–14 in August, 12–20 in September and 5–2 in October. This was the first time a Pirates team had finished in the second division during the Dreyfuss-Clarke Era.

Boston became the first team other than Pittsburgh, Chicago or New York since 1901 to claim the National League pennant. While the Pirates plunged to second-division status, the St. Louis Cardinals rose from their cellar-dwelling ways and finished in third place behind New York. Maybe Pittsburgh would have faired better in the standings if they had secured Johnny Evers and kept Jack Miller, Chief Wilson and Hank Robinson rather than trade them to St. Louis.

After the season ended, Dreyfuss confirmed that Konetchy had signed a contract to play for Pittsburgh's Federal League entry in 1915.[38] Dreyfuss stated that he wasn't going to let Koney escape without a fight. The Pirates owner wasn't doing this because he wanted Konetchy back on the Pittsburgh roster in 1915. Dreyfuss planned on making a fight for the first baseman based on principle only. He also was being a bit vindictive, given the fact that Konetchy had been a divisive force during the 1914 season. "There are defects in some players which it is impossible to detect until the men are working for you," said Dreyfuss. "When Koney appeared here as a Cardinal, he looked like a fine ball player, but it didn't take us long, once we had him on our roster, to discover that he had weaknesses that were fatal to a great performer. Way back last June, Clarke saw his mistake, and told me about it. 'It is no wonder St. Louis finished low with men like Koney and Mowrey on the roster,' said Fred to me. 'I wouldn't be surprised if we landed in the second division this year ourselves!'"[39]

Dreyfuss also believed that Konetchy had acted as an agent for the Federal League when he tried to enlist players such as Wilbur Cooper and Jimmy Viox for the renegade league.[40] Clarke and Dreyfuss both felt that Federal League meddling had been a major distraction throughout the 1914 season. Pittsburgh management believed that players were pre-occupied with all the generous monetary offers being thrown their way. This prevented them from concentrating on baseball. Discipline also wasn't doled out as freely on some teams since management feared disgruntled players would jump to the new league.[41]

Clarke was also criticized for being too lenient with his players in 1914. The press felt that since Clarke was no longer a member of the players' fraternity, he needed to be tougher when the team needed a kick in the behind.[42] The problem that arose during this unsettled period in baseball history was that ballplayers who believed they were not being treated fairly would consider the Federal League as a viable option. If Clarke didn't instill discipline and the team continued to lose, it was his fault. If he did make the players tow the line, causing them to jump, Cap also would be blamed. When it came to player relations, Clarke was in a no-win situation.

Clarke signed to be at the helm once again to steer the Pirates craft through choppy waters in 1915. His signing came as a surprise to many people who felt that Clarke would not be asked to come back after the team's unsatisfactory seventh-place finish in 1914. It had been a tough year for Cap who was bombarded with criticism from all sides. Unaccustomed to such treatment, Clarke didn't handle the censure of the scribes and fans very well. He had offered to resign from his post during the previous summer, but Dreyfuss refused to accept the document.[43] Pittsburgh's manager had a change of heart after the season as he decided to return and vindicate himself in 1915. "Everybody knows what we had a year ago, and what happened to it," said Clarke in discussing next season's plans. "Our team was a failure, and we have decided to reconstruct it. You can't build a team on old men, so we are going to give a lot of youngsters a chance. Of course, we have two or three veterans who will be retained, but that is because I do not consider that their usefulness in the big league is ended."[44]

Clarke's decision to return for the 1915 baseball season was commendable. However, it just wasn't practical. Gone were the days in Pittsburgh when Ginger Beaumont, Tommy Leach, Deacon Phillippe, Sam Leever and Claude Ritchey roamed the local baseball diamond. Clarke now had the likes of Doug Baird, Dan Costello, Wally Gerber and Bobby Schang to contend with. He believed that Pittsburgh could still compete for the pennant in 1915, even though the Pirates manager no longer had the horses to make a run at capturing the flag.

Veteran Doc Johnston was brought in to replace the departed Ed Konetchy at first base. Bill Hinchman was acquired from the minors to join Max Carey and a host of others in the outfield. Clarke planned on mixing in a dash of veterans with a number of rookies for the 1915 season. Honus Wagner was still on board, but age was beginning to slow down baseball's star performer. Clarke had hoped to ease Wagner's burden a bit by moving him to second or third base. This plan was scrapped after Wally Gerber failed at shortstop and Honus returned to the position which he manned superbly throughout most of his career.

Clarke did a sensational job of keeping his team in the hunt throughout most of the 1915 season. At the end of July, Pittsburgh stood in third place with a 47–45 record and trailed first-place Philadelphia by five games. The fact that Pittsburgh was still hanging around in the pennant race was amazing since Clarke still hadn't settled upon a definite lineup. He preferred to move his players around like pieces on a chess board, hoping to receive maximum results from a roster that was deficient in many areas.

Clarke had done it with smoke and mirrors up to this point. Everything came crashing down for the Pittsburgh Pirates in August as they struggled through the month, going 11–20 and dropping into seventh place. On August 3, Pittsburgh fans were able to get a glimpse of the old Fred Clarke one last time during a doubleheader loss at the hands of the Boston Braves. A confrontation occurred between Clarke and Johnny Evers after the Boston player was ejected by umpire Bob Emslie in the second game of the twin bill at Forbes Field.[45] Ralph Davis in *The Sporting News* concisely recorded the events of that encounter as Evers went over to the Pirates bench and approached Clarke:

> Leaving the field, [Evers] walked over to the Pirates' bench, ostensibly to get a drink. As he approached the water cooler he saw Clarke and some of the other Pirates laughing at him. Evers lingered, and Clarke finally appealed to Umpire Quigley to make him move on. As he did so, Evers filled a tin cup with water, and hurled it in Clarke's face. He then picked up a dirty sponge, which the players used for mopping perspiration, and hurled it at the Pirate manager.
>
> Clarke made allowance for Evers' excited condition, and kept his seat throughout this display of temper on the part of the Trojan, but as Evers started for the exit under the grandstand, to the side of the Pirates' bench, he called Clarke "yellow," and hurled several epithets at the local leader.
>
> Clarke was after him like a flash, and nailed him just under the stand. Grabbing him by the collar, the Pirate leader backed Evers up against the concrete wall and choked him until his tongue stuck out. Then he released him, and Evers hastened away.[46]

This truly was one of the last times that Pittsburgh rooters witnessed the competitive and fiery spirit which burned in Clarke's belly. The Pirates were well on their way to another second-division finish. One of the few bright spots of the 1915 team was the brilliant pitching of local youngster Al Mamaux, whose 21–8 record, supported by a miniscule 2.04, was the only positive result from another season of disappointment and anguish. The strain of managing from the bench had become too much for Clarke to bear. Clarke realized the time had finally come for him to walk away from the game that he loved so dearly. On September 8, 1915, Clarke announced that he was resigning from his post as manager of the Pittsburgh Pirates effective after the season's conclusion.

"I am getting out of baseball altogether and for good," commented Clarke about his retirement. "There is no jump to the Federal League attached to this move of mine, no dissatisfaction with my employer, or anything of that sort, but simply a desire on my part to prolong my life by giving up a position, the strain of which has been harder and harder ever since I quit my active career as a player."

"I stuck to baseball as a player as long as it was possible for me to do so," Clarke continued. "Then I became a bench manager, but life has never been the same since I quit the active life on the diamond. Managing from the bench may be easy for some folks, but not for me. I yearned for activity, I couldn't get it. I took a certain amount of exercise every day, but that wasn't enough."

"The strain began to tell in my health," Clarke added. "Two years ago my physicians advised me to quit, but I didn't want to retire. I wanted to stick to baseball, and I did it against their orders. Finally after last season I made up my mind I would try one more year of it, in an endeavor to make up for the failure of my 1914 team. I believed I could retire with a winner to my credit. At least, it seemed to be worth the trial, and I made it. I have failed again, but that does not alter in the least my determination to seek my farm in Kansas for the remainder of my days. It is useless to say that I am doing this without regret, for that would not be so. I have been in baseball for so long that it is second nature to me, and I will certainly miss the sport, at least for a long time."[47]

After Clarke made his retirement announcement, rumors began to surface which indicated that his decision was based on an unexpected salary cut due to the team's poor play over the past two seasons. This doesn't pass the smell test since Clarke was fairly well off financially. His decision to retire could be boiled down to two specific things. Clarke wanted to spend more time with his family and he no longer needed the strain of a job that would eventually damage his health.

Clarke retired from baseball with a lifetime batting average of .312. His highest seasonal mark at the plate came in 1897 when he hit .390 with the Louisville Colonels. The speedy left fielder stroked out 2,678 lifetime hits, scored 1,622 runs, smashed 361 doubles, hit 220 triples and stole 509 bases. Clarke also compiled an impressive managerial record of 1,602 wins against 1,181 defeats for Louisville and Pittsburgh from 1897 through 1915. He won four National League pennants and one World's Championship. In 1912, Clarke passed Cap Anson and Frank Selee to move into first place all-time for most wins by a baseball manager. Considered one of the best managers of his era along with John McGraw and Connie Mack, Clarke is one of the greatest player-managers in baseball history.

On September 23, the Pirates manager took the field one last time during Fred Clarke Day at Forbes Field.[48] He played four innings in left field and recorded one hit in two trips to the plate. During a special ceremony honoring Clarke, Mayor Joseph G. Armstrong presented Clarke with a bound book that contained the names of several thousand fans with their compliments and best wishes. Pittsburgh Pirates players presented a handsome hall clock to their manager as a token of gratitude.[49]

The city of Pittsburgh continued to celebrate Fred Clarke's career when a banquet in his honor was staged on October 4, 1915, where 500 members of the Stove League and their friends attended. Speeches were given by Mayor Armstrong, President Dreyfuss, Manager Clarke, Al Gumpert and other popular Pittsburgh citizens. Clarke received a souvenir program which contained

15. A Great Career Winds Down

a box score from his first National League game in Louisville during the 1894 season. Adoring fans also presented Clarke with a chest of silver and 50 young apple trees for his Kansas farm.[50] When Barney Dreyfuss finally addressed the crowd at the Hotel Schenley, he commented that Clarke would be hard to replace. Dreyfuss also summed up their long relationship in simple terms. "I hope I can get as good a man as Clarke," said he, "but I realize better than do any of you how hard that it is going to be. Fred and I have been associated together so long that we seem to have become a part of each other, and it will hardly seem like a Pirate team next season without him in charge. I know Fred always gave me the best he had and he is entitled to retire now if he desires to do so. I wish him great success and even more happiness on the farm than he has had in baseball."[51]

Pittsburgh fans totally agreed with Dreyfuss that it wouldn't seem like a Pirates team in 1916 without Fred Clarke in charge of the troops. While the former star seemed intent on making a smooth transition to the life of a full-time farmer, Clarke didn't realize when he walked away from the Pirates in 1915 that baseball was in his blood and leaving the game for good would prove a difficult task.

Chapter 16

Can't Get Baseball Out of His Blood

Before Fred Clarke could retire to his farm in Winfield, Kansas, he needed Barney Dreyfuss to do one more thing for him. Clarke had never been released during his 24 years in baseball. He wanted Dreyfuss and the Pittsburgh Pirates to give him his unconditional release, so that he could hang the document in his home. To do this, waivers had to be secured from every National League club. Out of deference for Clarke and the circumstances surrounding this request, every team in the league waived claim to the veteran manager.[1]

For better or worse, Clarke was now a civilian, free to do as he pleased as a newly retired baseball player. His brother-in-law, Chick Fraser, believed that Clarke would eventually go stir crazy being away from baseball. Fraser assumed the transition would be difficult for his longtime friend, even if Clarke himself thought the time was right to retire.[2] "I know him too well," said Fraser. "He has had a hard row of it in the last two years and doctors had advised him to quit, but as soon as that old sun beats its way around the Kansas hills next summer you can bet that he will feel the loneliness due to absence from the battle for the first time in 25 years. It has grown on him and love for the old game will be hard to shake off."[3]

Clarke knew that retirement would be difficult for him, since the former star had thrived under the competitive nature of baseball each year. Luckily, he had other hobbies in his life that could slightly satisfy the former manager's gung-ho nature. He had various responsibilities on the "Little Pirate Ranch" and could still indulge in activities such as hunting and trap shooting. Annette Clarke probably sensed that her husband would be spending more time doing these things in the near future; she bought her husband a shotgun for Christmas that was designed specifically to be used for trap shooting.[4]

This wasn't just any ordinary shotgun that Mrs. Clarke bought for her spouse. It was made to order to fit his measure. The gun was also engraved with a figure in the likeness of Clarke in a Pirate uniform and distinctive pose, done in gold and platinum. The gun was a single bore, 12-gauge made especially for work at the traps. It wasn't known exactly how much this extravagant gift cost, but it was priced in the neighborhood of $500.[5]

While Clarke was in Kansas raising cattle, farming his land, hunting, trap shooting and looking after his interests in one of the largest flour mills in that state, Dreyfuss was dealing with a crisis back in Pittsburgh. The Pirates had another horrible season in 1916 under the guidance of new manager Jimmy Callahan. At one point in the lost season, Callahan blamed Pittsburgh's bad showing on Clarke for not leaving him any players of major league caliber to work with.[6]

Dreyfuss took heat from both the press and fans, who believed the little magnate should follow Clarke's lead and retire. With this kind of mindset existing in Pittsburgh, it was only a matter of time before rumors surfaced that Dreyfuss planned on selling his baseball team. After the season, it was reported that a syndicate that included Fred Gwinner, former owner of the Federal League entry in Pittsburgh, oil tycoon Joe Trees and Clarke were prepared to buy the Pirates.[7] Dreyfuss quickly dismissed this story as being ridiculous and the owner made a statement denying that the Pittsburgh club was for sale. "What would I do if I got out of baseball?" he inquired of his interviewers. "It is a business to which I have devoted practically all of my life, and it is a pretty good business, at that. It may not always be ideally conducted, but I love it, and I don't have much intention of getting out of it."[8]

Clarke became associated with this rumor about a possible purchase of the Pittsburgh Pirates because he was known to be involved in business dealings with Trees. What baseball pundits failed to realize was that the Clarke-Trees connection existed through oil rather than baseball.[9] After he retired from baseball, Clarke finally decided to cultivate his oil-laden property. During the spring of 1916, Clarke made the rounds to fellow ranch owners and took up leases for oil and gas.[10] In September, Clarke was offered a half a million dollars for these leases, but he opted to remain independent from any big oil company.[11] This strategy proved to be brilliant when a nearby claim struck it rich in the fall. Writer A.R. Cratty explained how Clarke basically became a millionaire overnight.

> Cap was a free lance, but was acting under the direction of a developing company, though bound by only word of mouth. Clarke secured options in his own name. When accumulated these same reserves suddenly increased in value overnight, due to an oil strike adjacent. Clarke could have turned the leases over to a certain coterie of oil men and secured a profit of $90,000, but

he was loyal to his sponsors. He spurned transfer to any company other than the one which had urged his activity to land the agreements.

This corporation was led by Joes Trees, an oil baron, once famous as a tackle on a steel city gridiron gang. Trees had promised to drill on Clarke's own soil. This was done, and, instead of the usual one-eighth royalty given the land owner in oil sharing, F. Clifford, for his honorable conduct, was allowed in at a quarter split. The steel bit pierced oil-bearing strata on Clarke's Little Pirate Ranch, mother earth then gave her hoard of ages, and Clarke had the delight of seeing a dream of years fulfilled to the very letter. Now will you believe that Frederick Clifford Clarke, late steersman of the Pittsburgh base ball band, has become a millionaire?[12]

Clarke was worth about $250,000 before he struck it rich in oil. After the golden crude began to flow on his property, Clarke's asset value jumped well above the $1.0 million mark.[13] Through the years, Clarke had always made wise investments in stock and real estate. This fiscal prudence on Clarke's part paid off many times during his life and most baseball fans considered him the premier capitalist among all retired players.[14]

These same rooters also believed that Clarke would somehow return to baseball within an ownership capacity now that he was a millionaire. When Clarke visited Pittsburgh in January 1918, stories once again surfaced that he was interested in purchasing the Pittsburgh Pirates. Clarke scoffed at such talk, claiming that he was much too busy overseeing his oil and coal interests.[15] "I have seen too much of the business end of the club," said Clarke, "and know too well its uncertainties to care to take any chances along that line."[16]

In spite of Clarke's comments on this occasion, one had to wonder if he wasn't acting as a liaison to purchase the Pirates on behalf of a Ponca City oilman by the name of Lou Wentz. He was a Pittsburgh man who went to Oklahoma and forged a fortune in the oil-leasing business. Wentz was a fanatical Pirates fan who used to watch games at Exposition Park with glasses while he sat on top of Mount Washington. Wentz and Clarke became connected in 1915 through their dealings in the oil-drilling industry. Clarke claimed that Wentz confided in him that he wanted to purchase the Pirates after his first big oil strike. If Wentz succeeded in buying out Dreyfuss, he wanted Clarke to take over and run the baseball operation. Clarke went to talk to Dreyfuss in 1918 after it was learned that Barney was contemplating retirement.[17] He offered Dreyfuss $3 million to buy the Pirates, but Dreyfuss demurred. "Dreyfuss was convinced, but he kept hemming and hawing," Clarke related the story. "He had no objection to the price. Finally I said: 'Barney, you are on record claiming you want to retire, but I can see that isn't so. You could no more retire for good, and take this check, than you could think of going away to a desert island. This is the life you love.'"[18]

Dreyfuss had baseball in his blood, just like Clarke. The little Pirate magnate was being roasted by Pittsburgh writers and fans after his team had performed miserably in 1916, 1917 and 1918. Dreyfuss' head may have told him to sell the Pirates, but his heart wasn't in it. After being spurned by Dreyfuss in this effort to purchase the Pittsburgh Pirates, Clarke turned his attention to participating in trap shooting events across the country.

Clarke was still considered a novice trap shooter, but he was moving up the ranks quickly as he participated in as many events as possible. He made the journey to California to participate in the Los Angeles Gun Club competition on June 22, 1919. Former Chicago Cubs pitcher Orval Overall hosted the event within his capacity as president of the California-Nevada Association. In August 1919, Clarke was elected president of the Kansas State Sportsmen's Association with the 1920 State Tournament slated to be held in Winfield, Kansas. During the 1919 state event in Kansas, Clarke broke 439 out of 500 clay pigeons during the contest. The former Pirates manager was in a zone on the first day of competition, when his score was 93 out of 100.[19]

Even though Clarke was able to immerse himself in trap shooting competitions, Kansas ranch work and oil deals, baseball was still in his blood. He felt a burning desire to return to the game he loved. Efforts to buy the Pittsburgh Pirates had failed. He needed to find another way to get back in the game. An opportunity afforded itself when his old catcher George Gibson, from the 1909 World's Championship team, was named to manage the Pirates in 1920. Gibson asked Clarke to join the team as a coach for spring training at Hot Springs in 1921.[20] He gladly accepted.

Clarke joined the Pirates contingent in the Valley of Vapors and lent credible assistance to Gibson. He helped to train and coach the players. He also umpired games that were played between the regulars and the yanigans. Clarke offered sage advice to Gibson and proclaimed that Pittsburgh's roster was solid in every respect.[21] He gave special batting instruction to young first baseman Charlie Grimm that paid immediate dividends for the Corsairs in 1921.[22] Grimm saw his average rise from .227 in 1920 to .274 in 1921.

Clarke followed suit in 1922 and joined the Pirates in Hot Springs for spring training once again after he helped train the Kansas University baseball team for ten days.[23] As camp wound down, a group of old-timers played the Pittsburgh Pirates in a five-inning game on March 27. Clarke managed the team of rusty old men which included Hugh Duffy, Joe Kelley, Jimmy Burke, Bill Hinchman and Chick Fraser. Babe Adams pitched for Clarke's brigade against Earl Hamilton as the old-timers won the game, 11–7. Kelley hit a home run in the game and needed assistance rounding the bases. Hank O'Day was supposed to play in the game, but he had a change of heart and turned to the familiar role of umpiring the festivities.[24]

When Gibson was fired on June 30, 1922, and replaced by Bill McKechnie, Clarke once again came aboard to help another former player when requested. Clarke joined the Pittsburgh team for its final trip against New York during September in an effort to offer assistance to the rookie National League manager.[25] McKechnie, who played for Clarke from 1910 through 1912, was an average player, but he had an aptitude for picking up on the strategy of game situations that made him fine managerial timber. Clarke's support went all for naught as New York claimed the pennant and Pittsburgh finished in third place.

Clarke was able to offer such assistance when needed because his responsibilities at home had been lessened during the past few years. Youngest daughter Muriel graduated from Winfield High School as an honor student in 1922.[26] Helen and Muriel Clarke were both adults who were now ready to lead their own lives. This meant that Cap didn't need to be on hand to watch over his little girls any longer. This afforded Clarke the opportunity to do other things that no longer interfered with family obligations.

Clarke intended to join McKechnie and the Pittsburgh Pirates at Hot Springs for spring training in 1923. These plans were cancelled when Lucy Cutler Clarke passed away on January 4, 1923. Fred Clarke's 85-year-old mother was laid to rest at Winterset Cemetery next to his father.[27] It had been over fifty years since Clarke ran away from home to play baseball in Carroll, Iowa. Lucy Clarke had always supported her son even though she never considered baseball a good living for Fred and Josh. Clarke's mother constantly reminded him throughout his career about the evils of baseball and how she believed it was associated with gambling and horseracing.[28]

In the summer of 1923, Clarke was assigned a new responsibility by Dreyfuss, who wanted Clarke to find a new training area in California for the Pittsburgh Pirates in 1924.[29] They had trained at Hot Springs for every year but two since 1901, but Dreyfuss believed that it was time for a change. Since Clarke had been in California on many occasions during the past four years participating in trap shooting tournaments, Dreyfuss figured that the former manager was just the man for this particular job.

Clarke searched for two months before he found a suitable place in Paso Robles.[30] Dreyfuss trusted his former manager's instincts and declared that the Pirates would spend the 1924 spring training season in California. Clarke believed the facility in Paso Robles had better amenities than in Hot Springs. "I think the Pittsburgh Club has made an ideal selection," stated Clarke. "The Paso-Robles ball park is located only a half a mile outside the town and there is no street car running near it. That means that the players will be called upon to hike at least a mile every day, and that will do them a lot of good. Then there is the fine water on the spot, and all of the facilities that a big league club can desire."[31]

Clarke helped get the field ready and was on hand once the Pittsburgh squad reached California for spring training in 1924. Helping to train the troops in March was fine with Cap, but the former manager was setting his sights on more lofty goals in the near future. There were rumors that he was part of a syndicate that tried to buy the Philadelphia Phillies in 1924, but this proved to be false.[32] Clarke supposedly was looking into buying a minor league team. This never reached fruition either. As it turned out, celebratory events during the 1925 season acted as a means for Clarke to triumphantly return to Pittsburgh.

The National League decided to celebrate its Golden Jubilee by having each team play special games during the 1925 season in which a group of old-time players would compete against the squad's current aggregation. June 6 was the day chosen for Pittsburgh to participate in this celebration. A group of players from the turn of the century were invited to play in the Golden Jubilee game. Tommy Leach, Claude Ritchey, Honus Wagner, Ginger Beaumont, Kitty Bransfield, Tom McCreery, Chief Zimmer, Jack O'Connor, Deacon Phillippe, Jesse Tannehill, Sam Leever, Jack Chesbro and Fred Clarke all accepted invitations to partake in the gala event.[33]

Clarke came to Pittsburgh weeks before the game in order to get in shape. While in the Steel City training, Clarke also began having discussions with Dreyfuss about returning to the Pirates in some capacity. In June, Clarke was appointed to the post of team vice-president. It was also decided that Fred Clarke would act as an assistant to manager McKechnie and sit on the bench. He also was permitted to purchase an interest in the club in order to consummate the deal.[34]

Clarke's presence in the Pirates dugout did wonders for the Pittsburgh team.[35] He instilled a new fighting spirit in the squad as Pittsburgh crushed all comers on its way to winning the 1925 National League pennant. This team was built around solid hitters such as Kiki Cuyler, Pie Traynor, Glenn Wright, Clyde Barnhart, Max Carey, Eddie Moore and George Grantham. These heavy bats were supported skillfully by pitchers Ray Kremer, Lee Meadows, Emil Yde, Johnny Morrison and Vic Aldridge. Clarke was given much of the credit for Pittsburgh's success in 1925, as he was considered a significant factor in stabilizing the team.

Things had changed a bit since he last graced a major league dugout in 1915. Clarke believed that baseball had become too sociable over the past 10 years. "I was always friendly with other players off the field," claimed Clarke. "But there never was any sociable chatting on the field. We were enemies on the field and we never forgot that. If we bumped into a batsman and knocked him flat there were no apologies, and none were expected. The baseman made up his mind to take a firmer stand the next time. It was a contest, a battle all the way. And that made baseball greater. Nowadays, you frequently see a baserunner apologize after colliding with a baseman. That's polite, but not good baseball. I don't want the players to try injure each other, but it's a contest."[36]

The Pittsburgh Pirates showed that fighting spirit which Clarke preached throughout his career when they rallied from a three-game deficit to defeat the Washington Senators in the 1925 World Series. The Pirates captured the seventh game at Forbes Field under less than ideal conditions on October 15 when they defeated Washington, 9–7. Walter Johnson was ineffective for the Senators given the muddy and rainy conditions.

Johnson had baffled the Pirates in Games One and Four, but he wasn't equal to the task on this day. Max Carey and Kiki Cuyler were the Pirate heroes that wet, October day. Even though Carey played the game with broken ribs, he recorded four hits, scored three runs and drove home two Pirates players. Cuyler's two-run double in the eighth inning broke a 7–7 tie and secured Pittsburgh's second championship in the past 17 years. Clarke believed that this particular aggregation was better than any of his pennant squads from 1901, 1902, 1903 and 1909 because each player did everything well.[37] "I never was connected with a club on which there was such splendid spirit," proclaimed Clarke. "The will to win is ever present, and there is perfect harmony. The players all like their manager, and always carry out his orders to the best of their ability. It is hard to beat an outfit like the present Pirates."[38]

An event which potentially started some disharmony on the Pittsburgh team occurred when McKechnie appointed a committee of players to decide on how the winner's purse of World Series money should be divided. Initially, it was determined that Clarke would receive nothing since he had team stock. Carey made an appeal on Clarke's behalf, and through a second caucus, the Pirate vice-president was awarded $1,000 by a slim one vote margin. Clarke refused to take the money and sent it back to Dreyfuss with a note stating that it should be given to McKechnie instead. Clarke only accepted the cash bonus after Dreyfuss convinced him to do so.[39]

In October and November, rumors circulated once again that Clarke was part of a syndicate that intended to purchase the Pittsburgh Pirates. As before, Joe Trees was mentioned in connection with this tale along with State Senator John Harris, Pittsburgh Hockey Club President Henry Townsend and State Senator James Coyne.[40] Clarke refuted this tale and stated that neither he nor Trees were interested in buying the Pirates.[41] In December, Dreyfuss announced that Clarke would once again be aboard in 1926 acting as his assistant, chief scout and assistant to McKechnie.[42]

Pittsburgh was expected to claim the pennant once again in 1926. The core of the Pirate team was young players who hadn't reached their full potential just yet. The purchase of infielder Hal Ryhne and outfielder Paul Waner from San Francisco were the only off-season personnel changes made to the Pittsburgh squad. When spring training began in Paso Robles, Clarke quickly proclaimed that Waner was a future star after he watched the outfielder perform for a few days. "He still has a few rough spots to wear off, but he's fairly well finished right now," opined Fred. "He has all the earmarks of a real star."[43]

Clarke was dead-on in his assessment of the Ada, Oklahoma, product. Paul Waner hit .336 in 144 games and complemented star outfielder Kiki Cuyler quite well. The problem for McKechnie and the Pirates was that Max Carey and Clyde Barnhart, both star performers during the 1925 season, were horrible in 1926. Carey was afflicted with an illness prior to spring training and couldn't get on track once the season began. He batted .222 for the year while Barnhart struggled as well and hit a disappointing .192. McKechnie also had problems with discipline as he had to fine second baseman Eddie Moore and pitcher Emil Yde for indifferent play on the baseball field. Pitcher Vic Aldridge also was reprimanded when he broke team rules by showering and leaving the ballpark instead of remaining in the dugout after he pitched in the first game of a doubleheader.[44]

Despite the fact that Pittsburgh was experiencing internal issues, they were still holding down the top spot in the National League before a doubleheader in Boston on August 7. McKechnie's squad experienced the ultimate humiliation when the seventh-place Braves held Pittsburgh scoreless in both games. In between games, Clarke offered advice to McKechnie that started a chain reaction of events that brought the Pirates' season crashing down. Clarke had tired of watching Carey struggle in the field and at the plate. He believed that a lineup change was in order for the second game.

"Better get some one out there to play center field," said Clarke. "Max is having a hard time of it."

"I haven't got anybody," McKechnie replied.

"Put some somebody out there, even if it is a pitcher," suggested Clarke.[45]

Carey didn't hear this remark, but his good friend Carson Bigbee was nearby when Clarke gave his advice. Bigbee told Carey what had been said, and then both men approached elder statesman Babe Adams and asked his opinion. Adams replied that the manager should be permitted to manage without interference. Carey then approached McKechnie and requested that a team meeting be held. McKechnie initially agreed, but he eventually changed his mind and didn't sanction the meeting, which occurred in New York where a vote was taken by the players to determine if Clarke should be asked to leave the bench.[46]

It was possible that Clarke's comment could have been taken out of context. Clarke may have reasoned that placing a pitcher in Carey's outfield position wasn't demeaning since he had done the same thing with Jesse Tannehill while managing the Pirates in 1901 and 1902. This lost its plausibility when other events came to light. Eddie Moore supposedly had told Clarke to leave the bench on various occasions during the season when unsolicited advice was offered about the second baseman's play.[47] Moore ended up being the one to leave the Pittsburgh dugout when he was sold to Boston in July. There were other instances of Clarke bellowing out unwanted advice with his acid tongue. Some players eventually resented his presence on the bench as it tore apart team unity.[48]

When the player vote was taken in New York, it was decided by an 18 to 6 vote that Clarke would be permitted to remain on the bench. Emboldened by this sudden show of support, Clarke demanded that the perpetrators of this witch hunt be reprimanded. Dreyfuss was vacationing in Europe with his wife and daughter when this uprising occurred. Clarke and Dreyfuss' son Sammy were left in charge while he was away.[49]

On August 13, 1926, Sam Dreyfuss announced that Babe Adams and Carson Bigbee had been released. Max Carey was suspended and placed on waivers with Brooklyn being awarded the claim for his services.[50] Sam Dreyfuss made the announcement in Pittsburgh, but most believed that this decision had been made by Barney Dreyfuss while he was in Europe. Max Carey spoke on behalf of the three maligned players as he explained why the vote to remove Clarke from the dugout was taken.

"Anything that we did was done because we wanted to see the club win," said Carey. "After we lost that doubleheader in Boston, Manager McKechnie suggested that a meeting be held to discuss the welfare of the club. A time was set for the sessions, but about a half-hour before it was to be held McKechnie called it off. Later, Clarke appeared in the clubhouse, and said he would not appear again on the bench if he was not wanted. The next day a vote was taken by the players as to whether he should be asked to retire. That is all there is to it. But I feel that Manager McKechnie should make a statement, setting forth my part and that of the other older players in the matter. We simply wanted to get results. No team can thrive under two managers. That is not said with any special reference to Fred Clarke, for he and I are good friends, but it is a general baseball proposition that holds true on any club. There were conditions existing on our club, which were losing games for us."[51]

Clarke denied that he had interfered with McKechnie when the Pirates manager made decisions regarding the team. He also vehemently stated that no player had ever challenged him to leave the bench as alluded to in the Eddie Moore story.[52] Before this incident, which was referred to in Pittsburgh newspapers as the ABC Affair (named after Adams, Bigbee and Carey), Pittsburgh was in first place. When the dust settled at season's end, the Pirates finished in third place, 4½ games behind the first-place St. Louis Cardinals.

Max Carey debuted under Fred Clarke in 1910. During the 1926 season, Carey led a team rebellion against his former manager in which a player vote was taken to determine whether Clarke should be asked to leave the bench and relinquish his title as an assistant to Manager Bill McKechnie. The player ballot supported Clarke by an 18–6 vote. Carey, Carson Bigbee and Babe Adams were released for their involvement in what was called the ABC Affair.

Barney Dreyfuss wasn't done cleaning house when the 1926 season came to a merciful end. Veteran first baseman Stuffy McInnis, a player loyal to Clarke, was released since he had leaked the news about a player vote in New York to newspapers.[53] McKechnie's contract was not renewed for the 1927. He was criticized for not handling the whole crisis in a proper manner. While many fans in Pittsburgh speculated that Clarke would be named to replace McKechnie as Pittsburgh's manager, Donie Bush was named to manage the team in October.[54]

The final chapter regarding this uprising was written when Clarke mailed a letter of resignation from his Kansas farm.[55] On October 27, 1926, the club's board of directors accepted his resignation during a special meeting. This meant that Clarke was relinquishing his duties as vice-president and assistant manager. It was also determined that his small block of stock would be repurchased by the Pittsburgh club.[56] Clarke had severed all ties from the organization after years of loyal and dedicated service. In the end, it was an ugly incident that chased him away from major league baseball. The time for true retirement was at hand.

Chapter 17

A Full Life After Baseball

When Fred Clarke resigned from his post as vice-president of the Pittsburgh Pirates on October 27, 1926, he permanently walked away from major league baseball. There were persistent rumors that Clarke was a part of some syndicate that intended to purchase teams like the Philadelphia Phillies or St. Louis Cardinals. These reports usually were proven to have no foundation or basis. After the events surrounding the ABC Affair in Pittsburgh played out in ugly fashion, Clarke was probably happy to shake the dust of the Smoky City from his feet.

After a few months of the quiet, retired life on his Kansas ranch, Clarke became a grandfather for the first time on February 14, 1927. Fred Clarke Donahoe was born to daughter Helen and her husband Daniel Justin (Dee) Donahoe, Jr.[1] Helen had married Dee a few years prior and the couple began building a magnificent house in Ponca City, Oklahoma. Dee was the son of prominent Ponca City businessman Daniel J. Donahoe. Dee's father had made his mark through ranching, grain milling and real estate development. Daniel Donahoe, Sr., originally acquired his land by filing a successful land claim when the Cherokee Strip opened.[2] One had to wonder if Clarke and Donahoe crossed paths during the infamous Cherokee Strip run of 1893.

Clarke's daughter Muriel also walked away from the single life when she married a lawyer from Newkirk, Oklahoma, named Neal A. Sullivan in October 1928.[3] Four years later in March 1932, Sullivan assisted Clarke when the former Pirates manager acted as a receiver for the court in a dispute with Colonel Zack Miller of the famous 101 Ranch in Ponca City.[4] Miller was deeply in debt and District Judge Claude Duvall ordered that his personal property be auctioned off by Clarke so that creditors could be paid. Clarke was only responsible for private belongings as the court was overseeing the 101 Ranch's other financial responsibilities.[5]

Neal Sullivan and fellow lawyer R.O. Wilson, both attorneys for the receiver, visited Miller in order to discuss the parameters of this auction. The three men argued, and Miller claimed that Sullivan laughed at him. Colonel Miller grabbed his shotgun and fired one shot into the floor. This caused both lawyers to run from the house, although Wilson was still in the domicile when Miller fired the shot near his feet.[6] Police handled the situation and Clarke eventually was able to hold the auction. Clarke was then relieved of his duties by the court after completion of this particular task.

A tragic occurrence also tugged at Clarke's heart in early 1932 when longtime friend and associate Barney Dreyfuss passed away on February 5. Dreyfuss had entered Mt. Sinai Hospital in New York the previous December. He was operated on for a glandular problem on January 6 and seemed to be doing fine for a short time. His condition deteriorated and the problem was compounded when he caught pneumonia.[7] The little magnate was too weak to fight and succumbed at the age of 66. Dreyfuss had been in poor health since his son Sam Dreyfuss died unexpectedly on February 23, 1931.[8]

Barney Dreyfuss was laid to rest at West View Cemetery in Pittsburgh.[9] Tributes and accolades were paid to the man that had seen his Pittsburgh Pirates win six National League pennants and two World's Championships during the time he owned the team from 1900 until his death in 1932. Dreyfuss was instrumental in helping bring about peace between the American and National leagues after the 1902 season. He played a huge role in creating the concept of a World Series to be played by the champions of both leagues after the regular season. Star shortstop and longtime friend Honus Wagner lamented the loss. "I have lost a great friend," said Wagner. "I played for Mr. Dreyfuss three years in Louisville and 18 in Pittsburgh. Our friendship warmed through those years and I feel a big loss in his passing. His generosity was only one of the remarkable things about Mr. Dreyfuss."[10]

Clarke also lost a great friend when Dreyfuss passed away. Clarke's parting after the ABC Affair in 1926 was a bit strained, but this didn't mean that Fred no longer considered Dreyfuss a close friend. Dreyfuss sent Clarke tickets to the 1927 World Series between Pittsburgh and the New York Yankees. Clarke gladly obliged as he joined brother-in-law Chick Fraser while viewing the first two games in Pittsburgh. Clarke was in agreement with Wagner when he talked about Dreyfuss' generosity. What many people didn't know was that Dreyfuss always went above and beyond the call of duty when dealing with his players.

"He helped many of them and never said a word about it," recalled Clarke. "I learned about many of them after I had left Pittsburgh. But while I was there I know he was not hard-hearted. One day a regular came to me and complained Dreyfuss would not pay him what he asked. I had to agree the player was worth what he asked. But you do not argue with an owner, so I had to think of a scheme. 'Here's what you do,' I told the player. 'Go back in there. Tell Dreyfuss he is unfair, but you are not going to be unfair, and ask him for a blank contract, which you will sign, so that he can pay you as little as he wants.' The player came out grinning. Barney had filled in exactly the sum he demanded."[11]

Clarke owed Dreyfuss a debt of gratitude for helping to shape him into the man he had become. Dreyfuss gave Clarke the opportunity to play baseball in Louisville. He didn't directly choose Clarke to manage that team in 1897, but he was fully responsible for giving Fred the opportunity when both men matriculated to Pittsburgh in December 1899. While there was no doubt that Clarke had built his baseball career and monetary fortune through determination and hard work, Dreyfuss deserved a little credit for giving a scrawny kid from Iowa the chance to play major league baseball back in 1894.

Decades of sacrifice and hard work afforded Clarke and his wife the opportunity to enjoy the fruits of their labor as the years went by. Clarke was a millionaire and he decided to rest and enjoy life more during his golden years. The Clarkes traveled throughout the United States and sometimes spent the winter months in a climate which was warmer than the Kansas plains. Clarke also became involved with the local political scene near Winfield. Clarke supported candidates who upheld the ideals and values that he stressed throughout his life. Clarke also continued to attend the annual baseball meetings in New York just as he had done while managing Louisville and Pittsburgh. While at the meetings, Clarke was able to visit old friends from his playing days and new acquaintances such as Baseball Commissioner Kenesaw Mountain Landis.

A decision which Commissioner Landis made in 1944 before he passed away aided Clarke in reaching the pinnacle of baseball rewards in 1945. Landis appointed a special committee to look into selecting players for the Baseball Hall of Fame at Cooperstown, New York, who had been overlooked in regular voting by baseball writers.[12] In 1945, no player received the 75 percent threshold of votes needed to gain entrance through the writers' ballot that year. Clarke finished sixteenth in the balloting with 53 votes.[13] The Veterans Committee then took up the task of seeing if anyone deserved admission that year. This committee included Connie Mack, Ed Barrow, and Bob Quinn; veteran writers Sid Mercer and Melville Webb and National Baseball Museum officials Stephen C. Clark and Paul S. Kerr. John Heydler missed the meeting because he mistakenly did not receive an invitation and Mercer was unable to vote since he was ill.[14]

The Veterans Committee decided that ten players whose careers began during the nineteenth century were worthy of induction into baseball's hallowed

Hall of Fame. Roger Bresnahan, Dan Brouthers, Ed Delahanty, Hugh Duffy, Hughie Jennings, King Kelly, Jim O'Rourke, Wilbert Robinson, Jimmy Collins and Fred Clarke were chosen as the class of inductees for 1945. It seemed fitting that the men who managed each of the combatants in the first World Series were being enshrined together. Clarke had also battled against Jennings' Detroit Tigers in the 1909 Fall Classic and waged wars with Bresnahan and Robinson while they were members of John McGraw's New York Giants.

Clarke's enshrinement into the Baseball Hall of Fame guaranteed the former star outfielder immortality. As years passed by, his great accomplishments could only be related to a younger generation through the tales of old-timers who had seen Clarke play. Many would enter the Baseball Hall of Fame because they were great players. Others gained entrance since they were highly successful managers. Fred Clarke was one of the few to be enshrined into Cooperstown who could have made it on the merits of being either a player or a manager.

When Clarke was enshrined in 1945, stories about his perfect debut in 1894, the numerous pennants Pittsburgh won in 1901, 1902, 1903 and 1909, his hard-nosed style of play and complete dedication to baseball were resurrected from the history vaults. Clarke himself was a bit melancholy when he thought back to the good old days. A few years prior to his enshrinement, a fire on his Kansas ranch destroyed a huge portion of his house.[15] Clarke was disappointed that key mementos from his days as a baseball warrior were lost forever. "I felt bad over the loss of fishing tackle, motors, camping outfits and shooting trophies," said Clarke, "but even worse over the destruction of some of my valued baseball pictures, old friends and baseball enemies, many of whom have passed away."[16]

Clarke's run of bad luck continued during the fall of 1947 when he cheated death on three separate occasions. Clarke's first mishap occurred when he and Annette Clarke were fishing in northern Minnesota. A storm capsized the boat and the couple was thrown into the lake's icy water. Clarke quickly fought his way to the surface, but his wife was still underwater. Clarke frantically searched and found her clinging to a seat on the capsized boat. The couple hung on to the side of the boat for three hours before a rescue team reached them. Mrs. Clarke was looked after by a physician for a few days.[17] Fred Clarke was fine and had his own medicine to combat the effects of this ordeal. "There was nothing wrong with me that a few highballs wouldn't cure."[18]

Clarke was back on that same lake fishing the next day. When husband and wife returned to Winfield a few days later, Clarke used the second of his nine lives while on a quail hunt. When a friend's gun misfired, the bill of Clarke's hunting cap deflected the pellets harmlessly away. Clarke's last close

In 1945, Fred Clarke achieved baseball immortality when he was elected to the Baseball Hall of Fame by the Veterans Committee. Clarke was the second Pittsburgh Pirates player to be enshrined in Cooperstown.

call occurred when he returned home from that particular hunting trip. Clarke went to turn on his gas furnace, when it exploded and tossed him across the basement.[19] Clarke showed the depth of his levity after this haunting trifecta of horrible luck failed to do any damage. "Seems like you can't kill a good old man."[20]

This particular good old man was able to celebrate his golden wedding anniversary with wife Annette in 1948. The couple planned to have a big celebration commemorating their nuptials 50 years earlier in 1898. Friends and acquaintances were invited to the gala event. One person who was surprised that he received an invitation was former umpire Bill Klem.[21] Clarke and Klem had numerous battles during their time together in baseball. In spite of the many quarrels and arguments, Clarke sent Klem a Christmas card every year.[22] Klem considered his inclusion in this momentous occasion in Fred Clarke's life as the ultimate gesture. "You know," Bill said, "when you come right down to it, that's pretty nice."[23]

Clarke didn't walk away from baseball altogether after he left the Pittsburgh Pirates in 1926. In January 1937, Honus Wagner, commissioner of the National Semi-Pro Baseball Congress, appointed Clarke to be director of its national association.[24] He did this for many years. In 1951, Clarke was named the director of the National Association of Leagues and the nationwide player contract system.[25]

Under this new title, Clarke was responsible for acting as a liaison between this association and Organized Baseball. Making the names of exceptionally talented players under NBC contracts available to Organized Baseball was the foremost new function that Clarke had. He also was responsible for overseeing the various activities of leagues that were connected to the NBC. Clarke's baseball expertise wasn't restricted to being used on a large, grand national level. He also was involved locally within his title as president of the Winfield Kansas Baseball League for children.[26] During an interview with Joe King for *The Sporting News* in 1951, Clarke explained how this highly successful youth baseball program worked.

"The city furnishes the park and lighting, and the business men put up the money for baseballs, and to hire umpires. We draw four to five thousand people to many games, but do not charge admission. If all the balls which were fouled out of the park were lost, we could not afford to operate," said Clarke. "Therefore, we have an honor system which works. When a ball goes out, the boy who returns it gets a bottle of pop and has his name put on the honor roll. The kid with the most entries on the honor roll each week gets an autographed ball. Last year 847 balls were hit out, and 840 were returned. We lost only seven."[27]

Clarke also talked about the old days during this interview. He still believed that the game was better when he played baseball as compared to the current version which existed in 1951. When Clarke played, a hitter had to be good in order to hit a baseball which was considered dead during that era. When the livelier ball was introduced during the 1920s, slugging became more important than thinking when a player approached each and every at bat.

Clarke realized when he was a 52-year-old coach that hitting a baseball had become so much easier since it was more lively. "I wasn't a great slugger," the Hall of Famer reminisced, "and I recall I never hit a ball over the left field wall in Forbes Field from the time the present park was constructed in 1909 until I retired in 1915. But when I came back to Pittsburgh as coach, I walloped a dozen over the wall in hitting practice. Don't tell me I got that much stronger ten years later."[28]

Clarke also believed that current hitters were not as intelligent at the plate as those men who played during his era. "Hitters of today are absolutely not as smart as the old-timers," he commented. "We used to feint a fellow into throwing a certain pitch. Like a fighter looking for an opening. Backing away, walking up on the ball, crowding the plate, shifting stance and grip, always doing something to make the pitcher worry. But you sit behind the screen today and see pitchers make the batter hit at his weakness. Time after time, too. That is stereotyped hitting. You can put this down — and it's every bit as true now as then. The fellows who work the hardest last the longest."[29]

Clarke was also kind enough to name his all-time baseball team for King. Not surprisingly, all of the players but one were from Clarke's era. Cap chose Johnny Kling as his catcher, Bill Terry for first base, Nap Lajoie at second, Jimmy Collins at third and Honus Wagner was the obvious choice at shortstop. The outfield consisted of Tris Speaker, Hughie Duffy and Ty Cobb. His right-handed pitcher was Christy Mathewson and the left-hander was good old Rube Waddell.[30]

When Clarke did this interview in 1951, he still attended many of the old-timer events and reunions throughout the country. Clarke also was an original inductee into the Iowa Sports Hall of Fame in 1951.[31] As time went by, he spent more time on the Kansas ranch during his twilight years. There were fewer comrades from his days with the Pirates that Clarke could visit or call upon with each passing year. Five teammates from the glory years of 1901, 1902 and 1903 passed away during a period of six years: Claude Ritchey (1951), Deacon Phillippe (1952), Sam Leever (1953), Honus Wagner (1955) and Ginger Beaumont (1956).

By 1956, Clarke was in failing health himself. He broke his hip after a fall and had to be hospitalized.[32] After this mishap, the 83-year-old was forced to use a cane in order to move about.[33] The Hall of Famer experienced many other falls at his home over the next few years, but Clarke showed that he still had sense of humor in spite of this. "I don't get around like a man who once stole 66 bases a season," commented the former Pirate great.[34]

Throughout his retired life, Clarke remained a devoted Pittsburgh Pirates baseball fan. He stuck with the team through thick and thin and was one of their most ardent supporters. In 1960, Pittsburgh looked like the team to beat in the National League as they performed at a magical level throughout the year. Clarke believed that this was the year Pittsburgh would win its first pennant since 1927. Despite poor health which had afflicted him for the past five years, Clarke continued to root for his beloved Pittsburgh Pirates until his last dying breath.[35]

On Sunday, August 14, 1960, Fred Clarke passed away in a Winfield hospital from pneumonia. Clarke was survived by his wife, Annette Clarke, daughters Helen Donahoe and Muriel Sullivan, eight grandchildren and a great-grandson. A funeral mass to celebrate Clarke's life was held on August 17 at Holy Name Catholic Church in Winfield. Fred Clarke was laid to rest at nearby St. Mary's Cemetery.[36]

After Fred's death, Annette Clarke went to live with her two daughters in Oklahoma. She, too, was in failing health. She died on November 22, 1961, at the home of daughter Muriel in Newkirk.[37] She was laid to rest next to her husband in Winfield. Fred and Annette Clarke had been soul mates for more than 60 years. Their odyssey together began at the turn of the century during Clarke's days as a Louisville Colonel. Annette Clarke always supported her husband when any decision regarding his baseball career was made. Baseball had permitted Fred Clarke to make a living. His wife Annette made it possible for Clarke to make a life.

Two months after Fred Clarke passed away, the Pittsburgh Pirates claimed the baseball championship when they upset the mighty New York Yankees in a thrilling, seven-game, World Series. Pittsburgh was crowned champions when they won the final game in Pittsburgh, 10–9. One had to wonder if Clarke was supplying divine assistance when a double play ball jumped up and hit Yankee shortstop Tony Kubek in the throat during the eighth inning. By allowing the inning to continue, Pittsburgh scored five runs and took a 9–7 lead.

If the winds of fate weren't blowing from Winfield, Kansas, when that happened, Clarke certainly was offering a helping hand from above when Bill Mazeroski won the game in the bottom of the ninth inning with a solo home run. Clarke had won pennants in 1901, 1902, 1903 and 1909. He won a World Series in 1909 and was an assistant to Bill McKechnie when Pittsburgh defeated Washington in the 1925 Fall Classic. It seemed like the baseball gods were doing the famous Pirate one last favor when Pittsburgh claimed the title in 1960.

Fred Clarke's legacy still lives in baseball today. No other manager has won as many National League pennants for the Pittsburgh Pirates franchise. He oversaw the most powerful franchise in the National League from 1900 through 1909. He became a star outfielder and eventually gained election to the Baseball Hall of Fame. Clarke preached dedication and perseverance when he counseled his players. These were the traits that had allowed him to make his mark playing baseball. Hometown fans had always loved his aggressive nature while patrons in visiting ballparks detested Clarke's playing style.

Even the fans in Pittsburgh were belligerent toward Fred Clarke when he played for Louisville. They used to heckle and abuse him from the outfield bleachers. One day, when the Pittsburgh faithful were giving Clarke a particular rough time, he jokingly made a prophetic comment that eventually rang true in the hearts of Pittsburgh Pirates baseball fans.[38] "Never mind, some day I'll be managing your team, and then you'll all be for me," yelled Clarke as he turned to the bleacher fans.[39]

Once Fred Clarke showed the Smoky City patrons what he was capable of doing, Pittsburgh Pirates baseball fans certainly pulled for the Hall of Fame outfielder throughout his career. At times, Clarke did things that the rooting populace did not agree with. In spite of this, Pittsburgh fans treasured Clarke and he in turn loved playing for the Pirates. After Fred Clarke announced his retirement as team manager in 1915, writer Ralph S. Davis of *The Sporting News* capably assessed the accomplishments of the Kansas farmer during his time in Pittsburgh. "Clarke gave Pittsburgh the best baseball it ever experienced," stated Davis, "and his efforts have been appreciated here, although at times critics have found fault with Fred's managerial policy. However, they are all willing to concede that the city never boasted of a better ball player or a better manager."[40]

Appendix: Fred Clarke's Career Statistics*

Batting Record

Year, NL Team	G	AB	R	H	2B	3B	HR	RBI	BB	SB	AVG	OBP	SLG
1894, Louisville	76	314	55	86	11	7	7	48	26	26	.274	.337	.420
1895, Louisville	132	550	96	191	21	5	4	82	34	40	.347	.396	.425
1896, Louisville	131	517	96	168	15	18	9	79	43	34	.325	.392	.476
1897, Louisville	130	526	122	205	30	13	6	67	45	59	.390	.461	.530
1898, Louisville	149	599	116	184	23	12	3	47	48	40	.307	.373	.401
1899, Louisville	149	606	122	206	23	9	5	70	49	49	.340	.404	.432
1900, Pittsburgh	106	399	84	110	15	12	3	32	51	21	.276	.368	.396
1901, Pittsburgh	129	527	118	171	24	15	6	60	51	23	.324	.395	.461
1902, Pittsburgh	113	459	103	145	27	14	2	53	51	29	.316	.401	.449
1903, Pittsburgh	104	427	88	150	32	15	5	70	41	21	.351	.414	.532
1904, Pittsburgh	72	278	51	85	7	11	0	25	22	11	.306	.367	.410
1905, Pittsburgh	141	525	95	157	18	15	2	51	55	24	.299	.368	.402
1906, Pittsburgh	118	417	69	129	14	13	1	39	40	18	.309	.371	.412
1907, Pittsburgh	148	501	97	145	18	13	2	59	68	37	.289	.383	.389
1908, Pittsburgh	151	551	83	146	18	15	2	53	65	24	.265	.349	.363
1909, Pittsburgh	152	550	97	158	16	11	3	68	80	31	.287	.384	.373
1910, Pittsburgh	123	429	57	113	23	9	2	63	53	12	.263	.350	.373
1911, Pittsburgh	110	392	73	127	25	13	5	49	53	10	.324	.407	.492
1913, Pittsburgh	9	13	0	1	1	0	0	0	0	0	.077	.077	.154
1914, Pittsburgh	2	2	0	0	0	0	0	0	0	0	.000	.000	.000
1915, Pittsburgh	1	2	0	1	0	0	0	0	0	0	.500	.500	.500
Career Statistics	2246	8584	1622	2678	361	220	67	1015	875	509	.312	.386	.429

*Statistics courtesy of Retrosheet

Appendix

Managerial Record

Year, NL Team	G	W	L	PCT	RS	RA	STANDING
1897, Louisville	92	35	54	.393	458	604	Eleventh
1898, Louisville	154	70	81	.464	728	834	Ninth
1899, Louisville	156	75	77	.493	833	787	Ninth
1900, Pittsburgh	140	79	60	.568	733	612	Second
1901, Pittsburgh	140	90	49	.647	776	534	First
1902, Pittsburgh	142	103	36	.741	775	439	First
1903, Pittsburgh	141	91	49	.650	793	613	First
1904, Pittsburgh	156	87	66	.569	675	592	Fourth
1905, Pittsburgh	155	96	57	.627	692	570	Second
1906, Pittsburgh	154	93	60	.608	623	470	Third
1907, Pittsburgh	157	91	63	.591	634	510	Second
1908, Pittsburgh	155	98	56	.636	585	468	Second
1909, Pittsburgh	154	110	42	.724	701	448	First
1910, Pittsburgh	154	86	67	.562	655	576	Third
1911, Pittsburgh	155	85	69	.552	744	557	Third
1912, Pittsburgh	152	93	58	.616	751	565	Second
1913, Pittsburgh	155	78	71	.523	673	585	Fourth
1914, Pittsburgh	158	69	85	.448	503	540	Seventh
1915, Pittsburgh	156	73	81	.474	557	520	Fifth
Career Statistics	**2826**	**1602**	**1181**	**.576**	**12889**	**10824**	

Chapter Notes

Chapter 1

1. Marcus Lee Hansen, "Official Encouragement of Immigration to Iowa," *The Iowa Journal of History and Politics* 19.2 (1921): 159–195.
2. 1870 United States Federal Census, www.ancestry.com.
3. *Winterset, Iowa*, en.wikipedia.org.
4. *Ibid.*
5. Herman A. Mueller, *History of Madison County Iowa and Its People* (Chicago: S.J. Clarke, 1915), p. 174.
6. *Ibid.*
7. *Ibid.*
8. *Ibid.*, p. 115.
9. *Ibid.*
10. Charles T. G. Looney, *The Isabella Furnace*, Prepared for the Third Annual Conference of the Society for Industrial Archeology, April 1974.
11. *Ibid.*
12. "Mark Twain: Roughing It at Library Hall," *Pittsburgh Daily Gazette*, January 12, 1872.
13. George Thornton Fleming, *History of Pittsburgh and Environs*, Volume III (New York: American Historical Society, 1922), p. 658.

Chapter 2

1. Joe King, "The Wonder Man of Pittsburgh: Life Story of Fred Clarke, Famed Pirate," Part 1, *The Sporting News*, March 14, 1951, p. 16.
2. William G. Cutler, *History of the State of Kansas* (Chicago: A.T. Andreas, 1883).
3. *Ibid.*
4. *Ibid.*
5. *Ibid.*
6. *Ibid.*
7. *Ibid.*
8. *Ibid.*
9. 1880 United States Federal Census, www.ancestry.com.
10. *Ibid.*
11. Cutler, *History of the State of Kansas*.
12. King, "The Wonder Man of Pittsburgh," Part 1.
13. "Caught on the Fly," reprinted from *Udall Kansas News*, *The Sporting News*, March 11, 1905, p. 6.
14. *Ibid.*
15. Frederick G. Lieb, *The Pittsburgh Pirates* (1948; reprint Carbondale: Southern Illinois University Press, 2003), p. 60.
16. *Ibid.*
17. *Ibid.*
18. Bert McGrane, "Pop Anson, Marshalltown, 1951—Fred Clarke, Winterset, 1951—Red Faber, Cascade, 1951—Bob Feller, Van Meter, 1951," *Des Moines Register*, April 15, 1951.
19. *Ibid.*
20. "Fred Clarke's First Pair of Baseball Shoes," *Baseball Magazine*, February 1912, p. 74.
21. *Ibid.*
22. *Ibid.*
23. H.L. Constans, "The Pirate Chief: A Sketch of Fred Clarke and His Remarkable Record with the Pittsburgh Club," *Baseball Magazine*, June 1913, p. 87.
24. "Tips by the Managers," *The Sporting News*, December 15, 1906, p. 4.
25. *Ibid.*
26. Frederick G. Lieb, "Oilman Clarke Drills into Diamond Memories," *The Sporting News*, January 17, 1946, p. 13.
27. Lieb, *The Pittsburgh Pirates*, p. 60.
28. Lieb, "Oilman Clarke Drills."
29. *Ibid.*
30. *Ibid.*
31. *Ibid.*

32. *Ibid.*
33. *Ibid.*
34. *Ibid.*
35. *Ibid.*
36. *Ibid.*
37. Lieb, *The Pittsburgh Pirates*, p. 62.
38. *Ibid.*
39. *Ibid.*
40. *Ibid.*
41. *Ibid.*
42. Lieb, *The Pittsburgh Pirates*, pp. 62–63.
43. Barney Dreyfuss, "Making a Winner: Dreyfuss' Experience in the National League," reprinted from *Pittsburgh Press*, *The Sporting News*, November 30, 1901, p. 7.

Chapter 3

1. Lieb, *The Pittsburgh Pirates*, p. 63.
2. *Ibid.*
3. King, "The Wonder Man of Pittsburgh," Part 1.
4. Lieb, *The Pittsburgh Pirates*, p. 63.
5. *Ibid.*
6. *Ibid.*
7. Lieb, *The Pittsburgh Pirates*, p. 44.
8. *Ibid.*
9. Lieb, *The Pittsburgh Pirates*, pp. 45–46.
10. Lieb, *The Pittsburgh Pirates*, p. 45.
11. *Kentucky Derby—History of Racing*, www.kentuckyderby.info.
12. *Our History*, www.sluggermuseum.org.
13. Lieb, *The Pittsburgh Pirates*, p. 63.
14. "An Electric Storm Does a Large Amount of Damage at Louisville," *Decatur Weekly Republican*, June 28, 1894 (transcribed by Jenni Lanham for www.gendisasters.com).
15. Lieb, "Oilman Clarke Drills."
16. Lieb, *The Pittsburgh Pirates*, p. 63.
17. "The Latest News from All Points of the Compass," *The Sporting News*, July 14, 1894, p. 1.
18. *Ibid.*
19. McGrane, "Pop Anson, Marshalltown, 1951."
20. King, "The Wonder Man of Pittsburgh," Part 1.
21. O.P. Caylor, "The Outlook: Prospects of League Teams for 1895," *The Sporting News*, March 30, 1895, p. 5.
22. "Baseball Caught on the Fly," *The Sporting News*, May 25, 1895, p. 5.
23. "Baseball Caught on the Fly," *The Sporting News*, July 13, 1895, p. 5.
24. "Baseball Caught on the Fly," *The Sporting News*, September 29, 1894, p. 5.
25. Lieb, *The Pittsburgh Pirates*, pp. 63–64.
26. *Ibid.*
27. Bourbon, "Stucky Means Business: Louisville's President Refuses to Sell Any of His Players," *The Sporting News*, November 23, 1895, p. 6.
28. Dee Jay See, "Clarke's Discovery: How the Brilliant Outfielder Was Ushered into the League," *Sporting Life*, January 4, 1896, p. 3.
29. "The Gossip of the Players," *The Sporting News*, March 14, 1896, p. 3.
30. John J. Saunders, "Louisville Lines: The Colonels Give Evidence of Improvement," *Sporting Life*, August 1, 1896, p. 7.
31. John J. Saunders, "Louisville Lines: Hope of Escape from Last Place Abandoned," *Sporting Life*, August 15, 1896, p. 3.
32. F.E. Goodwin, "Cincinnati Chips: The Home Season of the Reds Now Over," *Sporting Life*, August 15, 1896, p. 11.
33. *Ibid.*
34. *Ibid.*
35. W.A. Phelon, Jr., "Chicago Gleanings: After Thoughts About the Recent League Meeting," *Sporting Life*, November 21, 1896, p. 7.
36. W.A. Phelon, Jr., "Chicago Gleanings: A Mournful Wail for Old-Time Base Ball," *Sporting Life*, December 19, 1896, p. 4.
37. Phelon, "Chicago Gleanings: After Thoughts About the Recent League Meeting."
38. "News and Comment," *Sporting Life*, December 26, 1896, p. 4.
39. John J. Saunders, "Louisville Lines: A Good Man Gone Wrong," *Sporting Life*, December 5, 1896, p. 9.
40. John J. Saunders, "Louisville Lines: Club Affairs Still Unsettled in the Falls City," *Sporting Life*, December 12, 1896, p. 4.

Chapter 4

1. John J. Saunders, "Louisville Lines: Rejoicing Over Clarke's Return to the Fold," *Sporting Life*, April 3, 1897, p. 4.
2. 1880 United States Federal Census, www.ancestry.com.
3. *Sporting Life*, "Merry Wedding Bells Ring Out for Pitcher Fraser of Louisville," March 27, 1897, p. 4.
4. *Ibid.*
5. "News and Comment," *Sporting Life*, September 25, 1897, p. 5.
6. John J. Saunders, "Louisville Lines: One More Swap of Horses in Mid-Season," *Sporting Life*, June 26, 1897, p. 4.
7. C.L. Moore, "Clark's Nerve: He Requested Pulliam to Call on Him," *The Sporting News*, March 20, 1897, p. 2.
8. C.L. Moore, "Is Competent: Fred Clark Will Make a Good Manager," *The Sporting News*, June 26, 1897, p. 7.
9. "Baseball News and Comment," *Sporting Life*, July 10, 1897, p. 5.

10. Joe King, "The Wonder Man of Pittsburgh: Life Story of Fred Clarke, Famed Pirate," Part 2, *The Sporting News*, March 21, 1951, p. 16.
11. Joe King, "The Wonder Man of Pittsburgh: Life Story of Fred Clarke, Famed Pirate," Part 3, *The Sporting News*, March 28, 1951, p. 21.
12. "Funny Base Stealers: How Fred Clarke and the Farmer Base Runner Fared," *Sporting Life*, November 6, 1897, p. 3.
13. *Ibid*.
14. W.A. Phelon, "Chicago Gleanings: The Ups and Downs of the Uncertain Colts," *Sporting Life*, July 10, 1897, p. 6.
15. John J. Saunders, "Louisville Lines: The Great Race Between the Second Division Clubs," *Sporting Life*, September 11, 1897, p. 7.
16. *Ibid*.
17. *Ibid*.
18. "News and Comment," *Sporting Life*, September 25, 1897, p. 5.
19. Charles L. Moore, "To Buy Stars: Louisville Will Soon Close a Big Deal," *The Sporting News*, November 27, 1897, p. 1.
20. "Baseball News and Comment," *Sporting Life*, October 16, 1897, p. 5.
21. "Gossip of the Players," *The Sporting News*, January 15, 1898, p. 2.
22. "Tips from Managers," *The Sporting News*, February 19, 1898, p. 2.
23. John J. Saunders, "Louisville Lines: Hope for Fred Clarke's Managerial Future," *Sporting Life*, July 16, 1898, p. 6.
24. John J. Saunders, "Louisville Lines: Manager Clark's Judgment Questioned," *Sporting Life*, May 21, 1898, p. 8.
25. John J. Saunders, "Louisville Lines: Elated Over the Recent Good Work of the Colonels," *Sporting Life*, August 21, 1898, p. 19.
26. Jack Saunders, "Louisville Lines: All Sorts of Hard Luck Pursuing the Colonels," *Sporting Life*, June 25, 1898, p. 6.
27. "Merry Wedding Bells: Ring Out for Ball Players Clarke and Anderson," *Sporting Life*, July 16, 1898, p. 6.
28. "Anson's Tribute to Cap," *Sporting Life*, August 20, 1898, p. 15.
29. *Ibid*.
30. "Gossip of the Players," *The Sporting News*, November 26, 1898, p. 2.
31. John J. Saunders, "Louisville Lines: Barney Dreyfuss to Take Hand in the Game," *Sporting Life*, November 26, 1898, p. 9.
32. *Ibid*.
33. "Can't Make a Deal: Louisville Attempts to Sell to New York in Vain," *Sporting Life*, December 31, 1898, p. 4.
34. Saunders, "Louisville Lines: Barney Dreyfuss."
35. "News and Comment," *Sporting Life*, December 31, 1898, p. 3.
36. "Baseball Caught on the Fly," *The Sporting News*, February 14, 1903, p. 5.
37. "Louisville Tears: Over the Frightful Deal in the Schedule," *Sporting Life*, April 1, 1899, p. 6.
38. *Ibid*.
39. John J. Saunders, "Balky Colonels: A Clique Against Manager Clarke in the Louisville Team Said to Exist," *Sporting Life*, June 3, 1899, p. 6.
40. John J. Saunders, "Louisville Lines," *Sporting Life*, August 12, 1899, p. 6.
41. John J. Saunders, "Louisville Lines: Misfortune Still Marks Colonels as Her Own," *Sporting Life*, August 19, 1899, p. 10.
42. John J. Saunders, "Louisville's Lament: The Premature Closing of the Local Season and the Courses Thereof," *Sporting Life*, September 9, 1899, p. 5.
43. *Ibid*.

Chapter 5

1. "News and Comment," *Sporting Life*, December 30, 1899, p. 4.
2. "Dreyfuss Has It: Pittsburgh's Club Will Be His Property in a Few Days," *Sporting Life*, November 4, 1899, p. 4.
3. *Ibid*.
4. Circle, "Pittsburgh Points: A Loophole Spoils the Sale," *Sporting Life*, November 11, 1899, p. 3.
5. *Ibid*.
6. *Ibid*.
7. Pirate, "Gigantic Deal: Star Colonels Sold to Pittsburgh Club," *The Sporting News*, December 16, 1899, p. 3.
8. *Ibid*.
9. "Robison Explains: Reasons Why St. Louis Has Bought No Players," *The Sporting News*, December 23, 1899, p. 4.
10. *Ibid*.
11. *Ibid*.
12. "The Trick Turned: Mr. Dreyfuss Will After All Remain in the League," *Sporting Life*, December 16, 1899, p. 4.
13. Circle, "Proud Pittsburgh: The Biggest Deal in Recent History Successfully Carried Out," *Sporting Life*, December 16, 1899, p. 4.
14. *Ibid*.
15. "Gossip of the Players," *The Sporting News*, December 23, 1899, p. 2.
16. C.B. Power, "Superb as a Player: But Fred Clarke Has Yet to Show Managerial Ability," *The Sporting News*, December 30, 1899, p. 5 (reprinted from the *Pittsburgh Leader*).
17. *Ibid*.

18. *Ibid.*
19. *Ibid.*
20. Al. E. Gheny, "Coming to a Head: Circuit Complications Will Soon Be Settled," *The Sporting News*, March 10, 1900, p. 2.
21. *Ibid.*
22. *Ibid.*
23. *Ibid.*
24. 1900 United States Federal Census, www.ancestry.com.
25. Al. E. Gheny, "Headless Horde: Pirates a Bunch of Brainless Players," *The Sporting News*, April 14, 1900, p. 5.
26. King, "The Wonder Man of Pittsburgh," Part 2.
27. *Ibid.*
28. Al E. Gheny, "Great Ball Town: Pittsburgh Crowd Averages 5,000 to a Game," *The Sporting News*, May 12, 1900, p. 7.
29. John E. Calvin, "Colts Lose Caste: Comiskey's Team Has the Call in Chicago," *The Sporting News*, May 12, 1900, p. 5.
30. *Ibid.*
31. Lieb, *The Pittsburgh Pirates*, p. 72.
32. *Ibid.*
33. King, "The Wonder Man of Pittsburgh," Part 3.
34. "Waddell Has Been Loaned to Milwaukee," *The Sporting News*, July 28, 1900, p. 1.
35. Al. E. Gheny, "Wager Big Money: Pittsburgh Sports Gamble on the Ball Games," *The Sporting News*, August 25, 1900, p. 4.
36. Lieb, *The Pittsburgh Pirates*, p. 71.
37. King, "The Wonder Man of Pittsburgh," Part 3.
38. Al. E. Gheny, "Bright Prospects: Pirates Should Soon Pass the Brooklyn Bunch," *The Sporting News*, September 29, 1900, p. 3.
39. Al. E. Gheny, "Base Ball Crazy: Pittsburgh Wild Over Pirates' Pennant Prospects," *The Sporting News*, September 15, 1900, p. 1.
40. "Dreyfus Will Punish Loafers: Dreyfus Scores His Players," *The Sporting News*, October 13, 1900, p. 1.
41. "Tips by the Managers," *The Sporting News*, October 27, 1900, p. 2.
42. Al. E. Gheny, "Utter Nonsense: Story That Writers Will Be Barred in 1901," *The Sporting News*, November 3, 1900, p. 2.
43. Pirate, "Proposed Trade: Kerr Offers Jesse Tannehill for Ed Scott," *The Sporting News*, December 29, 1900, p. 4.
44. "Gossip of the Players," *The Sporting News*, December 29, 1900, p. 2.

Chapter 6

1. "Said by the Magnates," *The Sporting News*, December 22, 1900, p. 2.
2. "Base Ball Caught on the Fly," *The Sporting News*, November 3, 1900, p. 5.
3. *The Sporting News*, December 29, 1900, p. 4.
4. Circle, "Pirates Picked: The New Pittsburgh Team Practically Made Up," *Sporting Life*, December 30, 1899, p. 11.
5. Lieb, *The Pittsburgh Pirates*, p. 75.
6. *Ibid.*
7. Duquesne, "Facts About Deal: How Barney Dreyfuss Beat Kerr and Auten," *The Sporting News*, March 2, 1901, p. 4.
8. *Ibid.*
9. *Ibid.*
10. Lieb, *The Pittsburgh Pirates*, p. 76.
11. Duquesne, "Pirates Are Sold: Kerr and Auten Retire from Pittsburgh Club," *The Sporting News*, February 23, 1901, p. 2.
12. *Ibid.*
13. Duquesne, "Magnates Absent: Dreyfus and Pulliam Not Back from Meeting," *The Sporting News*, March 9, 1901, p. 5.
14. Duquesne, "Dreyfus Hopeful: Pirates' President Confident of Holding His Job," *The Sporting News*, February 9, 1901, p. 4.
15. Hot Springs, "Signs Two Stars: McGraw Makes Birds of Donlin and Williams," *The Sporting News*, March 30, 1901, p. 5.
16. Duquesne, "Is Saying Little: But Barney Dreyfuss Is Considering Jimmy Williams' Case," *The Sporting News*, April 6, 1901, p. 2.
17. "Bad Effect on the Game: Reports of Contract Jumping by So Many Players." *Chicago Daily Tribune*, April 7, 1901.
18. Duquesne, "Pirates Pleased: No Training Point Equal to Hot Springs," *The Sporting News*, April 13, 1901, p. 5.
19. "Said by the Magnates," *The Sporting News*, April 13, 1901, p. 2.
20. "Base Ball Caught on the Fly," *The Sporting News*, March 16, 1901, p. 5.
21. "Gossip of the Players," *The Sporting News*, March 16, 1901, p. 2.
22. Duquesne, "Not Pennant Ball: The Brand the Pirates Have Been Playing," *The Sporting News*, May 11, 1901, p. 3.
23. King, "The Wonder Man of Pittsburgh," Part 2.
24. Duquesne, "Clarke Disabled: Pirates Feel the Loss of Their Leader," *The Sporting News*, May 18, 1901, p. 7.
25. King, "The Wonder Man of Pittsburgh," Part 2.
26. Duquesne, "First-Class Park: Pittsburgh to Have Better Grounds and Stands," *The Sporting News*, June 29, 1901, p. 4.
27. King, "The Wonder Man of Pittsburgh," Part 3.
28. King, "The Wonder Man of Pittsburgh," Part 2.

29. Duquesne, "Americans Agent: Charge of Disloyalty Made Against Ely," *The Sporting News*, August 3, 1901, p. 4.
30. Duquesne, "Atlantic City: Week of Pleasure Provided for the Pirates," *The Sporting News*, August 17, 1901, p. 5.
31. *Ibid.*
32. King, "The Wonder Man of Pittsburgh," Part 3.
33. *Ibid.*
34. Duquesne, "Nothing to Fear: If the Pirates' Regulars Are on Duty," *The Sporting News*, August 31, 1901, p. 4.
35. Duquesne, "Americans Agent: Charge of Disloyalty."
36. Duquesne, "Atlantic City: Week of Pleasure."
37. Duquesne, "Politic Pirates: Show Appreciation for Fans' Favors," *The Sporting News*, October 12, 1901, p. 2.
38. *Ibid.*
39. *Ibid.*
40. Lieb, *The Pittsburgh Pirates*, p. 85.
41. "Said by the Magnates," *The Sporting News*, December 28, 1901, p. 2.

Chapter 7

1. Duquesne, "Clarke Returns from Kansas," *The Sporting News*, January 11, 1902, p. 3.
2. *Ibid.*
3. "Tips by the Managers," *The Sporting News*, January 18, 1902, p. 2.
4. *Ibid.*
5. Duquesne, "Sure of Success: Dreyfus' Faith in Spalding Is Not Shaken," *The Sporting News*, February 1, 1902, p. 3.
6. Duquesne, "Holding Its Own: Base Ball Is Still the Popular Pastime," *The Sporting News*, January 25, 1902, p. 4.
7. Duquesne, "Will Not Retreat: Spaldingites Will Stick to Their Leader," *The Sporting News*, February 15, 1902, p. 3.
8. Duquesne, "Is Not Wavering: Barney Dreyfuss with Spalding to the End," *The Sporting News*, January 18, 1902, p. 3.
9. *Ibid.*
10. "Tips by the Managers," *The Sporting News*, January 25, 1902, p. 2.
11. Lieb, *The Pittsburgh Pirates*, p. 85.
12. *Ibid.*
13. *Ibid.*
14. "Spalding President of Baseball League — He Declares That Freedman Must Retire from Baseball," *New York Times*, December 14, 1901, p. 7.
15. *Ibid.*
16. Lieb, *The Pittsburgh Pirates*, p. 86.
17. *Ibid.*
18. Lieb, *The Pittsburgh Pirates*, pp. 86–87.
19. Lieb, *The Pittsburgh Pirates*, p. 87.
20. Duquesne, "Prefer American: Pittsburgh Patrons Sore on National League," *The Sporting News*, August 2, 1902, p. 6.
21. Duquesne, "Fast and Daring: Pirates' Base Running Dazes Opponents," *The Sporting News*, May 24, 1902, p. 6.
22. Duquesne, "Censured Clarke: Many of the Regular Patrons at Pittsburgh," *The Sporting News*, June 28, 1902, p. 5.
23. *Ibid.*
24. "Waddell May Be a Pirate," *New Castle (Pa.) News*, June 18, 1902.
25. *Ibid.*
26. John H. Gruber, "Remarkable Games: Waistedeep in Water," *The Sporting News*, December 28, 1916, p. 4.
27. *Ibid.*
28. *Ibid.*
29. "American League Begins War Upon Barney Dreyfuss," (Syracuse, N.Y.) *Post Standard*, August 24, 1902.
30. *Ibid.*
31. *Ibid.*
32. *Ibid.*
33. "Planning to Place Team to Oppose the Pirates," (Syracuse, N.Y.) *Post Standard*, August 24, 1902.
34. Duquesne, "To Jump in 1903: Two Pitchers Leave Pittsburgh with O'Connor," *The Sporting News*, August 30, 1902, p. 1.
35. Duquesne, "Beat the Pirates: Wallace's Great Fielding and Fine Batting," *The Sporting News*, October 18, 1902, p. 4.
36. Duquesne, "Saved His Stars: Dreyfuss Gives List of His 1903 Players," *The Sporting News*, October 11, 1902, p. 5.
37. Duquesne, "Beat the Pirates."
38. "Chesbro Leaves Pittsburgh," (Richmond, Va.) *Times*, October 15, 1902,
39. *Ibid.*
40. Duquesne, "Beat the Pirates."
41. Duquesne, "Leach's Loyalty: Says Dreyfuss Can Count on Him for 1903," *The Sporting News*, November 8, 1902, p. 6.
42. "Leach Secured by Pittsburgh," *Chicago Daily Tribune*, November 7, 1902.
43. "Dreyfuss Draws a Warm Retort," *Chicago Daily Tribune*, November 8, 1902.
44. Duquesne, "Traced to Somers: Advance Money Leach Secured from Johnson," *The Sporting News*, November 15, 1902, p. 2.
45. *Ibid.*
46. Duquesne, "Leach's Loyalty."
47. *Ibid.*
48. Duquesne, "Has His Own Ideas: But Barney Will Abide by Committee's Action," *The Sporting News*, December 27, 1902, p. 2.

Chapter 8

1. "Tips by the Managers," *The Sporting News*, October 25, 1902, p. 2.
2. Lieb, *The Pittsburgh Pirates*, pp. 93–94.
3. Duquesne, "American's Fault: Peace Conference Delayed on Flimsy Protest," *The Sporting News*, January 10, 1903, p. 2.
4. Lieb, *The Pittsburgh Pirates*, p. 93.
5. Lieb, *The Pittsburgh Pirates*, p. 94.
6. *Ibid.*
7. *Ibid.*
8. *Ibid.*
9. Lieb, *The Pittsburgh Pirates*, p. 95.
10. "Baseball Peace Assured," *New York Times*, January 23, 1903.
11. Francis C. Richter, ed. *Reach's Official American League Base Ball Guide for 1903* (Philadelphia: A.J. Reach, 1903), p. 126.
12. *Ibid.*
13. "Gossip of the Players," *The Sporting News*, March 7, 1903, p. 2.
14. "Gossip of the Players," *The Sporting News*, January 17, 1903, p. 2.
15. Ralph S. Davis, "Has Full Charge: Dreyfuss Does Not Interfere with His Manager," *The Sporting News*, March 21, 1903, p. 5.
16. "Base Ball Caught on the Fly," *The Sporting News*, May 23, 1903, p. 5.
17. Lieb, *The Pittsburgh Pirates*, p. 98.
18. "Base Ball Caught on the Fly," *The Sporting News*, July 4, 1903, p. 5.
19. *Ibid.*
20. "A Heavy Fine for Bowerman: Must Pay One Hundred Dollars for Assaulting Fred Clarke," *The Pittsburgh Press*, July 15, 1903, p. 1.
21. Ralph S. Davis, "Refuses to Talk: Dreyfuss Declines to Discuss Pulliam's Action," *The Sporting News*, July 4, 1903, p. 1.
22. Ralph S. Davis, "Are Unbeatable: Pirates Won Six Straight Shut Out Games," *The Sporting News*, June 13, 1903, p. 1.
23. Ralph S. Davis, "Doheny to Return: Pirates' Southpaw Sorry That He Deserted," *The Sporting News*, August 8, 1903, p. 4.
24. Ralph S. Davis, "In Better Shape: Pirates' Disabled List Grows Smaller," *The Sporting News*, August 15, 1903, p. 6.
25. *Ibid.*
26. Ralph S. Davis, "Big Hospital List: Most of the Champions in Bad Shape," *The Sporting News*, August 1, 1903, p. 4.
27. *Ibid.*
28. "Late News: Pirates Without Wagner," *The Sporting News*, September 12, 1903, p. 1.
29. "World's Series on Again—Boston Players Make Compromise with Killilea," *Chicago Daily Tribune*, September 26, 1903.
30. King, "The Wonder Man of Pittsburgh," Part 3.
31. Ralph S. Davis, "Pittsburgh's Pride: Phillippe's Grand Pitching in World's Series," *The Sporting News*, October 17, 1903, p. 1.
32. Ralph S. Davis, "Knocking Leever: Pitcher Charged with Having a Weak Heart," *The Sporting News*, October 24, 1903, p. 3.
33. "Tips by the Managers," *The Sporting News*, October 24, 1903, p. 2.
34. "Pittsburgh's Success in Championship Series with Boston Depends on These Men," (New York) *Evening Telegraph*, October 2, 1903.
35. "Pittsburgh Fans Are Wild," *Chicago Daily Tribune*, October 5, 1903.
36. "Pirates Win One More," *Chicago Daily Tribune*, October 7, 1903.
37. Lieb, *The Pittsburgh Pirates*, p. 102.
38. *Ibid.*
39. King, "The Wonder Man of Pittsburgh," Part 2.
40. "Mad Ball Player at Bay," *New York Times*, October 12, 1903, p. 12.
41. *Ibid.*
42. King, "The Wonder Man of Pittsburgh," Part 2.

Chapter 9

1. "Pittsburgh Players Each Receive $1,316," *Washington Times*, October 16, 1903.
2. "National League News," *Sporting Life*, March 26, 1904, p. 4.
3. Ralph S. Davis, "Had No Schedule: Johnson Not Ready to Discuss Dates," *The Sporting News*, January 30 1904, p. 2.
4. A.R. Cratty, "Pittsburgh Points: Capt. Clarke Improving His Idle Hours," *Sporting Life*, January 30, 1904, p. 5.
5. A.R. Cratty, "Pittsburgh Points: The Champions Now Preparing for a Fourth Pennant," *Sporting Life*, April 2, 1904, p. 10.
6. A.R. Cratty, "Pittsburgh Points: After Cap's Oil," *Sporting Life*, January 23, 1904, p. 4.
7. Ralph S. Davis, "Premiers' Leader: Will Finish His Career with Dreyfuss' Team," *The Sporting News*, February 13, 1904, p. 3.
8. *Ibid.*
9. "National League News," *Sporting Life*, February 27, 1904, p. 5.
10. *Ibid.*
11. "Tips by the Managers," *The Sporting News*, March 5, 1904, p. 2.
12. "National League News," *Sporting Life*, April 16, 1904, p. 4.
13. *Ibid.*
14. "Big Offer for Star Pitchers," *Chicago Daily Tribune*, May 10, 1904.
15. Ralph S. Davis, "Eyes Trouble Him: Phillippe Under Treatment by Specialist," *The Sporting News*, July 16, 1904, p. 5.

16. Ralph S. Davis, "Pirates' Chance: Play at Home Almost All of July," *The Sporting News*, June 18, 1904, p. 3.
17. Ralph S. Davis, "Clarke Disabled: Pirates Play Poorly Without Their Leader," *The Sporting News*, July 23, 1904, p. 6.
18. Ralph S. Davis, "In Sore Distress: Pirates Went East Without Three Stars," *The Sporting News*, August 6, 1904, p. 6.
19. Ralph S. Davis, "Plucky Pirates: Many of Champions' Stars Have Been Disabled," *The Sporting News*, September 17, 1904, p. 1.
20. "Leach, The Leader: In Temporary Command of the League Champions," *Sporting Life*, July 23, 1904, p. 3.
21. *Ibid.*
22. "Tips by the Managers," *The Sporting News*, April 2, 1904, p. 2.
23. Ralph S. Davis, "Help the Hitting: Best Suggestion Is to Amend Strike Rule," *The Sporting News*, October 22, 1904, p. 1.
24. A.R. Cratty, , "Sebring's Slide for His Happy Home in Williamsport," *Sporting Life*, August 16, 1904, p. 3.
25. *Ibid.*
26. Davis, "Plucky Pirates."
27. *Ibid.*
28. "Tips by the Managers," *The Sporting News*, December 17, 1904, p. 4.
29. A.R. Cratty, "Pittsburgh Points: Clarke's Big Hunt," *Sporting Life*, November 12, 1904, p. 6.
30. "Shakeup in Pittsburgh Town," *Chicago Daily Tribune*, December 11, 1904.
31. Ralph S. Davis, "Two Poor Trades: Made by Pittsburgh at Recent Meeting," *The Sporting News*, December 24, 1904, p. 5.
32. Ralph S. Davis, "Pirates' Line-Up: Training Squad Will Consist of 21 Players," *The Sporting News*, February 4, 1905, p. 3.
33. A.R. Cratty, "Pittsburgh Points: Veterans Want the Training Season Cut Down," *Sporting Life*, April 8, 1905, p. 12.
34. A.R. Cratty, "Pittsburgh Points: No Danger of Clarke Giving Up Pirate Leadership," *Sporting Life*, June 22, 1905, p. 11.
35. "Condensed Dispatches," *Sporting Life*, September 16, 1905, p. 25.
36. A.R. Cratty, "Pittsburgh Points: Clancy Declined Like a Flash," *Sporting Life*, July 22, 1905, p. 11.
37. "McGraw on Carpet: To Be Tried by the National Board of Directors," *Sporting Life*, June 3, 1905, p. 3.
38. *Ibid.*
39. *Ibid.*
40. *Ibid.*
41. *Ibid.*
42. *Ibid.*
43. A.R. Cratty, "Pittsburgh Points: Dreyfuss Turn-Down Resented," *Sporting Life*, June 10, 1905, p. 8.
44. *Ibid.*
45. "Pittsburgh Viewpoint: The New York Players Blamed for the Forfeiture," *Sporting Life*, August 12, 1905, p. 3.
46. *Ibid.*
47. *Ibid.*
48. Ralph S. Davis, "Fighting to the End: Pirates Inspired by Words of Their Leader," *The Sporting News*, September 30, 1905, p. 7.
49. Ralph S. Davis, "Lose Easy Games: Reasons Why Pirates Do Not Gain on Giants," *The Sporting News*, August 26, 1905, p. 2.
50. "National League News," *Sporting Life*, November 4, 1905, p. 9.

Chapter 10

1. Ralph S. Davis, "Something Doing: Every Minute National League Was in Session," *The Sporting News*, December 23, 1905, p. 6.
2. Ralph S. Davis, "Will Be a Pirate: Fred Clarke Signs Nealon to 1906 Contract," *The Sporting News*, November 11, 1905, p. 1.
3. *Ibid.*
4. "Tips by the Managers," *The Sporting News*, December 23, 1905, p. 4.
5. Ralph S. Davis, "Pirates' 1906 Pay: No Reduction in Salaries This Season," *The Sporting News*, January 13, 1906, p. 6.
6. A.R. Cratty, "Pittsburgh Points: Pirate's Spring Tour a Treat to Old-Timers," *Sporting Life*, March 10, 1906, p. 6.
7. A.R. Cratty, "Pittsburgh Points: On Walnut River," *Sporting Life*, January 6, 1906, p. 10.
8. *Ibid.*
9. "Tips by the Managers," *The Sporting News*, April 21, 1906, p. 4.
10. Ralph S. Davis, "Will Do His Best: Willis Glad to Get Away from Boston," *The Sporting News*, March 17, 1906, p. 7.
11. A.R. Cratty, "Pittsburgh Points: Paragraphers Come Close to Creating Trouble," *Sporting Life*, November 25, 1905, p. 6.
12. Ralph S. Davis, "Inspiring Sight: Exposition Park Packed on Opening Day," *The Sporting News*, April 28, 1906, p. 3.
13. *Ibid.*
14. Davis, "Will Do His Best."
15. Ralph S. Davis, "Caused Comment: Award of Catcher Phelps to Boston," *The Sporting News*, July 7, 1906, p. 3.
16. *Ibid.*
17. "More Friction: Caused by the Decision in the Phelps Case," *Sporting Life*, July 7, 1906, p. 8.
18. "Lest We Forget: Too Soon," *Sporting Life*, July 14, 1906, p. 11.

19. "More Friction: Caused by the Decision in the Phelps Case."
20. "Men and Measures," *Sporting Life*, July 21, 1906, p. 9.
21. "F. Clarke Rebels: Manager Comes to a Rupture with President," *Sporting Life*, October 13, 1906, p. 18.
22. Ralph S. Davis, "Still Friendly: Clarke and Dreyfuss Together in Chicago," *The Sporting News*, October 20, 1906, p. 3.
23. Ralph S. Davis, "Brush All Alone: John T. Cast Only Vote Against Pulliam," *The Sporting News*, December 22, 1906, p. 6.
24. *The Sporting News*, December 22, 1906, p. 1.
25. Veteran, "Talk of Transfer: Several of the Phillies May Be Traded," *The Sporting News*, October 27, 1906, p. 1.
26. A.R. Cratty, "Pittsburgh Points: An Old Guard Gone," *Sporting Life*, December 29, 1906, p. 9.
27. "Cheap Gamblers Roast Pirates: Victim of Gamblers," *The Sporting News*, April 27, 1907, p. 1.
28. *Ibid.*
29. A.R. Cratty, "In Pittsburgh: Southern Slab Stars Picked by a Posted Patron," *Sporting Life*, August 3, 1907, p. 4.
30. *Ibid.*
31. "Latest News: Pittsburgh's Protest — In Which Bresnahan's Leg-Guards Figure Largely," *Sporting Life*, May 18, 1907, p. 2.
32. *Ibid.*
33. "Latest News: President Pulliam Rules on Leg-Guard Question," *Sporting Life*, June 1, 1907, p. 1.
34. Ralph S. Davis, "Pirates' Hoodoos: Beaten in Opening Game of Second Trip," *The Sporting News*, July 11, 1907, p. 2.
35. A.R. Cratty, "In Pittsburgh: Fun with Doggy," *Sporting Life*, July 20, 1907, p. 4.
36. "The Joke on Barney," *Sporting Life*, December 31, 1904, p. 11.
37. Ralph S. Davis, "Strenuous Fight: Three Teams Contesting for Second Place," *The Sporting News*, September 5, 1907, p. 4.
38. *Ibid.*
39. "National League News," *Sporting Life*, August 31, 1907, p. 9.
40. A.R. Cratty, "In Pittsburgh: Took Affairs Too Easy," *Sporting Life*, September 14, 1907, p. 7.
41. *Ibid.*
42. A.R. Cratty, "In Pittsburgh: Yearned for Home," *Sporting Life*, October 19, 1907, p. 15.
43. "National League News," *Sporting Life*, September 21, 1907, p. 11.
44. "National League News," *Sporting Life*, November 2, 1907, p. 7.
45. A.R. Cratty, "In Pittsburgh: Some Patrons Will Miss a Regular Feature," *Sporting Life*, November 16, 1907, p. 8.
46. Ralph S. Davis, "No Chance of War: Base Ball's Annual Agitation Is Over," *The Sporting News*, November 7, 1907, p. 6.
47. A.R. Cratty, "In Pittsburgh: An American Star Finds a Silent Booster," *Sporting Life*, November 23, 1907, p. 7.

Chapter 11

1. A.R. Cratty, "In Pittsburgh: Unique Capture Made by the Pirates' Pilot," *Sporting Life*, November 9, 1907, p. 8.
2. Davis, "No Chance of War: Base Ball's Annual Agitation Is Over."
3. "A Player Shot: Pitcher Eels Injured While Hunting with Fred Clarke," *Sporting Life*, December 7, 1907, p. 3.
4. *Ibid.*
5. *Ibid.*
6. Ralph S. Davis, "Will Start Later: Season Will Not Begin Until April 16," *The Sporting News*, December 12, 1907, p. 3.
7. A.R. Cratty, "In Pittsburgh: Manager Clarke's Missive Confers Real Pleasure," *Sporting Life*, December 21, 1907, p. 3.
8. *Ibid.*
9. *Ibid.*
10. "Fred Clarke's Declaration," *Sporting Life*, September 21, 1907, p. 15.
11. Ralph S. Davis, "May Manage Reds: Garry Herrmann Negotiating with Leach," *The Sporting News*, January 16, 1908, p. 2.
12. *Ibid.*
13. *Ibid.*
14. "Ganzel Wins: Cincinnati Captain Will Be Manager Also," *Sporting Life*, January 25, 1908, p. 2.
15. Ralph S. Davis, "Tommy to Tarry: Pittsburgh Will Keep Diminutive Star," *The Sporting News*, January 23, 1908, p. 3.
16. "Ganzel Wins: Cincinnati Captain Will Be Manager Also."
17. Ralph S. Davis, "Ten Are Unsigned: Fifteen of the 1908 Pirates Under Contract," *The Sporting News*, February 13, 1908, p. 3.
18. *Ibid.*
19. Ralph S. Davis, "Not with Pirates: Later on Wagner May Join His Old Team," *The Sporting News*, April 16, 1908, p. 3.
20. Ralph S. Davis, "Want More Money: Wagner, Leach and Gibson Have Not Signed," *The Sporting News*, March 5, 1908, p. 3.
21. Ralph S. Davis, "Blow to Pirates: Hans Wagner Will Rest for Season," *The Sporting News*, March 19, 1908, p. 3.
22. *Ibid.*

23. Ralph S. Davis, "Not Appreciated: Wagner Driven Out of Game by Roasts," *The Sporting News*, April 2, 1908, p. 3.
24. "Gossip of the Players," *The Sporting News*, April 16, 1908, p. 4.
25. A.R. Cratty, "In Pittsburgh: Col. Dreyfuss Doles Out Some Philosophy," *Sporting Life*, February 13, 1908, p. 8.
26. A.R. Cratty, "In Pittsburgh: High Tribute Is Paid to Sporting Life," *Sporting Life*, March 14, 1908, p. 14.
27. A.R. Cratty, "In Pittsburgh: Weird Gossip About Hans Wagner's Shift," *Sporting Life*, May 2, 1908, p. 7.
28. Ralph S. Davis, "Plucky Pirates: Have Had All Kinds of Bad Luck," *The Sporting News*, June 11, 1908, p. 2.
29. Ralph S. Davis, "Playing to Form: Pirates Make Good Showing in East," *The Sporting News*, June 18, 1908, p. 2.
30. Wm. F.H. Koelsch, "New York News: Gov. Hughes' Success and Its Probable Effect," *Sporting Life*, June 20, 1908, p. 3.
31. A.R. Cratty, "In Pittsburgh: There Is Rejoicing Over Willis' Recovery," *Sporting Life*, June 27, 1908, p. 5.
32. A.R. Cratty, "In Pittsburgh: They Are Bewailing the Miserable Weather," *Sporting Life*, May 30, 1908, p. 7.
33. "Rumored That Wagner Will Retire: Wagner May Quit Pirates," *The Sporting News*, July 16, 1908, p. 1.
34. *Ibid*.
35. Ralph S. Davis, "Strenuous Race: Pirates Lead National by Small Margin," *The Sporting News*, July 23, 1908, p. 2.
36. *Ibid*.
37. Ralph S. Davis, "Lost First Place: Pirates Hope to Soon Regain Lead," *The Sporting News*, September 3, 1908, p. 3.
38. Ralph S. Davis, "Fought to Finish: Pirates Lost 1908 Pennant in Last Game," *The Sporting News*, October 8, 1908, p. 4.
39. Francis C. Richter, ed. "National League: The Complete 1908 Record," *Sporting Life*, October 17, 1908, p. 8.
40. *Ibid*.
41. Davis, "Fought to Finish: Pirates Lost 1908 Pennant in Last Game."
42. Ralph S. Davis, "Passing on Plans: Dreyfuss' Time Taken Up with Architects," *The Sporting News*, November 5, 1908, p. 2.
43. "A Successful Pittsburgh Innovation," *Sporting Life*, November 14, 1908, p. 4.
44. A.R. Cratty, "In Pittsburgh: There Is No Resentment for Pirates' Failure," *Sporting Life*, October 17, 1908, p. 10.
45. A.R. Cratty, "Pirate Points: Barney Dreyfuss' Ideas About Managers," *Sporting Life*, December 12, 1908, p. 8.

Chapter 12

1. Ralph S. Davis, "Ready Next June: Pirates Will Have New Home in 1909," *The Sporting News*, October 29, 1908, p. 7.
2. *Ibid*.
3. Michael Gershman, *Diamonds: The Evolution of the Ballpark* (Boston: Houghton Mifflin, 1993), p. 89.
4. A.R. Cratty, "Pirate Points: A Busy Winter for Barney Dreyfuss," *Sporting Life*, November 7, 1908, p. 3.
5. Ralph S. Davis, "Wintering Well: Clarke and His Players Enjoy Off Season," *The Sporting News*, December 3, 1908, p. 2.
6. Ralph S. Davis, "Will Not Retire: Wagner and Clarke to Remain with Pirates," *The Sporting News*, October 15, 1908, p. 6.
7. *Sporting Life*, "Fred Clarke's Luck: The Pittsburgh Manager May Strike Oil on His Kansas Ranch," February 27, 1909, p. 18.
8. Ralph S. Davis, "Pirates Signing: Eleven of Clarke's Players Are Under Contract," *The Sporting News*, January 28, 1909, p. 2.
9. *Ibid*.
10. Ralph S. Davis, "Slow in Starting: Pirates Will Be Late in Spring Stunts," *The Sporting News*, March 4, 1909, p. 6.
11. *Ibid*.
12. Ralph S. Davis, "Returned to Camp: Pirates Left Hot Springs for Four Games," *The Sporting News*, April 8, 1909, p. 2.
13. Ralph S. Davis, "Good Youngsters: Miller Boys Making Good with Pirates," *The Sporting News*, April 29, 1909, p. 6.
14. *Ibid*.
15. *Ibid*.
16. Gershman, *Diamonds: The Evolution of the Ballpark*, p. 89.
17. David Cicotello and Angelo J. Louisa, eds., *Forbes Field: Essays and Memories of the Pirates' Historic Ballpark, 1909–1971* (Jefferson, NC: McFarland, 2007), p. 16.
18. *Ibid*, p. 17.
19. Ralph S. Davis, "Test for Pirates: Play Cubs Five Games This Week," *The Sporting News*, July 1, 1909, p. 2.
20. Ralph S. Davis, "Storke in Shape: Responded to Hurry Call from Clark," *The Sporting News*, May 20, 1909, p. 2.
21. "Latest News: Herrmann on the Case of Fred Clarke," *Sporting Life*, June 26, 1909, p. 2.
22. *Ibid*.
23. *Ibid*.
24. "Explanation Asked: Chairman Herrmann After Fred Clarke for Recent Roast," *Sporting Life*, June 19, 1909, p. 2.
25. *Ibid*.
26. "Makes Peace: Fred Clarke Not to Be

Disciplined by the National League," *Sporting Life*, July 3, 1909, p. 1.

27. "Clarke to Retire: Veteran Pittsburgh Leader to Live on a Ranch in Kansas," *Sporting Life*, June 19, 1909, p. 2.

28. *Ibid.*

29. Ralph S. Davis, "Pirates Beaten: Lost First Series at Forbes Field," *The Sporting News*, July 8, 1909, p. 2.

30. *Ibid.*

31. "Said by the Magnates," *The Sporting News*, March 4, 1909, p. 4.

32. "Passing of Pulliam," Francis C. Richter, *Sporting Life*, August 7, 1909, p. 3.

33. *Ibid.*, p. 1.

34. *Ibid.*, p. 3.

35. "Wagner Weeps: Because He Could Not Attend the Funeral of Harry Pulliam," *Sporting Life*, August 7, 1909, p. 3.

36. Ralph S. Davis, "Byrne's New Berth: Bobby Has Added to the Speed of the Pirates," *The Sporting News*, August 26, 1909, p. 2.

37. A.R. Cratty, "In Pittsburgh: A Team Trade That Stirred Up Fans," *Sporting Life*, September 4, 1909, p. 7.

38. Ralph S. Davis, "Finish at Boston: Four Easy Games for Speedy Pirates," *The Sporting News*, September 2, 1909, p. 2.

39. "National League News," *Sporting Life*, September 18, 1909, p. 24.

40. A.R. Cratty, "Pirates Points: Chicago Tactics Fail to Please Pittsburghers," *Sporting Life*, September 25, 1909, p. 12.

41. Ralph S. Davis, "Clarke Will Stay: Says He Will Pilot Pirates Next Season," *The Sporting News*, October 14, 1909, p. 2.

42. *Ibid.*

43. *Ibid.*

44. A.R. Cratty, "In Pittsburgh: Dreyfuss and Clarke Will Remain Together," *Sporting Life*, December 25, 1909, p. 10.

45. Charles H. Zuber, "Clarke and Wagner: To Retire Together from Base Ball, Is an Allegation on 'Inside Information' Made by a Veracious Cincinnati Scribe," *Sporting Life*, September 25, 1909, p. 12.

46. King, "The Wonder Man of Pittsburgh," Part 2.

47. Ralph S. Davis, "Pittsburgh Packed: Fans Eager to See Games in Smoky City," *The Sporting News*, October 14, 1909, p. 1.

48. King, "The Wonder Man of Pittsburgh," Part 2.

49. *Ibid.*

50. "The Leaders' View," *Sporting Life*, October 23, 1909, p. 7.

51. "Honors at Forbes Field," *Sporting Life*, October 23, 1909, p. 7.

52. Ralph S. Davis, "Cheering Reports: Clarke and Wagner Sure to Be in Harness Again," *The Sporting News*, December 16, 1909, p. 2.

Chapter 13

1. A.R. Cratty, "In Pittsburgh: Dreyfuss and Clarke Will Remain Together," *Sporting Life*, December 23, 1909, p. 10.

2. *Ibid.*

3. *Ibid.*

4. *Ibid.*

5. *Ibid.*

6. "Clarke's Move: Will Give Farming a Rest for a Time," *Sporting Life*, January 15, 1910, p. 6.

7. "Three More Years: Will Fred Clarke Manage Barney Dreyfuss' Pittsburgh Team," *Sporting Life*, February 12, 1910, p. 2.

8. "National League Notes," *Sporting Life*, January 29, 1910, p. 13.

9. "Caught on the Fly," *The Sporting News*, February 10, 1910, p. 6.

10. "Tips by the Managers," *The Sporting News*, February 17, 1910, p. 4.

11. A.R. Cratty, "In Pittsburgh: Are Seen Harbingers of the Coming Race," *Sporting Life*, February 19, 1910, p. 12.

12. Ralph S. Davis, "Why Willis Went: Clarke's Methods of Punishing Irresponsibility," *The Sporting News*, February 24, 1910, p. 1.

13. *Ibid.*

14. Ralph S. Davis, "First Stage Over: World's Champions Begin Final Preparation," *The Sporting News*, March 24, 1910, p. 1.

15. Ralph S. Davis, "What Clarke Says: Pirates' Condition Worse Now Than at Start," *The Sporting News*, May 19, 1910, p. 1.

16. Ralph S. Davis, "Record May Fall: Pittsburgh to Turn Out as One Man on Thursday," *The Sporting News*, April 21, 1910, p. 1.

17. Davis, "What Clarke Says: Pirates' Condition Worse Now Than at Start."

18. *Ibid.*

19. Ralph S. Davis, "Fans Wonder When: World's Champions' Slump Has 'Em Guessing," *The Sporting News*, June 9, 1910, p. 1.

20. Ralph S. Davis, "Laugh Goes Round: Ridiculous Yarns to Account for Pirates' Slump," *The Sporting News*, June 16, 1910, p. 1.

21. Ralph S. Davis, "Rule, Dead Letter: Lid Off as to Player Limit in Both Big Leagues," *The Sporting News*, September 1, 1910, p. 1.

22. *Ibid.*

23. "Clarke Quits!: The Pirate Leader Will Play No More," *Sporting Life*, September 10, 1910, p. 3.

24. *Ibid.*

25. *Ibid.*

26. "The Proper Course," *Sporting Life*, September 10, 1910, p. 4.

27. Ralph S. Davis, "Cammy Acts Ugly: Pittsburgh Pitcher Makes Fuss Over Doubtful Bonus," *The Sporting News*, October 13, 1910, p. 1.
28. *Ibid*.
29. *Ibid*.
30. *Ibid*.
31. Ralph S. Davis, "Pirates Disperse: Some Few Playing Successful Barnstorming Engagement," *The Sporting News*, October 20, 1910, p. 1.
32. *Ibid*.
33. A.R. Cratty, "Pittsburgh Points: Cool Waves," *Sporting Life*, September 10, 1910, p. 3.
34. "National League Notes," *Sporting Life*, April 16, 1910, p. 4.
35. "National League Notes," *Sporting Life*, May 21, 1910, p. 11.
36. "Clarke's Invention: The Patent Office Acts Favorably on a New Property Trunk," *Sporting Life*, February 11, 1911, p. 1.
37. "National League Notes," *Sporting Life*, May 13, 1911, p. 9.
38. Ralph S. Davis, "Rumors Baseless: Pittsburgh Flooded with False Tales of the Pirates," *The Sporting News*, November 3, 1910, p. 1.
39. "National League Notes," *Sporting Life*, December 24, 1910, p. 10.
40. Ralph S. Davis, "Will Keep Cammy: Howard Will Play for Clarke or Not at All," *The Sporting News*, February 9, 1911, p. 1.
41. Ralph S. Davis, "Fred a Boy Again: Base Ball Fever Attacks the Pirate Manager," *The Sporting News*, February 2, 1911, p. 1.
42. Ralph S. Davis, "Hans Is Patriotic: Wagner Will Serve as Juror During March," *The Sporting News*, February 16, 1911, p. 3.
43. Ralph S. Davis, "Pirates Well In: Clarke Has All Desirables Undercover," *The Sporting News*, February 23, 1911, p. 1.
44. "National League Notes," *Sporting Life*, April 22, 1911, p. 9.
45. "Clarke's Code: Few but Drastic Rules for Control of Pittsburgh Players," *Sporting Life*, April 15, 1911, p. 10.

Chapter 14

1. A.R. Cratty, "Pirate Points: Club Officials Joyous Over the Outlook," *Sporting Life*, April 15, 1911, p. 9.
2. Ralph S. Davis, "Smoky City Eyes: See Pirates Against Real Team and Are Pleased," *The Sporting News*, May 4, 1911, p. 2.
3. Ralph S. Davis, "Picks His Pirates: Clarke Decides on Crew Before Quitting Springs," *The Sporting News*, April 6, 1911, p. 2.
4. "Fred Clarke's Record: The Pittsburgh Manager Makes Ten Putouts in Left Field in One Game," *Sporting Life*, May 6, 1911, p. 1.
5. Ralph S. Davis, "It Is Up to Leach: Did He Reveal the Story of His Differences," *The Sporting News*, June 29, 1911, p. 3.
6. *Ibid*.
7. "Caught on the Fly," *The Sporting News*, July 6, 1911, p. 4.
8. "National League News," *Sporting Life*, November 21, 1908, p. 10.
9. Ralph S. Davis, "Will Do a Garrison: Pirate Plans for Pennant Are Made Known," *The Sporting News*, July 27, 1911, p. 3.
10. Rube Marquard, en.wikipedia.org.
11. Ralph S. Davis, "Ah! Here's O'Toole: Makes His First Start During Eastern Invasion," *The Sporting News*, August 17, 1911, p. 3.
12. Ralph S. Davis, "Talks of His Prize: Dreyfuss Thinks O'Toole Worth Every Cent Paid," *The Sporting News*, August 3, 1911, p. 3.
13. A.R. Cratty, "Pirate Points: Unpleasant Echoes of the Great O'Toole Deal," *Sporting Life*, September 9, 1911, p. 24.
14. Ralph S. Davis, "Bench for Clark: Pirate Leader Thinks He Gets Better Results," *The Sporting News*, August 10, 1911, p. 3.
15. King, "The Wonder Man of Pittsburgh," Part 3.
16. Ralph S. Davis, "Pittsburgh's Kick: Pirate Fans Have Again Proved Rank Quitters," *The Sporting News*, October 5, 1911, p. 2.
17. "Caught on the Fly," *The Sporting News*, July 20, 1911, p. 4.
18. Ralph S. Davis, "Scuttled the Cubs: Bold Pirates Wreck Chance's Pennant Craft," *The Sporting News*, September 21, 1911, p. 2.
19. Ralph S. Davis, "Slip Away Unsung: Pittsburgh Draws Curtain on 1911 Baseball Season," *The Sporting News*, October 12, 1911, p. 5.
20. "Clarke Is Done: Will Play No More After This Season," *Sporting Life*, September 23, 1911, p. 6.
21. *Ibid*.
22. Fred Clarke, "Hunting Big Game with Big League Players: A Record of My Recent Excursion in the Wilds of Minnesota," *Baseball Magazine*, February 1912, p. 14.
23. *Ibid*.
24. *Ibid*., p. 17.
25. *Ibid*., p. 18.
26. "Quaker Quips: Local Jottings," *Sporting Life*, March 30, 1912, p. 11.
27. A.R. Cratty, "Sun Glasses," *Sporting Life*, February 10, 1912, p. 14.
28. "National League News in Short Metre," *Sporting Life*, March 2, 1911, p. 10.
29. "Clarke's Chaps: Look Pretty Good to the Team Handler," *Sporting Life*, April 6, 1912, p. 12.

30. "National League News in Short Metre," p. 12.
31. Ralph S. Davis, "Dreyfuss in Doubt: Does Not Seem Enthusiastic Over Miller at First," *The Sporting News*, April 11, 1912, p. 2.
32. A.R. Cratty, "Pirate Points: No Man's Position Said to Be Cinched," *Sporting Life*, March 16, 1912, p. 9.
33. Ralph S. Davis, "Alibi of Pirates: Team Misses the Services of Both Donlin and Wagner," *The Sporting News*, May 9, 1912, p. 3.
34. Ralph S. Davis, "Pirates Cruise On: First Squad Under Clarke Goes to West Baden," *The Sporting News*, March 7, 1912, p. 5.
35. A.R. Cratty, "Pirate Points: Many Angles of the Deal with Chicago," *Sporting Life*, June 15, 1912, p. 2.
36. A.R. Cratty, "Leach Not Missed," *Sporting Life*, June 29, 1912, p. 2.
37. Ralph S. Davis, "Pirates Have Hope: Think Western Clubs May Pull Giants Down," *The Sporting News*, July 4, 1912, p. 1.
38. Ralph S. Davis, "Clarke Will Play: He Might Be in Now but for a Broken Finger," *The Sporting News*, June 13, 1912, p. 2.
39. David J. Davies, "One Happy Player: Marty O'Toole Glad First Big League Year's Over," *The Sporting News*, October 10, 1912, p. 6.
40. *Ibid.*
41. Ralph S. Davis, "One Lie Is Nailed: Fred Clarke Will Continue as Pirate Leader," *The Sporting News*, October 10, 1912, p. 2.

Chapter 15

1. "Pittsburgh Pencillings: Col. Dreyfuss Delighted with Cap Clarke's Signing," *Sporting Life*, October 5, 1912, p. 17.
2. *Ibid.*
3. *Ibid.*
4. Ralph S. Davis, "Mrs. Britton's No: It Stood in Way of Ed Koney Being a Pirate," *The Sporting News*, December 19, 1912, p. 2.
5. "Huggins' Plan: Cardinals' Manager Will Remain Active," *Sporting Life*, December 28, 1912, p. 7.
6. *Ibid.*
7. Ralph S. Davis, "He Won't Worry: Dreyfuss Stands Pat on His Holdout Bunch," *The Sporting News*, February 27, 1913, p. 3.
8. Ralph S. Davis, "Clear Lady Owner: Pirate Club Owners Did Not Say She Interfered," *The Sporting News*, December 26, 1912, p. 2.
9. Ralph S. Davis, "Roger Kills Deal: Signing with Cubs Has Double Interest to Cards," *The Sporting News*, January 16, 1913, p. 1.
10. "Clarke's Capture: The Famous Pirate Chief Purchases a Farm Which Was Once the Site of a Fake Gold Mining Town," *Sporting Life*, February 22, 1913, p. 9.
11. Ralph S. Davis, "Crafty Mr. Clarke: Plans to Put Something Over on Red Sox," *The Sporting News*, March 13, 1913, p. 7.
12. Ralph S. Davis, "Jinx Bunches Hits: Pirates Chortled Before They Were Out of Woods," *The Sporting News*, March 27, 1913, p. 3.
13. "National League News in Short Metre," *Sporting Life*, April 12, 1913, p. 6.
14. Ralph S. Davis, "Again They Call Them Buccos Bold: Pirates Have Been Showing Some Old Stuff," *The Sporting News*, July 24, 1913, p. 3.
15. "Latest News by Telegraph Briefly Told," *Sporting Life*, June 14, 1913, p. 1.
16. Ralph S. Davis, "Rookie Luhrsen Wants His Rights: Learns Major League Umpires Miss Good Ones," *The Sporting News*, September 18, 1913, p. 2.
17. Ralph S. Davis, "Pirate Fans Can't Be Comfortable: Show a Regular Mrs. Worry Disposition," *The Sporting News*, October 30, 1913, p. 3.
18. "Manager Clarke Signs: Latest News by Telegraph Briefly Told," *Sporting Life*, November 22, 1913, p. 2.
19. *Ibid.*
20. Ralph S. Davis, "Clarke Will Make Some More Deals: After One Big Trade, Fred Is Still Unsatisfied," *The Sporting News*, December 25, 1913, p. 2.
21. "Some Big Deals Made: Tinker Is Sold for $25,000," *The Sporting News*, December 18, 1913, p. 3.
22. "Clarke Makes Best Deal: The Pittsburgh Pirates Are Vastly Strengthened," *Sporting Life*, December 20, 1913, p. 9.
23. *Ibid.*
24. *Ibid.*
25. "National League News in Short Metre," *Sporting Life*, December 20, 1913, p. 14.
26. *Federal League*, en.wikipedia.org.
27. *Ibid.*
28. *Ibid.*
29. Ralph S. Davis, "Mowrey Signs Up with the Pirates: Thus Exploding Another Fed Report," *The Sporting News*, January 22, 1914, p. 2.
30. Ralph S. Davis, "Pirates Will Keep Fans Interested: Contests with American Teams Are Planned," *The Sporting News*, February 26, 1914, p. 3.
31. Ralph S. Davis, "Dreyfuss Got By with Legal Bone: Rule of Interference Pulls Him Out of the Hole," *The Sporting News*, April 9, 1914, p. 2.
32. Davis, "Pirates Will Keep Fans Interested."
33. "National League News in Short Metre," *Sporting Life*, February 14, 1914, p. 10.

34. Ralph S. Davis, "First in League, First with Fandom: Pittsburgh One Team That Is Clear of Feds," *The Sporting News*, April 30, 1914, p. 2.
35. Ralph S. Davis, "They All Can Point Faults in Pirates: Players Too Particular as to What They Hit," *The Sporting News*, June 11, 1914, p. 3.
36. Ralph S. Davis, "O'Toole Soon Will Be on Move Again: Returned to the Pirates by Giants but Not to Stay," *The Sporting News*, October 22, 1914, p. 2.
37. F. C. Richter, "Philly Pointers," *Sporting Life*, August 15, 1914, p. 7.
38. Ralph S. Davis, "Koney Played Fed Spy for Months: Fred Clarke Soon Got on to His First Sacker," *The Sporting News*, November 26, 1914, p. 2.
39. *Ibid.*
40. *Ibid.*
41. Ralph S. Davis, "Pirates Not Only Ones Who Can Quit: Fans Are Guilty of What They Blame Players For," *The Sporting News*, June 25, 1914, p. 3.
42. *Ibid.*
43. Ralph S. Davis, "Pirates Now Find They Have Nemesis: No, It Is Not a New Kind of Charley Horse," *The Sporting News*, August 13, 1914, p. 2.
44. Ralph S. Davis, "Clarke Favors Cut and Will Make It: Intimation He Won't Wait Until May Either," *The Sporting News*, December 17, 1914, p. 2.
45. Ralph S. Davis, "Evers More Silly Than Dangerous: Damage Done to Himself and Not His Ball Team," *The Sporting News*, August 12, 1915, p. 2.
46. *Ibid.*
47. Ralph S. Davis, "Clarke Pines for More Active Life: Reason for Giving Up His Berth with Pittsburgh," *The Sporting News*, September 16, 1915, p. 2.
48. Ralph S. Davis, "Pittsburgh's Big Event Yet to Come: Great Preparations for Banquet to Fred Clarke," *The Sporting News*, September 30, 1915, p. 3.
49. *Ibid.*
50. Ralph S. Davis, "Dreyfuss Plans to Shake Up Pirates: No Hint, However, as to What Changes May Be," *The Sporting News*, October 14, 1915, p. 6.
51. *Ibid.*

Chapter 16

1. Ralph S. Davis, "Clarke Works for Future of Pirates: Tries Out Rookies in Closing Days of Season," *The Sporting News*, September 23, 1915, p. 3.
2. James Jerpe, "On and Off the Field," *The Sporting News*, September 23, 1915, p. 4.
3. *Ibid.*
4. "Caught on the Fly," *The Sporting News*, January 13, 1916, p. 6.
5. *Ibid.*
6. Ralph S. Davis, "Adams Finds Fame Is a Fleeting Thing: Former Idol of Pittsburgh Fans Draws His Release," *The Sporting News*, August 10, 1916, p. 3.
7. Ralph S. Davis, "Dreyfuss Spoils a Fresh Line of Dope: He Won't Sell Out Nor Will He Fire Callahan," *The Sporting News*, October 26, 1916, p. 3.
8. *Ibid.*
9. *Ibid.*
10. A.R. Cratty, "Fred Clarke, the Ex-Manager Believed to Be Worth One Million Dollars as the Result of Lucky Discoveries in Oil," *Sporting Life*, January 13, 1917, p. 4.
11. "Caught on the Fly," *The Sporting News*, September 14, 1916, p. 4.
12. Cratty, "Fred Clarke, the Ex-Manager Believed to Be Worth One Million Dollarsas the Result of Lucky Discoveries in Oil."
13. *Ibid.*
14. *Ibid.*
15. Ralph S. Davis, "Injections of Cheers for Pirate Fandom: Visiting Moguls All Take Bright View of Future," *The Sporting News*, January 31, 1918, p. 5.
16. *Ibid.*
17. King, "The Wonder Man of Pittsburgh," Part 2.
18. *Ibid.*
19. "Some High Line Shooters," *Baseball Magazine*, August 1919, p. 244.
20. Ralph S. Davis, "Gibby Enthuses as Rooks Show Paces: Practically Every Veteran Finds He Has Real Rival," *The Sporting News*, March 24, 1921, p. 3.
21. Ralph S. Davis, "Pirates Will Finish Training En Route: Regulars on Road Until Opening Day in Cincinnati," *The Sporting News*, March 31, 1921, p. 5.
22. Ralph S. Davis, "Pirates Absolutely Right for a Start: That's the Verdict as Team Ends Training Session," *The Sporting News*, April 14, 1921, p. 3.
23. "Fred Clarke to Coach: Former Manager of Pirates to Help Prepare Kansas Nine," *New York Times*, February 26, 1922, p. 25.
24. "Caught on the Fly," *The Sporting News*, April 6, 1922, p. 6.
25. Ralph S. Davis, "Here's Reason for Success of Giants: McGraw's Team Fortified Itself with an Early Lead," *The Sporting News*, September 21, 1922, p. 3.
26. *Winfield, Kansas, High School 1922 Lagondan Yearbook*, www3.old-yearbooks.com.

27. *Winterset Cemetery, Winterset, Madison County, Iowa*, www.interment.net.
28. Jerpe, "On and Off the Field."
29. Ralph S. Davis, "Two Bound to Make M'Graw Miserable: Pirates and Reds Making Giants Fight for Their Lives," *The Sporting News*, August 30, 1923, p. 3.
30. Ralph S. Davis, "One Thing Pirates Won't Argue About: They Know Well Ahead Who Will Be Their Manager," *The Sporting News*, October 18, 1923, p. 3.
31. *Ibid.*
32. "Caught on the Fly," *The Sporting News*, November 13, 1924, p. 8.
33. Ralph S. Davis, "And Dreyfuss Did It All Himself: Pirates Will Spend More for Rail Fare Than Any Other Club," *The Sporting News*, February 12, 1925, p. 2.
34. Ralph S. Davis, "Clarke Goes Back with His Old Team: Former Manager to Serve as an Assistant to Dreyfuss," *The Sporting News*, June 18, 1925, p. 3.
35. Ralph S. Davis, "There's Something to Those Pirates: They Have Beaten Back Gamely and Are Dangerous," *The Sporting News*, June 25, 1925, p. 1.
36. J. Roy Stockton, "Veteran Deplores Waning of Old Fighting Spirit on Diamond," *The Sporting News*, September 24, 1925, p. 3.
37. Ralph S. Davis, "Pirates Best Team Ever, Says Clarke: Beats Anything Pittsburgh Had in Four Other Flag Years," *The Sporting News*, October 8, 1925, p. 1.
38. *Ibid.*
39. Ralph S. Davis, "Murder Will Out, Even with Pirates: Misplaced Zeal Trio Does Some Talking for the Press," *The Sporting News*, October 7, 1926, p. 1.
40. "Caught on the Fly," *The Sporting News*, October 22, 1925, p. 6.
41. Ralph S. Davis, "Clarke Not Likely to Desert Pirates: Veteran Denies That He Is After Interest in Robins," *The Sporting News*, November 12, 1925, p. 1.
42. Ralph S. Davis, "Clarke to Return as M'Kechnie's Aid: Announcement Belies Reported Rift Over Management," *The Sporting News*, December 17, 1925, p. 1.
43. Ralph S. Davis, "Fred Clarke Put His Seal on Waner: Recruit Takes Veteran Back to the Days of Ginger Beaumont," *The Sporting News*, March 18, 1926, p. 2.
44. Ralph S. Davis, "M'Kechnie Wields an Iron Fist to Restore Champions to Order: Rigid Disciplinary Rule Being Followed," *The Sporting News*, July 29, 1926, p. 1.
45. "Carey Wages Fight in Rebellion Ouster," *The Sporting News*, August 19, 1926, p. 1.
46. Ralph S. Davis, "Guillotine Quickly Puts Down Anti-Clarke Rebellion: Carey's Head Falls with Two Other Vets," *The Sporting News*, August 19, 1926, p. 1.
47. Davis, "Murder Will Out, Even with Pirates."
48. *Ibid.*
49. Davis, "Guillotine Quickly Puts Down Anti-Clarke Rebellion."
50. *Ibid.*
51. *Ibid.*
52. Davis, "Murder Will Out, Even with Pirates."
53. Ralph S. Davis, "Donie Bush Named to Pacify Pirates: M'Kechnie's Successor Has Fine Record in Indianapolis," *The Sporting News*, October 28, 1926, p. 1.
54. *Ibid.*
55. "Caught on the Fly," *The Sporting News*, November 4, 1926, p. 8.
56. Ralph S. Davis, "Dreyfuss Figures His House in Order: Resignation of Clarke Comes with Bush's Signing," *The Sporting News*, November 4, 1926, p. 1.

Chapter 17

1. *Conway's of Ireland*, www.fritziinc.com.
2. *Ibid.*
3. 1930 United States Federal Census, www.ancestry.com.
4. "Colonel Miller Held for Hearing," *Appleton* (Wis.) *Post Crescent*, March 25, 1932 (reprinted in *Old Timers Gazette*, Volume 3, compiled by Mollie Stehno for www.kaycounty.info).
5. "Defiant Zack Arraigned in Assault Case," *Sheboygan* (Wis.) *Press*, March 25, 1932 (reprinted in *Old Timers Gazette*, Volume 3, compiled by Mollie Stehno for www.kaycounty.info).
6. "Zack Miller Guards Home with Shotgun," *Appleton* (Wis.) *Post Crescent*, March 24, 1932 (reprinted in *Old Timers Gazette*, Volume 3, compiled by Mollie Stehno for www.kaycounty.info).
7. Ralph S. Davis, "Death Removes Barney Dreyfuss, Owner of Pittsburgh Pirates, Dean of Major Magnates and Father of Modern World's Series," *The Sporting News*, February 11, 1932, p. 5.
8. *Ibid.*
9. Lieb, *The Pittsburgh Pirates*, p. 243.
10. "Tributes Paid to Dreyfuss Emphasize Sportsmanship," *The Sporting News*, February 11, 1932, p. 5.
11. King, "The Wonder Man of Pittsburgh," Part 2.
12. Frederick G. Lieb, "Ten More Old-Time Stars Added to Game's Shrine: Duffy, Clarke and Bresnahan Among Players Honored by Spe-

cial Board," *The Sporting News*, May 3, 1945, p. 7.
13. Arthur Flynn, "94 Nominated, None Gains Hall of Fame," *The Sporting News*, February 1, 1945, p. 5.
14. Lieb, "Ten More Old-Time Stars Added."
15. Lieb, "Oilman Clarke Drills."
16. *Ibid.*
17. Bill Bryson, "Fred Clarke: Indestructible," *Baseball Digest*, March 1948, p. 45.
18. *Ibid.*
19. *Ibid.*
20. *Ibid.*
21. Frank Graham, "You Umpire for the Ball," *Baseball Digest*, October 1948, p. 80.
22. *Ibid.*
23. *Ibid.*
24. "Clarke in Baseball Post: Ex-Leader of Pirates to Direct National Semi-Pro Title Play," *New York Times*, January 5, 1937, p. 26.
25. King, "The Wonder Man of Pittsburgh," Part 3.
26. *Ibid.*
27. *Ibid.*
28. King, "The Wonder Man of Pittsburgh," Part 1.
29. *Ibid.*
30. King, "The Wonder Man of Pittsburgh," Part 3.
31. McGrane, "Pop Anson, Marshalltown, 1951."
32. "Fred Clarke Hospitalized," *New York Times*, December 6, 1956, p. 63.
33. Frederick G. Lieb, "Pittsburgh Mourns Early-Star Fred Clarke: Hall of Fame Picket Skippered Buccos to Four Pennants," *The Sporting News*, August 24, 1960, p. 13.
34. *Ibid.*
35. *Ibid.*
36. "Fred Clarke, Big League Star, Dies," (Danville, Va.) *Bee*, August 15, 1960, p. 20.
37. "Obituaries," *The Sporting News*, November 22, 1961, p. 32.
38. Ralph S. Davis, "Clarke Pines for More Active Life: Reason for Giving Up His Berth with Pittsburgh," *The Sporting News*, September 16, 1915, p. 2.
39. *Ibid.*
40. *Ibid.*

Bibliography

Books

Cutler, William G. *History of the State of Kansas*. Chicago: A.T. Andreas, 1883.
Fleming, George Thornton. *History of Pittsburgh and Environs*. Volume III. New York: American Historical Society, 1922.
Lieb, Frederick G. *The Pittsburgh Pirates*. 1948. Reprint, Carbondale: Southern Illinois University Press, 2003.
Looney, Charles T.G. *The Isabella Furnace*. Prepared for the Third Annual Conference of the Society for Industrial Archeology, April 1974.
Mueller, Herman A. *History of Madison County Iowa and Its People*. Chicago: S.J. Clarke, 1915.
Richter, Francis C., ed. *Reach's Official American League Base Ball Guide for 1903*. Philadelphia: A.J. Reach, 1903.

Newspapers and Periodicals

Appleton (Wis.) *Post Crescent*
Baseball Digest
Baseball Magazine
Boston Globe
Chicago Daily Tribune
Cincinnati Commercial
(Danville, Va.) *Bee*
Decatur (Ill.) *Weekly Republican*
Des Moines Register
Iowa Journal of History and Politics
New Castle (Pa.) *News*
(New York) *Evening Telegraph*
New York Journal-American
New York Times
Pittsburgh Daily Gazette
Pittsburgh Dispatch
Pittsburgh Leader
Pittsburgh Press
(Richmond, Va.) *Times*
Sheboygan (Wis.) *Press*
Sporting Life
The Sporting News
(Syracuse, N.Y.) *Post Standard*
Udall Kansas News
Washington Times

Bibliography

Statistical Information

www.baseball-reference.com
www.retrosheet.org
Sporting Life
The Sporting News

Informational Websites

chroniclingamerica.loc.gov
en.wikipedia.org
news.google.com
pqasb.pqarchiver.com
probaseballarchive.com
www.ancestry.com
www.fritziinc.com
www.gendisasters.com
www.interment.net
www.kancoll.org
www.kaycounty.info
www.kentuckyderby.info
www.la84foundation.org
www.paperofrecord.com
www.sabr.org
www.sluggermuseum.org
www.3.old-yearbooks.com
www.worldvitalrecords.com

Index

Numbers in ***bold italics*** indicate pages with photographs.

Abbaticchio, Ed 114, 121, 140, 144
ABC Affair 204–205, 207–208
Abstein, Bill 130, 139–140, 145, 154–155
Ada, Oklahoma 203
Adams, Charles "Babe" 120, 145, 148–151, 155, 159, 165, 168, 171, 178, 185, 188, 190, 199, 203–205
Akron, Kansas 95, 100, 110
Akron, Ohio 177
Albany, New York 112
Aldridge, Vic 201, 203
Allegheny, Pennsylvania 46, 73, 102
Allegheny River 72
American Association 19, 166, 167
American League 3, 48, 56–57, 61, 63, 65, 69–71, 73–81, 84, 87, 89, 95, 98, 124, 127, 147, 149, 154, 167, 188, 208
Anderson, Goat 116
Andover, Massachusetts 85, 87
Anson, Adrian "Cap" 7, 21–22, 36, 194
Arbuckle Building 42
Armstrong, Mayor Joseph G. 194
Atlantic City, New Jersey 44, 118
Atlantic League 32
Auburn, New York 32
Auten, Phil 42, 54–56

Baird, Doug 192
Baker, Frank 173
Baltimore, Maryland 188
Baltimore and Ohio Railroad Company 137
Baltimore Orioles 22, 41, 56–57, 104
Banker's team 67
Barbeau, Jap 139–140, 144, 146
Barnhart, Clyde 201, 203
Barnie, Bill 18, 22
Barrow, Ed 11–13, 32, 209
Barrow, George 13
Baseball Hall of Fame 209–211, 213–215
Baseball Magazine 173
Bausewine, George 106
Beaumont, Clarence "Ginger" 44, 50, 57–58, 63, 72, 75, 84, 88, 90, 106–107, 113–115, 192, 201, 213
Beckley, Jake 7
Bellaire, Ohio 81
Belmont Racetrack 141
Bennett Park 149–150
Bigbee, Carson 203–205
Blackwell, Oklahoma 138
Boston, Massachusetts 1, 22, 56, 87–91, 94, 105, 111, 203
Boston Americans 57, 87–94, 109, 112–113, 147, 165
Boston Beaneaters 24, 36, 61, 69–70, 84, 87–88, 109, 111, 114–115
Boston Braves 174, 178, 189–190, 192, 203–204
Boston Doves 132–133, 156
Boston Red Sox 178, 183
Boston Rustlers 167, 169, 171
Bowerman, Frank 7, 83–84
Brain, Dave 106, 109
Bransfield, Kitty 54, 58, 63, 72, 86, 90–91, 99–101, 115, 128, 130, 140, 187, 201
Brashear, Roy 71
Bresnahan, Roger 116–118, 181–182, 210
Bridgeville, Pennsylvania 146
Bridwell, Al 162
Britton, Helen Hathaway Robison 182
Brooklyn, New York 82, 188
Brooklyn Bridegrooms 21, 26
Brooklyn Robins 186, 204
Brooklyn Superbas 48, 50–51, 54, 59, 63, 69–70, 72–73, 96, 120, 169, 171

237

238 Index

Brouthers, Dan 210
Brown, Buster 173
Brown, Mordecai "Three Finger" 133
Brown, Tom 22
Brown College 97
Browning, Pete 20
Brush, John T. 39, 68–70, 73, 80, 83, 143
Buffalo, New York 49, 64, 188
Burke, Jimmy 73, 199
Bush, Donie 206
Butler, Artie 183, 186
Butler County, Pennsylvania 32, 71
Byrne, Bobby 140, 144–145, *146*, 149, 155, 159, 165, 172, 174–176, 183–184

California-Nevada Association 199
Callahan, Jimmy 197
Camnitz, Howard 120, 129, 135, 145, 147–148, 150, 155–156, 159, *160*, 161–164, 168, 171, 178, 182, 184, 188
Campbell, Vin 156, 158, 174
Cantillon, Joe 71, 77–78
Carey, Max 166, 169–170, 174, 176, 186, 192, 201–204, *205*
Carnegie, Pennsylvania 32, 50, 67, 97, 144
Carnegie Technical Schools 137
Carpenter, Bill 119
Carr, Louie 60
Carroll, Iowa 12, 200
Case, Charlie 97, 102
Cave Hill Cemetery in Louisville 144
Chance, Frank 143
Chancellorsville Battlefield 100
Chesbro, Jack 42, 44, 50, 57, 63, 72–79, 81–82, 84–85, 88, 93, 127, 201
Chicago, Illinois 27–29, 33, 36, 38, 41, 43, 56, 58–59, 77, 114, 118, 133, 136, 155, 159, 161–162, 166, 172–173, 188
Chicago Colts 21, 32

Chicago Cubs 69–71, 82, 85–87, 95, 97, 107–108, 113, 116, 118, 120, 124, 130, 132–134, 136, 142–145, 157–159, 166, 172, 174, 176–177, 182, 184, 189–190, 199
Chicago Orphans 33, 39, 41, 47–48, 58, 61, 71
Chicago White Sox 97, 108, 124
Chicago White Stockings 49, 69
Childs, Clarence "Cupid" 47–48
Church of the Annunciation in Chicago 36
Churchill Downs 20
Cincinnati, Ohio 24–26, 36, 47, 64, 80, 112, 125, 129, 141, 162
Cincinnati Reds 22–24, 26, 34, 39, 47, 54, 57, 68–70, 80, 82, 97, 99–101, 108, 112–113, 124–126, 141, 165, 167, 175, 186
Clancy, Bill 102
Clark, Stephen C. 209
Clarke, Anna 5, 7
Clarke, Annette Bertilla (Gray) 29–30, 34, 36, 39, 46, 66, 96, 110, 118, 123, 129, 142, 147, 164, 173, 183, 196–197, 209–210, 212, 214
Clarke, Charley 5
Clarke, Edgar 5
Clarke, Grace 5
Clarke, Hattie 5
Clarke, Helen Louise (Donahoe) 39, 46, 66, 200, 207, 214
Clarke, Joshua 11, 37, 122–123, 173, 200
Clarke, Lucy 5
Clarke, Lucy (Cutler) 5–6, 11, 121, 173, 200
Clarke, Mabel 10
Clarke, Mattie 5
Clarke, Muriel (Sullivan) 96, 200, 207, 214
Clarke, Sarah 11
Clarke, William 5–11, 13, 121
Clarke, William, Jr. 5
Clemente, Roberto 3

Cleveland, Ohio 64, 76, 172
Cleveland Naps 98, 122, 124
Cleveland Spiders 38, 41
Clingman, Billy 27, 45
Clyburn Place, Chicago 29
Clymer, Otis 102, 108, 114, 116–117
Cobb, Ty 147–149, 151, 173, 213
Cole, Leonard "King" 177
Collins, Jimmy 24, 87, 89, 210, 213
Columbia League 187
Columbus, Ohio 64
Columbus–Grand Rapids baseball team 39
Columbus Senators 190
Comiskey, Charley 7, 23
Conant, W.R. 109
Conn, Dr. J.E. 123
Conroy, Wid 73, 75–76, 81, 85
Cooper, Wilbur 185–186, 189, 191
Cooperstown, New York 209–211
Costello, Dan 192
Cowley, Matthew 9
Cowley County, Kansas 9–11, 95, 100, 123
Coyne, James 202
Crandall, Otis 162
Crane, Sam 59
Cratty, A.R. 197
Cross, Lave 7, 20
Cunningham, Elmore "Bert" 24, 42, 118
Cup Series 51–52
Cutler, William G. 9
Cuyler, Kiki 201–203

Dahlen, Bill 72
Dailey, Con 21
Dalrymple, Abner 7
Danvers, Massachusetts 93
Davies, David J. 178
Davis, Alphonzo "Lefty" 59–61, 73, 75, 79, 85
Davis, Ralph S. 85, 100, 193, 215
Delahanty, Ed 20, 210
Denver Grizzlies 120
Des Moines, Iowa 6, 11, 26, 33, 99, 114, 121–122
Des Moines Champs 122

Index

Des Moines City League 12
Des Moines Mascots 12, 14
Des Moines Register 11
Des Moines Stars 12–14
Detroit, Michigan 80, 149–150
Detroit Tigers 32, 75, 124, 147–151, 153, 155
Dexter, Charlie 27, 37
Dexter, Kansas 9
Dillon, Pop 44
Dinneen, Bill 87, 89–91
Doheny, Ed 59, 72, 82, 84–87, 91–94
Dolan, Albert "Cozy" 184–186
Donahoe, Daniel J. 207
Donahoe, Daniel J., Jr. "Dee" 207
Donahoe, Fred Clarke 207
Donlin, Mike "Turkey" 99, 174, 176
Donovan, Patsy 32, 44–45, 47, 54, 55, 71
Donovan, William "Wild Bill" 148, 150
Dooin, Charley 119
Dougherty, Patsy 87–88
Dreyfuss, Barney 2, 3; death 208–209; early years as Pittsburgh Pirate owner 43–45, 47–49, 51, 53–57, 60, 63–65, 68–71, 73–78; after Fred Clarke's resignation 196–202, 204–205; Pittsburgh ownership from 1903 through 1908 79–85, 87–88, 93–97, 99–102, 104–110, 112–116, 119, 120–128, 130–131, 133; Pittsburgh ownership from 1909 through 1915 137–139, 141–145, 150–155, 158–159, 161, 163–168, 170, 175–189, 191–192, 194–195; principal owner of Louisville Colonels 37–42; treasurer of Louisville Colonels 16, 18–19, 23, 25–26, 30
Dreyfuss, Sam 204, 208
Duffy, High 95, 199, 210, 213
Dungan, Sam 21
Dunn, Jack 109

Duquesne Gardens 67
Duvall, Judge Claude 207

East Liberty, Pittsburgh 89
Eastern League 102, 130
Ebbets, Charles 70, 80, 144, 186
Eclipse Park 20, 40
Edison, Thomas 162
Eels, Harry 122–123
Ehret, Red 34
Ely, Fred "Bones" 44, 55, 58–61, 63
Emslie, Bob 106, 193
Erie, Pennsylvania 64
Etna, Pennsylvania 7
Evers, Johnny 133, 143, 172, 189, 191–193
Ewing, Buck 22, 35
Exposition Park 47–48, 63–64, 71–72, 75, 84, 89–90, 98, 106, 115, 120, 132, 134–135, 137, 140–142, 188, 198

Falkenberg, Cy 82
Fall Classic 88, 95, 147, 171, 210, 214
Falls City Slugger 20
Federal League 3, 187–189, 191, 193, 197
Federal Patent Office 162
Ferris, Hobe 89
Ferry, Jack 171
Flaherty, Patsy 42, 97, 102, 104–105, 108, 114
Flynn, Jack 154–156, 158, 162
Forbes, General John 141
Forbes Field 141–143, 146–147, 151, 158, 164, 172, 193–194, 213
Fort Duquesne 141
Fort Pitt 141
Foster, John 59, 186
Fox, George 42
Fraser, Charles "Chick" 27, 29–30, 35, 38, 46, 95–97, 100, 114, 118, 172–173, 189, 196, 199, 208
Fraser, Mina (Gray) 29–30, 36, 46, 96, 172–173
Freedman, Andrew 37–38, 68–70, 80
Freeman, Buck 87
French and Indian War 141

Frisco Railroad 64
Frock, Sam 156
Galveston, Texas 22
Galvin, Jimmy 7
Ganley, Robert 113, 116
Ganzel, John 59, 71, 125
Gehrig, Lou 1
Gerber, Wally 192
Geyer, Rube 173
Gibson, George 102, 113, 118, 121, 127, 145, 158–159, 172, 174, 182, 199
Gilmore, James A. 187
Gold Ore farm 182–183
Graham, Peaches 173
Grantham, George 201
Gray, Ellen 34
Gray, John 34
Gray, Mary 34
Griffin, Rev. E.M. 29, 36
Griffith, Clark 33, 85
Grim, John 22
Grimm, Charlie 199
Gruber, John 72
Gumpert, Al 194
Gwinner, Fred 197

Hahn, Noodles 51
Hallman, Billy 116
Hamilton, Billy 20, 22
Hamilton, Earl 199
Hanlon, Ned 96, 124
Hanover Bank of New York 76
Harmon, Bob 186–187, 189
Harper, Jack 108–109
Harris, John 202
Hart, James 39, 70
Harvard University 130
Hastings, Nebraska 13–14
Havana, Cuba 55
Heinz, Henry John 7
Hendrix, Claude 171, 173, 175, 183–185, 188
Herrmann, August "Garry" 80, 108, 112–113, 124–126, 141–142, 186
Herron Hill, Pittsburgh 108
Herzog, Charley "Buck" 167, 186
Heydler, John 142–144, 209
Hickman, Charlie 59
Hill, Bill 27, 34–35, 118
Hillerich, John "Bud" 20

Index

Hinchman, Bill 192, 199
Hofman, Art "Solly" 177
Holmes, James "Ducky" 7, 14, 24, 158
Holy Name Catholic Church in Winfield 214
Hooker, Joseph 100
Hornsby, Rogers 1
Horrigan, John J. 25
Hot Springs, Arkansas 55–56, 81, 96, 101, 116, 120, 138, 142, 155–156, 164, 174–175, 183, 188, 199–200
Howard, Del 100–102, 108–109, 140
Howarth, Oberlin 93
Hoy, Dummy 34–35
Huggins, Miller 125, 182, 186
Hughes, Tom 87, 89, 91
Hulswitt, Rudy 98
Hunter, Newt 165
Hunter County, Kansas 9
Huntington Avenue Baseball Grounds 93
Hyatt, Ham 158

Ida Grove, Iowa 122–123
Indianapolis, Indiana 49, 188
Iowa Sports Hall of Fame 213
Iowa: The Home for Immigrants 5

Jackson, Stonewall 100
James, J.R. 64
Jennings, Hughie 54, 147, 210
John Carlson's band 36
Johnson, Ban 56, 61, 65, 69, 73–77, 80–81, 113, 144
Johnson, Walter 202
Johnston, Doc 192
Johnstone, James 105
J.P. Baden mill 174

Kane, Jimmy 130
Kane, John 125
Kansas City, Missouri 25, 49, 188
Kansas City Blues 159
Kansas State Sportsmen's Association 199
Kansas University 199

Keeler, Willie 31
Kelley, Joe 199
Kelley, Mike 42
Kelly, Billy 167–168, 174, 186
Kelly, King 210
Kennedy, Bill "Brickyard" 81–82, 86, 90
Kerr, Paul S. 209
Kerr, William 41–44, 47, 51, 54–56, 63
Killen, Frank 26
Killilea, Henry 87
Kiner, Ralph 3
King, Joe 212–213
Kittridge, Malachi 39, 45
Klem, Bill 105, 131, 172, 212
Kling, Johnny 213
Knell, Fred 22
Knowles, Fred 70
Konetchy, Ed 3, 181–182, 186–189, 191–192
Kremer, Ray 201
Krueger, Otto 100
Kubek, Tony 214

Lajoie, Nap 213
Lally, Bud 26–27
Landis, Kenesaw Mountain 209
Lange, Bill 36
Latimer, Cliff "Tacks" 42, 68
Latrobe, Pennsylvania 114
Leach, Tommy 32, 39, 42–44, 57–58, 60, 72, 74–77, 80, 84, 86, 88, 98, 106–107, 109, 111, 113–114, 116, 121, 124–125, **126**, 127, 139, 145, 148–149, 159, 162, 165–167, 169, 176–177, 192, 201
Leavitt, Charles Jr. 141
Lee, Watty 96
Leever, Sam 44, 50, 57, 63–64, 68, 72, 75, 81–82, 84–85, 87–91, 97, 100–102, **103**, 113, 120, 129, 144–145, 159, 162, 165–166, 192, 201, 213
Leifield, Albert "Lefty" 102, 113, 119–120, 129, 135, 142, 144–145, 149–150, 159, 162, 168, 171, 176–177
Lindaman, Vive 109

Little Pirate Ranch 99, 114, 123, 129, 131, 173, 196, 198
Little Rock, Arkansas 9
Little Rock Travelers 122
Lobert, Hans 125
Locke, William Henry 100, 128–129, 144, 182
Loftus, Tom 71
Long, Herman 7
Los Angeles, California 71
Los Angeles Gun Club 199
Louisville, Kentucky 1, 3, 18–27, 29, 35, 37, 39–40, 47, 67, 79, 115, 119, 127, 140, 144, 152–153, 195, 208–209
Louisville Colonels 2, 16–30, **31**, 32–43, 45, 50, 83, 87, 97, 118, 122–123, 152–153, 158, 175, 194, 209, 214–215
Louisville Times 23
Luby, Joseph 29
Lutenberg, Luke 22
Lynch, Mike 97, 102, 104–105

Mack, Connie 48–49, 57, 71, 194, 209
Macon, Georgia 25
Maddox, Nick 120, 129, 145, 149, 159
Madison, Art 42
Madison County, Iowa 6
Magee, Mayor W.A. 142, 147
Mamaux, Al 193
Marquard, Rube 167, 171
Martin, Frank 33
Mathewson, Christy 104, 106, 134, 145, 173, 213
Mayer, Casper P. 146
Mazeroski, Bill 3, 214
McBride, George 106
McCarthy, Alex 165, 174–176, 182–183, 186
McCloskey, John 14, 16, 18, 22, 24, 26
McCormick, Harry "Moose" 99–100
McCreery, Tom 24, 44, 201
McDermott, Mike 23
McFarland, Herm 26
McGinnity, Joe "Iron Man" 14, 104–105
McGraw, John 56–57, 84,

Index

104–107, 131–132, 143, 158, 162, 172, 182, 186, 190, 194, 210
McGreevey, Mike "Nuff Ced" 90
McGunnigle, Bill 26, 30, 34, 118
McInnis, Stuffy 205
McKechnie, Bill 162, 199–206, 214
McKeesport, Pennsylvania 140
McLean, Larry 125
McQuillan, George 184, 188
McRoy, Robert 77
Meadows, Lee 201
Memphis, Tennessee 2, 16, 26
Mercer, Sid 209
Merkle, Fred 133, 143, 186
Miller, Doggy 118
Miller, George L. 138
Miller, Jack "Dots" 140, 143, 145, 157–159, 162–165, 172, 174–176, 182–183, 185–186, **187**, 191
Miller, Roscoe 96
Miller, Ward 139
Miller, Zack 207–208
Milwaukee, Wisconsin 25, 38, 39
Minneapolis, Minnesota 123
Minneapolis Millers 38, 166, 168
Missouri Pacific Railroad 64
Mitchell, Mike 125, 176, 184
Mobile, Alabama 15
Moeller, Danny 130
Montgomery, Alabama 14–16
Montgomery Colts 14–15
Montreal Royals 102
Moore, C.L. 30–31
Moore, Eddie 201, 203–204
Moren, Captain John 110–111, 147
Morin, John M. 142
Morgan, J. Pierpont 76
Morgan, Jacob 6
Morrison, Johnny 201
Mt. Sinai Hospital in New York 208

Mount Washington, Pittsburgh 198
Mowrey, Mike 187–189, 191
Mueller, Herman 6
Mullin, George 97, 148–149
Murphy, Charles 144, 182, 189
Murphy, Morgan 22
Murray, Billy 119, 168

National Association of Leagues 212
National Commission 112, 141
National League 2–3, 16–17, 19, 21–23, 29, 33–34, 36, 38, 40–43, 45–46, 50, 55–57, 59, 61–63, 65, 68, 70–73, 78–79, 82–84, 89, 94, 96, 100, 102, 104–105, 111, 114, 116, 118, 123, 131, 133–136, 138, 140–145, 152, 155–156, 159, 164, 166–167, 171–172, 174–178, 181, 184–185, 188–189, 194–196, 200–201, 203, 208, 214
National League Golden Jubilee 201
National Semi-Pro Baseball Congress 212
Nealon, James Joseph 108–109, 111–113, 116, 119–121, 140
Nebraska State League 13–14
Needham, Tom 132
Neville Street in Pittsburgh 161
New Jersey Supreme Court 55
New Louisville Jockey Club 20
New Orleans, Louisiana 15, 22
New York, New York 1, 9, 24, 37, 59, 64, 68–70, 75–76, 79–80, 85, 99–100, 104–105, 107–109, 113–114, 131, 152, 155, 162, 181–182, 186, 203–205, 208–209
New York Americans 75, 81
New York Athletic Club 144

New York Evening Telegraph 89
New York Giants 14, 24, 27, 33, 37, 59, 61, 68–70, 83–87, 95, 97, 99, 104–108, 113, 116, 118, 124, 130–134, 143, 145, 147, 157–158, 162, 166–167, 169, 171–172, 174, 177–178, 182, 184–185, 189–191, 200, 210
New York Highlanders 82
New York Sun 74
New York Yankees 208, 214
Newark, Delaware 139
Newkirk, Oklahoma 207, 214
Nichols, Charles 7
Nicola Building Company 141
Noble, L. Clarence 7

Oakes, Rebel 182
Oakland, Pittsburgh 66, 137
O'Brien, George 118
O'Brien, John 42
O'Brien, Tom 50, 55–56
O'Connor, Jack 7, 48, 58, 73–77, 79, 85, 127, 154, 201
O'Day, Hank 133, 199
Ohio-Pennsylvania League 140
Ohio River 72
101 Ranch 138, 207
Organized Baseball 187, 212
O'Rourke, Jim 210
O'Toole, Marty 167–169, 171, 174–176, 178, **179**, 180, 184–185, 190
Overall, Orval 199

Pacific Coast League 108
Paducah, Kentucky 19
Paso Robles, California 200, 203
Paterson, New Jersey 31–32
Peitz, Heinie 100–102, 112–113
Peppers, Harrison 16
Pfeffer, Fred 22
Pfeister, Jack "The Giant Killer" 134
Phelan, Richard "Dad" 12, 33
Phelon, W.A. 33

Phelps, Eddie 79, 86, 89, 91, 97, 100–101, 112–113
Philadelphia, Pennsylvania 46, 56, 59–60, 63, 67, 99, 114, 116, 119, 185
Philadelphia Athletics 57, 71, 173
Philadelphia Phillies 20–21, 26, 61–63, 69–70, 84, 97–98, 100, 113–114, 119, 130, 158, 166, 171, 174, 184, 190, 192, 201, 207
Phillippe, Charles "Deacon" 38, 42–44, 50, 63, 67, 72, 75, 80–82, 84–91, *92*, 94–95, 97, 102, 113–114, 120, 130, 145, 147, 159, 162, 165, 175, 192, 201, 213
Pittsburgh, Pennsylvania 2–3, 7–8, 36–37, 41–43, 45–47, 54–55, 60–61, 63, 66–68, 71, 73–81, 89–90, 95, 101, 106–107, 109–110, 114–117, 119–122, 124, 126–135, 137, 139–141, 145, 147, 149–154, 157–159, 161–162, 167–169, 172, 174–176, 180–181, 183–185, 187–188, 191–192, 194–195, 197–199, 201, 204, 206–209, 213, 215
Pittsburgh-Chronicle-Telegraph 50
Pittsburgh Dispatch 178
Pittsburgh Gazette 82
Pittsburgh Hockey Club 202
Pittsburgh Leader 44
Pittsburgh Pirates 2–3, 26, 32, 41–50, 52–59, 61, *62*, 63–83, *84*, 85–102, 104, 106–121, 124–146, 148–178, 180–204, 206–215
Plaggmann, Harry 110
Polo Grounds 83, 104, 116, 133, 162
Ponca City, Oklahoma 198, 207
Powell, Bill 159
Power, C.B. 44, 45
Princeton University 96
Providence Grays 130
Pulliam, Harry 19, 27, 29–30, 33–34, 42–43, 54–55, 64, 68, 70, 73, 79–80, 82–83, 100, 104–105, 113, 118–119, 133, 138, 143–144, 153
Punxsutawney, Pennsylvania 48

Quaker City team 67
Quigley, Ernie 193
Quinn, Bob 209

Railroad Club 64
Raymer, Fred 58–59
Reach, Alfred J. 70
Reese, Bonesetter 86
Regan, Mike 90
Reulbach, Ed 143
Rhyne, Hal 202
Richardson, Danny 22
Ritchey, Claude 34–35, 42, 44, 50, 58, 62–63, 86, 89, 91, 101, 106–107, 113–115, 128, 192, 201, 213
River Coal Company 110
Robinson, Hank "Rube" 178, 185–186, 191
Robinson, Wilbert 210
Robison, Frank De Haas 39, 43, 80
Robison Street 106
Robitaille, Chick 97, 102
Rochester Bronchos 102
Rogers, Jim 30
Rogers, Colonel John I. 70
Roosevelt, President Theodore 76
Roswell, New Mexico 100
Royal Rooters 90
Rueben Quinn Club 110
Ruppert, J.V. 182
Rusie, Amos 27, 37
Ruth, Babe 1
Ryan, Jimmy 33

St. Joseph, Missouri 14
St. Joseph Saints 14–15
St. Louis, Missouri 43, 47, 56, 120, 129, 135, 145, 155, 182, 188, 190
St. Louis Browns 154
St. Louis Cardinals 43, 51, 55, 69, 71, 80, 106, 116, 120, 122, 129, 140, 144–146, 155, 166, 181–182, 186–187, 189–191, 204, 207
St. Louis Perfectos 39, 41
St. Mary's Cemetery in Winfield 214
St. Paul, Minnesota 164, 168
St. Paul Saints 154, 167–168, 174, 179, 186
San Francisco, California 71, 108, 112, 120
San Francisco Seals 203
Saratoga Racetrack 141
Savannah, Georgia 17, 20, 25, 124
Savannah Modocs 16
Scanlan, Doc 96
Schang, Bobby 192
Schenley Estate 137
Schenley Park 137
Schlei, George "Admiral" 125
Schulte, Frank 176
Scott, Ed 51
Sebring, Jimmy 79, 85–86, 88, 91, 99, 102
See, De Jay 25
Selee, Frank 194
Shannon, Spike 131–132
Sharpe, Bud 156
Sheehan, Tommy 109, 113
Shugart, Frank 23–24
Simon, Mike 162, 174, 188
Smith, Frank 108–109
Smith, Harry 57, 74, 76, 80, 86
Smith, Heinie 35
Smith, Ollie 124
Snodgrass, Fred 173, 186
Soden, Arthur 70
Somers, Charles 73–77
South End Grounds 171
Southern League 14, 16, 24
Spalding, Albert 64, 69–70
Speaker, Tris 183, 213
Sporting Life 3, 25
The Sporting News 3, 13, 100, 193, 212, 215
Stafford, Jimmie 35
Stahl, Chick 87, 90
Stargell, Willie 3
Starr, Charlie 128
Steele, Elmer 171
Steinfeldt, Harry 113
Storke, Alan 121, 130, 144, 146
Stove League 194
Stuart, William "Chauncey Bill" 95

Index

Stucky, Dr. Thomas Hunt 24, 30, 33–34, 37, 152
Sullivan, Neal A. 207–208
Sullivan, Ted 112
Summers, Ed 149
Sunday, Billy 7
Swacina, Harry 127, 130, 140

Tammany Hall 69
Tannehill, Jesse 44, 50–52, 54–55, 58, 61, 63, 72–79, 81–82, 84–85, 88, 93, 127, 201, 203
Taylor, Billy "Will" 37
Tenney, Fred 70, 133
Terry, Bill 213
Tessie 90
Thomas, Roy 130
Thompson, Gus 82
Thompson, Sam 7, 20
Tinker, Joe 176, 186
Toledo Mud Hens 122
Tomasco's orchestra 30
Toronto Maple Leafs 186
Townsend, Henry 202
Traynor, Pie 201
Trees, Joe 197, 198, 202
Tristam, Fred 64
Turner, Tuck 20
Twain, Mark 7
Twitchell, Larry 22, 124

Udall, Kansas 11, 38, 182
Ulora, Minnesota 173
Union Depot Station 89, 99
United States League 187

Vanderbilt University 156
Van Dusen, Sydney 64
Veil, Bucky 82, 86, 89
Veterans Committee 209, 211
Viox, Jimmy 175, 186, 188, 191

Wabash Railroad 64
Waddell, Rube 32, 39, 42, 44, 48–50, 53–54, 58, 68, 71–72, 77, 97, 166, 213
Wadsworth, John 16
Wagner, John Henry "Honus" 3, 31–32, 34–35, 37, 39, 41–44, 50, 57–58, 60–61, 63, 67–69, 72, 74, 80, 83–87, 89–91, 97–98, 107, 111, 113, 118–120, 127–129, 131–132, *134*, 135–136, 138, 140, 144–145, 147, 149–151, 157–159, 162–165, 172, 174–176, 183, 192, 201, 208, 212–213
Wallace, Bobby 55
Walnut River 9, 110, 121
Waner, Lloyd 3
Waner, Paul 3, 202–203
Warner, Jack 24, 83
Washington, D.C. 22, 32
Washington Nationals 30, 40–41
Washington Senators 116, 202, 214
Weaver, Farmer 22
Webb, Melville 209
Wentz, Lou 198
Werden, Perry 7, 45
West Baden, Indiana 29, 35, 129
West Point, Illinois 5
West View Cemetery in Pittsburgh 208
Western Association 14–15
Western League 12, 32, 38, 120
Western Pennsylvania League 67
Western Union 40
Weyhing, Gus 20
Wheeling, West Virginia 64, 120
White, Kirby 156, 162
Whittington Park 95
Wichita, Kansas 123
Wilhelm, Irving "Kaiser" 82, 84, 86
Williams, Jimmy 44, 50–51, 56–57, 63
Willis, Vic 109–111, 113, 120, 129, 133, 138–139, 143, 145, 148–150, 155–156
Wilson, Art 186
Wilson, Bill 35, 118
Wilson, Hack 1
Wilson, Owen "Chief" 122, 130, 145, 156, 169, 174, 176, 186, 191
Wilson, R.O. 208
Winfield, Kansas 9–11, 41, 78, 95, 107, 110–111, 121, 123, 128–129, 131, 154, 173–174, 182–183, 196, 199, 209–210, 214
Winfield High School 200
Winfield Kansas Baseball League 212
Winterset, Iowa 5–6, 9
Winterset Cemetery 200
Winterset Madisonian 6
Winterset News 6
Winterset Sun 6
Wood, Smoky Joe 183
Woods, Walt 38, 42
Woodside, J.P. 64
Worcester, Massachusetts 54
World Series 87–88, 91–94, 97, 103, 114, 147–148, 150–152, 154–155, 163, 165, 171, 175, 178, 183, 202, 208, 210, 214
Wright, Glenn 201

Yde, Emil 201, 203
Young, Cy 87–89, 91, 97
Young, Nick 64, 69–70
Youngstown, Ohio 86

Zimmer, Charles (Chief) 39, 42, 44–45, 49, 58, 201

www.ingramcontent.com/pod-product-compliance
Ingram Content Group UK Ltd.
Pitfield, Milton Keynes, MK11 3LW, UK
UKHW041939140426
5217IPUK00014B/556